Lloyd J. C

THE
PREACHER'S
COMMENTARY

JOSHUA

John A. Huffman, Jr.

THOMAS NELSON PUBLISHERS
Nashville

THE PREACHER'S COMMENTARY SERIES, Volume 6: *Joshua*. Copyright © 1986 by Word, Inc.

Published in Nashville, Tennessee, by Thomas Nelson, Inc.

The Bible text in this series is from the *Holy Bible, New King James Version,* copyright © 1979, 1980, 1982, by Thomas Nelson, Inc. Publishers. All rights reserved. Used by permission. Brief Scripture quotations within the commentary text are also from the *Holy Bible, New King James* Version, unless otherwise identified.

Library of Congress Cataloging-in-Publication Data

The preacher's commentary (formerly The communicator's commentary).

   Includes bibliographical references.
   Contents: v. 6. Joshua/John A. Huffman, Jr.
   1. Bible. O.T.—Commentaries. I. Ogilvie, Lloyd John. II. Huffman, John A., Jr., 1936–

BS1151.2.C66 1986   221.7'7   86–11138
ISBN 0-7852-4779-3

Printed in the United States of America

1 2 3 4 5 6 7 — 08 07 06 05 04

To the people of
St. Andrew's Presbyterian Church
of Newport Beach, California
with whom I am endeavoring daily
to flesh out God's lifestyle of promise

CONTENTS

Editor's Preface		*7*
Introduction		*13*
An Outline of Joshua		*17*
1.	A Lifestyle of Promise (1:1–9)	*19*
2.	A People Mobilized for Action (1:10–18)	*35*
3.	So God Can Use Anyone (2:1–24)	*49*
4.	The Crossover People (3:1–17)	*63*
5.	The Importance of Memories (4:1–24)	*75*
6.	A Time for Renewed Commitment (5:1–15)	*87*
7.	Jericho—A Model for Victory (6:1–20)	*99*
8.	Two Different Gods? (6:21–27)	*111*
9.	Achan and Ai—Learning How to Avoid Spiritual Defeat (7:1—8:35)	*123*
10.	Deception, Gullibility, and Integrity (9:1–27)	*139*
11.	When on God's Side (10:1–15)	*153*
12.	Completing the Conquest (10:16—12:24)	*167*
13.	The Archives Speak (13:1—19:51)	*183*
14.	Creating Two Kinds of Cities (20:1—21:45)	*207*
15.	An Altar of Rumor (22:1–34)	*221*
16.	The Covenant at Risk (23:1–16)	*237*
17.	The Bottom-Line Choice (24:1–33)	*251*
Bibliography		*265*

EDITOR'S PREFACE

God has called all of His people to be communicators. Everyone who is in Christ is called into ministry. As ministers of "the manifold grace of God," all of us—clergy and laity—are commissioned with the challenge to communicate our faith to individuals and groups, classes and congregations.

The Bible, God's Word, is the objective basis of the truth of His love and power that we seek to communicate. In response to the urgent, expressed needs of pastors, teachers, Bible study leaders, church school teachers, small group enablers, and individual Christians, the Preacher's Commentary is offered as a penetrating search of the Scriptures of the Old and New Testament to enable vital personal and practical communication of the abundant life.

Many current commentaries and Bible study guides provide only some aspects of a communicator's needs. Some offer in-depth scholarship but no application to daily life. Others are so popular in approach that biblical roots are left unexplained. Few offer impelling illustrations that open windows for the reader to see the exciting application for today's struggles. And most of all, seldom have the expositors given the valuable outlines of passages so needed to help the preacher or teacher in his or her busy life to prepare for communicating the Word to congregations or classes.

This Preacher's Commentary series brings all of these elements together. The authors are scholar-preachers and teachers outstanding in their ability to make the Scriptures come alive for individuals and groups. They are noted for bringing together excellence in biblical scholarship, knowledge of the original Hebrew and Greek, sensitivity to people's needs, vivid illustrative material from biblical, classical, and contemporary sources, and lucid communication by the use of clear outlines of thought. Each has been selected to contribute to this series because of his Spirit-empowered ability to help people live in the skins of biblical characters and provide a "you-are-there" intensity to the drama of events of the Bible which have so much to say about our relationships and responsibilities today.

The design for the Preacher's Commentary gives the reader an overall outline of each book of the Bible. Following the introduction, which reveals the author's approach and salient background on the book, each chapter of the commentary provides the Scripture to be exposited. The New King James Bible has been chosen for the Preacher's Commentary because it combines with integrity the beauty of language, underlying Hebrew and Greek textual basis, and thought-flow of the 1611 King James Version, while replacing obsolete verb forms and other archaisms with their everyday contemporary counterparts for greater readability. Reverence for God is preserved in the capitalization of all pronouns referring to the Father, Son, or Holy Spirit. Readers who are more comfortable with another translation can readily find the parallel passage by means of the chapter and verse reference at the end of each passage being exposited. The paragraphs of exposition combine fresh insights to the Scripture, application, rich illustrative material, and innovative ways of utilizing the vibrant truth for his or her own life and for the challenge of communicating it with vigor and vitality.

It has been gratifying to me as Editor of this series to receive enthusiastic progress reports from each contributor. As they worked, all were gripped with new truths from the Scripture—God-given insights into passages, previously not written in the literature of biblical explanation. A prime objective of this series is for each user to find the same awareness: that God speaks with newness through the Scriptures when we approach them with a ready mind and a willingness to communicate what He has given; that God delights to give communicators of His Word "I-never-saw-that-in-that-verse-before" intellectual insights so that our listeners and readers can have "I-never-realized-all-that-was-in-that-verse" spiritual experiences.

The thrust of the commentary series unequivocally affirms that God speaks through the Scriptures today to engender faith, enable adventuresome living of the abundant life, and establish the basis of obedient discipleship. The Bible, the unique Word of God, is unlimited as a resource for Christians in communicating our hope to others. It is our weapon in the battle for truth, the guide for ministry, and the irresistible force for introducing others to God.

A biblically rooted communication of the gospel holds in unity and oneness what divergent movements have wrought asunder. This commentary series courageously presents personal faith, caring for individuals, and social responsibility as essential, inseparable dimensions of biblical Christianity. It seeks to present the quadrilateral gospel in its fullness which calls us to unreserved commitment to Christ, unrestricted self-esteem in His grace, unqualified love for others in personal evangelism, and undying efforts to work for justice and righteousness in a sick and suffering world.

A growing renaissance in the church today is being led by clergy and laity who are biblically rooted, Christ-centered, and Holy Spirit-empowered. They have dared to listen to people's most urgent questions and deepest needs and then to God as He speaks through the Bible. Biblical preaching is the secret of growing churches. Bible study classes and small groups are equipping the laity for ministry in the world. Dynamic Christians are finding that daily study of God's Word allows the Spirit to do in them what He wishes to communicate through them to others. These days are the most exciting time since Pentecost. The Preacher's Commentary is offered to be a primary resource of new life for this renaissance.

It has been very encouraging to receive the enthusiastic responses of pastors and teachers to the twelve New Testament volumes of the Preacher's Commentary series. The letters from communicators on the firing line in pulpits, classes, study groups, and Bible fellowship clusters across the nation, as well as the reviews of scholars and publication analysts, have indicated that we have been on target in meeting a need for a distinctly different kind of commentary on the Scriptures, a commentary that is primarily aimed at helping interpreters of the Bible to equip the laity for ministry.

This positive response has led the publisher to press on with an additional twenty-three volumes covering the books of the Old Testament. These new volumes rest upon the same goals and guidelines that undergird the New Testament volumes. Scholar-preachers with facility in Hebrew as well as vivid contemporary exposition have been selected as authors. The purpose throughout is to aid the preacher and teacher in the challenge and adventure of Old Testament exposition in communication. In each volume you will meet Yahweh, the "I AM!", Lord who is Creator, Sustainer, and Redeemer in the unfolding drama of His call and care of Israel. He is the Lord who acts, intervenes, judges, and presses His people into the immense challenges and privileges of being a chosen people, a holy nation. And in the descriptive exposition of each passage, the implications of the ultimate revelation of Yahweh in Jesus Christ, His

Son, our Lord, are carefully spelled out to maintain unity and oneness in the preaching and teaching of the gospel.

In this volume on Joshua, Dr. John Huffman has written an outstanding commentary with you in mind. He writes for leaders in today's church—for clergy and laity who seek to lead in a way that is consistent with God's paradigms and principles.

John Huffman recognizes the man Joshua as one of God's paradigms for leadership. In Dr. Huffman's very skilled hands, the book named in honor of Joshua becomes a textbook for the Christian leader. Current practices of management, planning, and motivation are weighed in the biblical balance. As the scriptural mandate and model for leadership emerge, Dr. Huffman spells out clearly the implications for us today. He illustrates vividly how you and I may exhibit God-motivated excellence in our leadership responsibilities.

Our desire to be maximum in our leadership as teachers and preachers and communicators is also the longing of our listeners for their opportunities at home, in the church, at work, and in the community. This commentary shows us how to communicate the Book of Joshua in a way that meets the deepest needs and most urgent questions of people today. John Huffman exemplifies deep exposition that is practical, pastoral, and personal.

This commentary is practical. Careful explanation of the text, coupled with application drawn from rich experience, enhances the contemporary relevance of this commentary. Dr. Huffman's thorough research and prayerful study underlie the text in a way that will enrich your own life and help you in your teaching and preaching of the Book of Joshua. The creative outlines of passages and the wealth of illustrations, stories, and anecdotes will be an inspiring resource in your own efforts to communicate the message of Joshua in a memorable, life-changing way.

This commentary is also pastoral. Dr. Huffman writes with a pastor's heart. In reading you will feel as if you were sharing a warm conversation with a concerned friend, discussing openly the challenges of your life and ministry. Dr. Huffman's pastoral sensitivity pulsates through the medium of the written word. Your needs, hopes, and hurts, and those of people you seek to lead, are addressed with empathy and solid biblical insight.

And this commentary is personal. As you read, you will get to know John Huffman. You will experience his struggles; you will celebrate his victories. This is relational communication at its finest—the Word of God revealed through human intimacy.

I consider it a great privilege to know John as a personal friend, covenant brother, and prayer partner. Several years ago, we both were part of a support group of pastors here in Southern California that met regularly for mutual encouragement, vision, and prayer. I have come to know John as a man of Christ with immense ability and gifts.

John Huffman is an exemplary communicator. I know the careful planning, prayerful study, and imaginative writing that go into his biblical sermons. This has made him one of America's most distinguished preachers and pastors. It also explains the outstanding growth of his church in size and effectiveness. He is the senior pastor of the St. Andrew's Presbyterian Church, Newport Beach, California. John has guided this pivotal parish as a leading congregation recognized for its dynamic worship, innovative programs, mission giving, evangelism outreach, social involvement, and caring fellowship.

In addition to being a very impelling preacher and teacher, John is a faithful pastor and a strong administrator. He takes in stride the multiplicity of demands of the parish and yet maintains the priority of study and prayer so crucial to effective leadership. His printed weekly sermons are read by thousands across the nation, and his books have gained wide popularity. He is in demand as a preacher, conference speaker, and leader of church renewal. His balanced biblical theology and his bold, Christ-centered vision have made him an esteemed church statesman and strategist.

With enthusiasm and gratitude, I commend to you this excellent commentary on Joshua.

—LLOYD J. OGILVIE

INTRODUCTION

This commentary is designed to help you communicate the time-less messages revealed in Joshua to contemporary men and women. The history of ancient Israel is taken seriously. A true communication of God's Word cannot concentrate on the superficial perusal of Scripture that makes trite applications for today. What applications are made must emerge from a serious interaction with the text.

This commentary is geared primarily for communicators who are entrusted with the responsibility of facing men and women with a fresh Word of God relevant to today's living. This is not a technical commentary. There are many of those on Joshua available. Others are better equipped than I am to research and write such detailed critical evaluations of the available Hebrew manuscripts. To prepare sermons and popular teaching without consulting some of these is to shortcut an important part of the homiletical process. There are also a few books of sermons dealing primarily with the first twelve chapters. But there is a large gap in the literature between the technical commentaries at one extreme and the occasional book of several sermons at the other extreme. There is a need for supplementary homiletical material to fill this gap.

I have endeavored to help supplement this limited material in a way in which the contemporary needs of those to whom we minister are taken seriously. Some passages of Joshua are dealt with in detail. At other points, I move quite quickly over chapters that may give important historical details but offer little to the contemporary communicator. I have found that the writing of this book has been a natural outgrowth of my own weekly sermon preparations. As such, I trust that you will experience at least some of the joy I did in both preaching from Joshua and endeavoring to share the fruits of that preaching effort with you.

Joshua begins with a rearticulation of his divine call to be a successor to Moses, which is previously recorded in Numbers

27:18–23, and concludes with the record of his death. Joshua's biography presents the chronological parameters within which this fascinating history of the conquest is written. This book has great value for its historical insight into spiritual truth, its practical application of that truth, and its prophetic and typological glimpse into the future of God's redemptive plan for human history.

There is substantial disagreement among scholars as to the authorship and dating of Joshua. Some see it as being written after centuries of oral tradition, having its primary expression as a historical support for the reform of King Josiah in the latter part of the seventh century B.C. This critical approach sees Joshua as a continuation of the Pentateuch and links the six books together as the Hexateuch.

Other scholars give Joshua an earlier date, seeing it as a book that looks forward, written from the perspective of the beginning days of Israel's history in her national homeland. Some go as far as to ascribe the authorship of most of this book to Joshua himself, noting that the author was apparently an eyewitness of some of the events and that the use of personal pronouns and the phrase "to this day" suggests autobiographical writing.

It must be noted that nowhere in the Bible is the author of Joshua identified. I am inclined toward an early authorship of a pre-Davidic date, although not necessarily as early as the actual time of Joshua. Fortunately, the authorship and date of this book does not present a major problem to the communicator unless an endeavor is made to question the historical authenticity of the events recorded. I believe this is unacceptable to the evangelical preacher and teacher based on the internal claims of the text that this is a historical book describing actual events. Archaeological research has done much to confirm the authenticity of this history. Excavations have established that several important Canaanite cities were destroyed in the latter half of the thirteenth century B.C., the probable period of the Israelite conquest.

I have divided Joshua into seventeen chapters, each with its own internal subdivisions which are designed to be an outline for a series of messages or teaching themes. This is done so that you can compare the content of your own individual research and reflection with mine and find what will help you best communicate the major but often neglected themes of this important book. I urge you to consider preaching or teaching a series that will ultimately take you through the entire book. I did this over a period of eighteen months, preaching seventeen sermons in clusters of four to six weeks at a time.

My prayer is that this volume will help stimulate your preaching and teaching out of Joshua, giving you insights, suggestions for outlining, practical illustrations, awareness of major themes, and help from my own experience. I hope that God will use this commentary to touch your life and, through you, communicate these truths from Joshua to those for whom you bear preaching and teaching responsibility.

I want to express my deepest appreciation to three people who have been of enormous help in enabling me to complete this project. My administrative assistant, Toni Wood, has encouraged me from the very beginning with her enthusiastic work in typing the various drafts of the manuscript, leading ultimately to publication. My mother, Dorothy Huffman, has shared her gift for detail in proofreading the various drafts. Dr. Gary Pratico, formerly of Harvard University and now of Gordon-Conwell Divinity School, has given freely of his scholarly suggestions.

The St. Andrew's Presbyterian Church congregation of Newport Beach deserves my warmest thanks as that part of God's family that was so open to having me share the results of my Joshua study in seventeen sermons spread out over a year and a half.

I am so grateful for the understanding spirits of my daughters—Suzanne, Carla, and Janet—who brought me moments of refreshment for my work. And my wife, Anne, has not only been a thoughtful partner in ministry but has, through her own theological reflection and pastoral care, stimulated me to continuing growth toward my goal of being a responsible pastor, preacher, administrator, and family man.

AN OUTLINE OF JOSHUA

I. A Lifestyle of Promise: 1:1–9
    A. Living Life with Your Back to the Past: 1:1–2
    B. Claiming the Promises while Meeting the Conditions: 1:3–9

II. A People Mobilized for Action: 1:10–18
    A. A Profile of a Leader: 1:10–15
    B. A Profile of a People: 1:16–18

III. So God Can Use Anyone: 2:1–24
    A. God Working through the Ordinary and the Unlikely: 2:1–7
    B. Rahab—A Worthwhile Model: 2:8–24

IV. The Crossover People: 3:1–17
    A. Those Crossover Times: 3:1–4
    B. An Action Pattern for a Crossover People: 3:5–17

V. The Importance of Memories: 4:1–24
    A. Memory Stones: 4:1–14
    B. What Do These Stones Mean? 4:15–24

VI. A Time for Renewed Commitment: 5:1–15
    A. When God Acts, People Take Notice: 5:1
    B. Reconsecration Precedes Forward Action: 5:2–10
    C. Alert to Change: 5:11–12
    D. Every Leader Needs to Be Led: 5:13–15

VII. Jericho—A Model for Victory: 6:1–20
    A. Our God Is a God of Strange Strategies: 6:1–5
    B. The Result of True Worship Is Obedience: 6:6–19
    C. God Gives Victory to His Obedient People: 6:20

VIII. Two Different Gods? 6:21–27
    A. The Problem
    B. Four Observations

IX. Achan and Ai—Learning How to Avoid Spiritual Defeat: 7:1— 8:35
    A. Vulnerability at the Moment of Success: 7:1–6
    B. Turning Defeat into Victory: 7:7–13
    C. The Profound Effect of the Disobedience of One: 7:14–18

      D. A Scenario That Leads to Personal Defeat: 7:19–23

      E. The Severity of God's Judgment: 7:24–26

      F. A Hopeful Conclusion: 8:1–35

  X. Deception, Gullibility, and Integrity: 9:1–27

      A. Deception: 9:1–13

      B. Gullibility: 9:14–15

      C. Integrity: 9:16–27

  XI. When on God's Side: 10:1–15

      A. You Will Face Opposition: 10:1–5

      B. You Will Discover That God Keeps His Covenant: 10:6–11

      C. You Have Supernatural Resources: 10:12–15

  XII. Completing the Conquest: 10:16—12:24

      A. A Life of Ongoing Warfare: 10:16–21

      B. A Spiritual Battle to Death with Christ as Victor: 10:22–42

      C. A Spiritual Home Base: 10:43

      D. The Responsibility of Completing the Conquest:
         11:1— 12:24

  XIII. The Archives Speak: 13:1—19:51

      A. We Never Fully Arrive in This Life: 13:1–7

      B. God Gives and Holds Accountable: 13:8—14:5

      C. Faithfulness to the Covenant: 14:6—15:19

      D. Women's Rights: 15:20—17:13

      E. The Alternative to Complaining about One's Lot in Life:
         17:14–18

      F. The Disposition of the Remaining Land: 18:1—19:51

  XIV. Creating Two Kinds of Cities: 20:1—21:45

      A. A Place of Legal Safety: 20:1–9

      B. A Place of Spiritual Community: 21:1–45

  XV. An Altar of Rumor: 22:1–34

      A. Transitions: 22:1–9

      B. Rumors: 22:10–29

      C. Peacemaking: 22:30–34

  XVI. The Covenant at Risk: 23:1–16

      A. The Promise of Faithfulness: 23:1–13

      B. The Consequences of Unfaithfulness: 23:14–16

  XVII. The Bottom-Line Choice: 24:1–33

      A. The Facts: 24:1–13

      B. The Choice: 24:14–15

      C. The Results: 24:16–33

CHAPTER ONE—A LIFESTYLE OF PROMISE
JOSHUA 1:1–9

Scripture Outline

> Living Life with Your Back to the Past (1:1–2)
>
> Claiming the Promises while Meeting the Conditions (1:3–9)

Every so often, a coach, a teacher, or a pastor comes across a young person with great promise.

The coach detects unusual coordination combined with strong-willed determination. He pictures a future All-American. She visualizes a future Olympic gold medalist. The work begins.

When a teacher spots that gifted youngster, a special joy leaps within his or her heart. No, not everyone has to be a great scholar. But there is something extraordinary about this student. The teacher sees the promise of a valedictorian, a Phi Beta Kappa, a Ph.D., or simply a human being with a real hunger for truth.

Every so often, I spot a young person who shows great potential for the ministry. I get so excited that I have to hold myself back. God deserves the best in His full-time service. The ministry is not for those who can't do anything else. So I try to plant a little seed and encourage that person. I say, "You have great promise. No, don't go into the ministry because I'm pushing you. Please take time to listen for the call of God. However, as I see it, you do have great potential." My hope is that the young person will pick up the suggestion and give it serious consideration.

God is not an elitist. He doesn't single out some superhuman characters as special. He sees promise in us, and He's in the business of helping us discover and live a lifestyle of promise.

Joshua is one of the most fascinating books in the Bible. At one level, it relates the story of an ancient Hebrew leader and the people whom God called him to lead into the Promised Land. At another level, it's a personal story. It's the story of promise and of the great expectations that God has for us. It's as if God takes on the qualities of the perceptive coach, teacher, or pastor who becomes excited about what we can become if we use the gifts He's given to us. The study of this book helps us see ourselves in this light. It makes us question whether or not we are living up to our potential and God's promise.

These opening verses of Joshua offer explosive potential to both nonbelievers and believers. A nonbeliever must confront the fact that he or she is not in vital conversation with the living God. If there has not been repentance for sin, trust in the crucified and risen Christ, and the reception of His gift of salvation, there is not spiritual life.

A starting point of any Biblical study must be whether or not one is spiritually alive to receive God's message from His Word. It is especially important that the communicator who is preaching and teaching from the Old Testament keep the person and work of Jesus Christ central. The gospel must be articulated again and again. The invitation to receive God's gift of forgiveness, right now, needs to be the underlying, wooing message to the nonbeliever who is exposed to our preaching and teaching. We offer a lifestyle of promise that cannot be realized by anyone living outside the circle of God's love and grace.

At the same time, we offer specific encouragement and challenge to those who identify themselves as Christians. Ours is a lifestyle of promise as God wills it to be. The reality is that many of us believers back off from the promises. We live lives of discouragement. Too often we are defeated by temptation, suffering, or the casual blandness of our existence. Joshua models for us—both in the experiences of this Old Testament hero and the complex history of the community he was called to lead into the Promised Land—what it is to flesh out this promise. Joshua helps us see what God is immediately able to do to realize this promise in us. The question is, once we have observed what this involves, are we willing to act upon the promise?

LIVING LIFE WITH YOUR BACK TO THE PAST

1:1 After the death of Moses the servant of the LORD, it came to pass that the LORD spoke to Joshua the son of Nun, Moses' assistant, saying: **2** "Moses My servant is dead. Now therefore, arise, go over this Jordan, you and all this people, to the land which I am giving to them—the children of Israel.

—Joshua 1:1–2

A lifestyle of promise involves living life with our backs to the past.

It was probably intimidating to have been a second lieutenant to Moses, which Joshua had been during the forty years following the Exodus from Egypt. This young man first appears as an Israelite general in the battle against Amalek (Ex. 17:8–16) and then as Moses' "assistant" (Ex. 24:13; 32:17). In Exodus 33:11, Joshua is described as "a young man."

His primary exploit during the wilderness experience was serving as one of the twelve spies sent out to survey the Promised Land (Numbers 13 and 14). He came back along with Caleb, presenting a minority report. Although he foresaw it as an enormous task, Joshua believed that God would enable them to capture the land. The other ten filed their majority report and saw no possibility of victory; their report was adopted. Joshua and Caleb had failed.

As the forty years of wandering in the wilderness pass, Joshua goes on with his routine work at the side of the real leader, Moses. Although designated in advance to be Moses' successor (Num. 27:18–33), Joshua sees himself as an assistant, as a servant. Moses is seen as the great *"servant"* of the deity; but Joshua is seen as the youthful servant waiting on Moses and is called *"Moses' assistant"* (1:1). One Jewish prophetic tradition even emphasizes Moses' superiority and Joshua's inferiority.[1]

Now Joshua faces a crisis. For reasons of age and disobedience, Moses is not allowed to enter the Promised Land and dies. Joshua mourns his death, and as he lingers in grief over the memory of Moses, the Lord addresses Joshua directly with these words: *"Moses My servant is dead. Now therefore, arise, go over this Jordan, you and all this people, to the land which I am giving to them—the children of Israel"* (v. 2). God has seen promise in Joshua and has chosen and prepared him for this moment. God's timing is always correct, but I have to believe that Joshua was not so certain.

Joshua could have lived forever with a second-lieutenant mentality, forever living in the past, lingering in his grief, and musing on what could have been if Moses was still there. But God abruptly disturbed his backward focus and startled him into his privilege of living in the present and future by saying, "Joshua, you have great promise. Quit mourning. Moses is dead!" It was at this point that Joshua began to realize the enormous potential God had invested in him through those many years of preparation.

More than thirteen hundred years later, Jesus rearticulated the same principle, saying, "No one, having put his hand to the plow, and looking back, is fit for the kingdom of God" (Luke 9:62). A few years later, the apostle Paul put the same comment in different words, writing from prison in Rome to the church at Philippi: "Forgetting those things which are behind and reaching forward to those things which are ahead, I press toward the goal for the prize of the upward call of God in Christ Jesus" (Phil. 3:13–14).

How many of us carry our childhood insecurities into adult life? A woman I know appears to have everything going for her. She is a competent fifty-year-old who has lived a full life of rich, deepening experiences. A casual observer would see her as a fulfilled woman who has already realized some of the great promises that are hers. Little does anyone know that inside her is a recurring, repetitive, inferiority-complex mental cassette tape of the ugly-duckling adolescent, who will never forget what it was to be the chubby little kid with braces, thick glasses, acne, and a ponytail. She was teased a lot then, and she's never gotten over it. Today, she can't really see the promise that is hers as a magnificent, God-gifted woman.

I can still see one of my childhood friends now. He didn't grow as fast as the rest of us. So he managed our high-school basketball team because he couldn't play. There wasn't any job that was too small for him to do; he just wanted to be accepted. How insensitive we were—big lugs, guys who happened to grow a little bit faster. Teasingly, we would throw our sweaty attire at him as we picked up fresh towels and headed for the showers. He compensated by studying extra hard. When he grew up physically during the summer between his junior and senior years, the girls got interested. In fact, they dropped some of us as they stumbled over themselves, noticing him for the first time. He pursued a double major in college and went on to one of the finest medical schools in the country. He's now a noted surgeon and on the faculty of that same school. He is a respected Christian leader, as well as a highly recognized surgeon. I have to believe that deep inside him there are still the stinging memories of the insensitive put-downs we flung his way. In some complex manner, he probably still struggles a bit with self-esteem. Even some of the successes might have been motivated by memories of inferiority.

I say this perhaps because I have the same kinds of memories. These same fellows with whom I ran did a job on my brain, too. Unmercifully, they would tease me about my big rear end, my huge nose, and my curly hair. I hated the way I looked. Occasionally, I'd slick my hair down with sugar water so that it would be straight like the other "cool guys." How silly I must have looked—especially when the flies were attracted to my sticky, sweet thatch! It was only a few years ago that I realized that my buddy who teased me the most about my nose was guilty of projection. His was bigger. He had simply taken the offensive and focused the attention on me to remove it from himself. And here I am in midlife still orchestrated by some deep, inner insecurity from my childhood and adolescence.

My college roommate graduated number one in his class. He has his Ph.D. in philosophy from Yale. He is brilliant! He is also one of the kindest persons I have ever met, but I'm still intimidated by his brains. Three earned graduate degrees later, I am still not sure of my abilities.

Does this ring any bells? We are Christian communicators, endeavoring to share God's Word with other human beings. But we see other Christian leaders who seem to be so much more talented. We say to ourselves, if only I had his voice, her brains, his connections, her influence, his reputation, that pulpit. I'm not that gifted. I can't write or preach as well as those other people. I cringe every time I observe someone yawn during one of my sermons. It hurts to see a parishioner glance at his wristwatch and even shake it somewhat unobtrusively—down goes my self-esteem.

God looks us directly in the eyes and says, "You've got great promise!" We shift our eyes away. The old tapes begin to roll. "God doesn't really know me. Look at all the things I've done wrong. I don't really have what it takes." We go on comparing ourselves to other people.

Joshua must have admired Moses. Moses was a great man; he was one in a million. No doubt he considered himself to be inferior to the great lawgiver. Moses was not only Joshua's mentor; he would go down in both religious and secular history as one of the greatest leaders ever to appear.

Charles Haddon Spurgeon notes that if we mingle with our inferiors we are apt to grow vain. If we are closely associated with superior minds, there is a far greater probability that we will become depressed and will think less of ourselves than true humility might require. True humility is, after all, only a right estimate of our own powers.[2] Joshua must have been despondent under a pressing sense of his own deficiencies. He needed to hear God say, "Joshua, Moses My servant is dead! For years, I've been preparing you for this moment. I saw great promise in you a long time ago.

23

Quit comparing yourself. Live in the present, in the future, not in the past."

These opening two verses stress the importance of living with our backs to the past. To me, these words of God to Joshua have to be among the most important in all the Bible. Let those words *"Moses My servant is dead. Now therefore, arise"* roll over again and again in your mind and in your ministry. Are we willing to live with our backs to the past? Are we willing to challenge our people to live with their backs to the past?

To do this, we need to remember so that we can forget. We have the privilege of remembering the grace of our Lord Jesus Christ and all that God has done for us. This is the focus of worship and why we observe Advent and Lent. This is why we celebrate the sacrament of the Lord's Supper. These reminders help us to engage in a special concentration on the life, death, and resurrection of Jesus Christ. We are called to remember that all of our sins, all of our shortcomings, and all the sins and shortcomings of the people to whom we preach and teach were nailed to the cross. We remember in a way that enables us to forget.

We need to forget the failures that encourage low self-esteem. There's Joshua, whipping himself. He has the forty-year-old memory of when they wouldn't believe his report. He and Caleb were losers. How could he ever be a leader? He hadn't been persuasive in the one great opportunity he had had. It was hard for him to see that God had plans for him now. He had to forget his past failures.

We are also urged to forget our past successes. We can learn from both failure and success; but, at the same time, even our past successes can hold us in bondage. Joshua could have built a sense of false self-esteem, reminding himself that he was one of the two faithful spies. He could have minimized his potential for promise by reminding himself that he had been right when the other ten had been wrong. How sad it is to be held in the bondage of either past failures or successes.

I'm trying my best to etch in my memory the finality of the past: *"Moses My servant is dead!"* Don't ever forget that phrase. Along with burying Moses, preside over other funerals. Bury the memories of past failures and successes that can destroy your lifestyle of promise. We have the privilege of urging those to whom we are endeavoring to communicate God's grace to make a funeral pyre of those inner cassettes, drench them with gasoline, set a flame to them, bury the ashes. Remember that anyone who is in Christ is a new creature; old things have passed away. Everything is new in Jesus Christ.

CLAIMING THE PROMISES WHILE MEETING THE CONDITIONS

3 Every place that the sole of your foot will tread upon I have given you, as I said to Moses. 4 From the wilderness and this Lebanon as far as the great river, the River Euphrates, all the land of the Hittites, and to the Great Sea toward the going down of the sun, shall be your territory. 5 No man shall be able to stand before you all the days of your life; as I was with Moses, so I will be with you. I will not leave you nor forsake you. 6 Be strong and of good courage, for to this people you shall divide as an inheritance the land which I swore to their fathers to give them. 7 Only be strong and very courageous, that you may observe to do according to all the law which Moses My servant commanded you; do not turn from it to the right hand or to the left, that you may prosper wherever you go. 8 This Book of the Law shall not depart from your mouth, but you shall meditate in it day and night, that you may observe to do according to all that is written in it. For then you will make your way prosperous, and then you will have good success. 9 Have I not commanded you? Be strong and of good courage; do not be afraid, nor be dismayed, for the LORD your God is with you wherever you go."

—*Joshua 1:3–9*

God not only startles Joshua out of his backward musings, but He also now confronts him with some exhilarating promises for the present and future. These promises do not exist in a vacuum. They carry with them some conditions.

It's important for us as communicators to convey to the people we serve the double edges of the gospel. One is the edge of promise—the other is the edge of condition. To express the idea in a slightly different way, the coin of God's promise to us has two sides—one is the side of privilege; the other is that of responsibility. Or picture the lifestyle of promise as a strong rope. Two strands give it strength. One is the strand of the creative potential God invests in us. The other is the strand of our discipline in living up to that potential. Let's examine these two dimensions of promise and conditions as God revealed them to Joshua and in turn, through His Word, to us.

First, a lifestyle of promise involves *claiming God's specific promises*. God has made some tremendous promises to us. We need to know what they are, for then we are privileged to claim them. This particular text lists three promises that we can claim and that we can urge others to claim.

1. *Claim God's will for your life*. For Israel, this was a promise of land. God was giving territory to His people. He said to Joshua, "Moses My servant is dead. Now therefore, arise, go over this Jordan, you and all this people, to the land which I am giving to them—the children of Israel" (1:2). He went on to specify what this meant in terms of borders.

Israel has two sets of borders. One is that in which her own people live. This set of borders has expanded, shrunk, expanded, and shrunk in a cyclical fashion throughout the past three thousand years. The other set of borders is that which represents the Land of Promise. The Book of Joshua illustrates both types of boundaries.

The first set, which encompassed the land from Dan to Beer-Sheba and from the Mediterranean to the Jordan River, was the basic area of the conquest. In His will, God envisioned more, but Israel was capable of frustrating the will of God by disobedience. Israel never has fully claimed the promise of God's will.

For us, God's promise is not necessarily one of physical territory. His promise is that we can be in the center of His will. We have the privilege of claiming God's will for our lives.

God's promise may actually be physical property as it was for Joshua. In the late 1930s, Henrietta Mears, who was in charge of Christian education for the First Presbyterian Church of Hollywood, California, took the promises of thirty-three hundred years earlier as God's promise to her. This visionary woman believed that God wanted a retreat center in the mountains near Los Angeles for children, teenagers, and adults. This retreat would enable people to get a little closer to God and then return to their city homes, having had their lives transformed by Christ and renewed in the Holy Spirit.

She found a piece of land, but it was one that would take a miracle to obtain. She put on her hiking boots and walked all over the acreage she believed would be the best place. She didn't have the money. There were many obstacles in her way which seemed like giants to her. She and her colleagues felt like grasshoppers before those giants. They prayed together, and she continued to pray and hike alone. God honored her prayers and gave her the

ForHis Kingdom

land He wanted her to have. Christ's church is blessed today because she was willing to claim the promise of Israel.

We can hear stories like this and strike out in prayers of fantasy that are not God's desires for us. In 1978, I moved from pastoring the First Presbyterian Church of Pittsburgh, Pennsylvania—a 205-year-old congregation that was housed in a magnificent Gothic cathedral at the heart of that great industrial city. It was also blessed with a three-hundred-acre, year-round camp in the rolling hills of the Ligonier Valley, sixty minutes east of Pittsburgh. The move was a difficult one for our family. We had put out a "fleece." We believed that God had led us to Newport Beach to the young St. Andrew's Presbyterian Church.

Within the early months of our ministry in California, it became quite apparent that we would need a building program. Our committee set its eyes on fourteen acres of prime land on a bluff overlooking the Coast Highway, Newport Harbor, and the Pacific Ocean. For two years, I jogged the paths through Castaways Point, praying that if it was God's will He would give that land to St. Andrew's for a new church. I could picture a magnificent campus on this land with a cross raised high above the Coast Highway. We prayed hard. We claimed the land and worked to get it. At the same time, we continually reminded ourselves as a congregation that if God should say *No!* we'd sing the Doxology. It was a sad day when we received word from the Irvine Company that they were withdrawing their option to sell us the land. Because of a commitment they had made months before, papers had already been drawn up for us, and we were ready to present our first installment on the purchase price. But suddenly the doors had closed.

I can vividly remember the dreams we had for that land. I can feel even now the pain experienced when the doors slammed shut in our faces. I can also remember the trust and even the new beginning that was ours as we stood during all three services on that Sunday morning and sang the Doxology. And we've never once looked back (even though months later, when we were in complicated negotiations with our neighbors and the city over the redevelopment of our present property, both the mayor and the president of the Irvine Company made overtures that would have enabled the reconsideration of that site). God had said *No!* He had closed the doors at a time we had wanted them to be opened. As great as the disappointment had been, it is clear now that our church is stronger for having stayed at our present site. Many of the divisions have healed. God has given us additional land surrounding our present site and the additional buildings He wants us to have. We are claiming the land, subordinating our will to His will.

How do we know when we get ahead of God, presumptuously claiming what He doesn't want us to have? How can we as communicators know the will of God for our lives, so we don't claim the wrong things? How do we help our people discover the will of God for their lives?

Perhaps you're quite familiar with this five-step plan that helps us discover God's will. A brief review is always helpful. First, read the Scriptures. They are clear on so many matters. It is always God's will that we share the message of Christ's love by both our actions and our words. It is always God's will that we be Christ-centered fathers and mothers. His Word reminds us in the majority of situations what His will is.

Second, pray. It is amazing what God whispers to us when we are in open communication with Him.

Third, counsel with godly friends. God has a way of speaking truth through a multitude of counselors.

Fourth, check out the external circumstances. When doors remain closed that you have tried to open, believe that God has a lock on those doors. Look for new doors.

Fifth, when you have exhausted these first four steps of reading the Scriptures, praying, counseling, and checking the external circumstances, and you find the doors are neither opened nor closed, and you're still not sure what to do, then do what you want to do. We need to get this message across in all of our communication. God is in the business of granting the desires of our hearts if our hearts are transparently open to Him. We don't need to live with guilt if we happen to enjoy doing what we are doing. But it's important that we make this the last step in our pilgrimage to discover God's will rather than the first step. When we run our own desires through the grid of steps one through four, then we are able to claim God's will with energy and with enthusiasm.

2. *Claim the power and the presence of the Lord.* God said to Joshua, *"No man shall be able to stand before you all the days of your life; as I was with Moses, so I will be with you. I will not leave you nor forsake you"* (1:5).

No one could ask for a more fantastic promise than this. God will never leave us or forsake us. Essentially, God is saying, "I will not drop you in the middle of a project I've given to you." God is not in the business of deserting His people when we get in trouble, if we are honestly endeavoring to do His will.

God does close doors. The promise of His power and presence does not preclude occasional disaster and frequent tribulation. Our faith will be tested, and we may go through great suffering. Our lives will involve hard work. God's power will be with us through the good and the bad times. His presence will continually sustain us.

Life wasn't easy for Joshua. He claimed God's power and pres-✶ ence through both good and bad times.

Ironically, my phone rang while I was writing these very words. It was a dear friend whose life I've always seen as charmed by affluence, power, financial success, physical beauty, and an attractive family—weepingly shared with me the shock of bankruptcy combined with the discovery of her husband's cancer. She said, "The worst part of all is that right when I need Him, God has deserted me. I don't feel His presence anymore when I pray." I was able to give her the assurance of His promise, even when she didn't feel His power and presence.

Joseph claimed these promises even when he was betrayed by his brothers and thrown into the pit. God was there, and Joseph claimed His power and presence. He refused to be blackmailed by Potiphar's wife. It would seem that God should have handed him a bouquet right then and there, but He didn't. Joseph went to jail and languished there for a crime he hadn't committed. We know that God's power was with him, and His presence sustained him in that prison experience.

3. *Claim God's prosperity and success.* The Scripture says that as you claim the promises, *"you will make your way prosperous, and then you will have good success"* (v. 8). Our tendency is to decode this into narcissistic terms. But let's trust God for more than that. God doesn't function in cosmetic terms. He's not in the business of tummy tucks and nose jobs or of making life easy. He's in the business of transforming us into His image. He's in the business of ✶ helping us to serve Him, meeting the deepest needs of others who hurt, who are in pain, who need deliverance from sin, who need their bodies healed and their minds restored. This is success. This is prosperity. God is in the business of helping us to lead people to a personal, vital relationship with Him, the Savior Lord. ✶ *Seek first His Kingdom.*

As communicators, it is our responsibility to get across to our people, who live in a world of competitive success values, the biblical understanding of success. Somehow we have to help them realize that if God has given them good minds, and they use those minds to simply display their intelligence, they are not successful.

Those minds are God's gifts to be used to His glory. If they have been given the gift of making money, and they are hoarding that money for themselves, they are not successful. In fact, they are failures. We need to be prophetic in teaching and preaching this message. If they have been given good looks or a popular personality and are well known and well liked, they are not necessarily successful. We must challenge them to use these promising gifts to the honor of the Lord. Then they will know true success. And we have the sacred privilege and responsibility of humbly modeling these biblical values for them.

After claiming God's specific promises, we come to a second criterion for a lifestyle of promise—meeting *the conditions God has set on these promises.*

Condition one: Study the Scriptures.

God said, *"This Book of the Law shall not depart from your mouth, but you shall meditate in it day and night"* (v. 8). How many mistakes I have made because I tried to find God's will for my life without consulting the "Guide Book." How much pain we have experienced at those points in which we have not consulted the Word of God. It's important that we share some of those experiences with our people. Let them identify with some of these failures. I believe that we are to model the right kind of lives. I believe we are also to be willing to lead from weakness as well as from strength. We—and our people—know that we are human. Somehow some of us have bought into the concept that the leader must always do business from strength. Fortunately, God keeps biblical models in front of us—warts and all. It is good for us occasionally to do some reality testing of the lives of biblical heroes. There isn't a perfect one. These are men and women who made mistakes. The Holy Spirit has inspired uncensored biographies describing what happens to godly people when they fail to take seriously God's Word.

I have a chronic tendency to buy consumer goods and use them without reading the owner's manual. (In fact, I have an expandable file into which I put all those manuals.) Then I wonder why the item I've purchased doesn't function the way I had expected it to function. It's usually because I haven't serviced it the way it was meant to be serviced or used it the way it was meant to be used. I've been foolish. David wrote, "I have laid up thy word in my heart, that I might not sin against thee" (Ps. 119:11, RSV). We need to study the Scriptures, and we need to urge our people to study the Scriptures.

Condition two: Obey God.

God puts this as an important condition. He says that we are *"to do according to all the law which Moses My servant commanded you; do not turn from it to the right hand or to the left, that you may prosper wherever you go"* (v. 7).

This is a tough life. We want all the goodies, but we don't want the sacrifice. We are called to expendability and to lives of obedience. There's too much of American Christianity today that is geared to getting what we want to satisfy our own personal pleasures.

I'm convinced that our people are hungry to hear an honest word from us. I believe they're tired of blaming God for everything that goes wrong in their lives. The problem is that they've been sold a false bill of goods. They are bombarded with religious teaching in the media and in the popular self-help books that convince them that God is some kind of a genie whose sole purpose is to bring us personal pleasure. It is easy to compartmentalize one's life—obeying God where obedience comes easy and doing what one wants to do in those areas in which obedience would demand self-denial.

Let's be honest with ourselves and with those with whom we share God's Word. Let's not be afraid to declare that if a person has done something wrong and is paying the price for it he or she has no right to blame God for the pain.

This could be a moment of truth for someone, a very liberating moment of truth. It may not be that this person intended to do anything wrong. It's simply that he or she did do something wrong—not seeking God's wisdom. He needs to ask His forgiveness for that. God wants to forgive and give us a fresh start. We have to be loving enough to urge those who are called to serve Him not to blame God for action taken without seeking His wisdom.

Along a similar line, if someone has done something wrong in specific disobedience to God's Word, we have to teach that person not to blame Him for his or her trouble. We have to have the courage to call others to repentance. Ours is the responsibility of exhorting our people to express their sorrows to God and request His forgiveness. They need to know that God's promises carry with them specific conditions.

Obedience is the most significant of these conditions. We are called to model for our people what it is to thank God even for the disasters, knowing that whatever pain we experience in this life is insignificant in comparison with the unending pain of alienation from God in the life to come.

Not only can we point to the results of disobedience in our own lives, we can also give illustration after illustration of what happened to the people of God in the Scriptures when they disobeyed. Moses thought he could beat the system. He was going to deliver his people from bondage with his own strength. In trying to accomplish something good, he did some things that were both foolish and wrong. In a burst of anger, he killed an Egyptian slave-master. He had failed to wait upon the Lord. His timing was wrong, so he had to flee to a foreign country. During those forty years in the backside of the desert, the arrogance and the pride of his first forty years in the court of Pharaoh were driven from him.

Almost everyone has been to the backside of the desert. Share the pain that comes from getting ahead of God. I've done some foolish things. I've disobeyed; I've been wrong. I've failed to meet certain conditions. Wherein I have disobeyed, my lifestyle has been one of unfulfilled promise. The good news is: It is never too late to come back and be renewed by the power of God.

Condition three: Be strong and of good courage.

God stated this condition bluntly, *"Be strong and of good courage"* (1:6); *"Only be strong and very courageous"* (v. 7); *"Have I not commanded you? Be strong and of good courage; do not be afraid, nor be dismayed, for the LORD your God is with you wherever you go"* (v. 9).

When we have met the conditions of studying the Scriptures and of obeying the Lord, then we have the right to live without fear. Somehow we have to communicate that this is what is meant by the "peace of God which passes all understanding." We know people who run scared all through life even though they have many things going for them. If we have checked out the validity before God of what we are doing, then we have the privilege of letting life flow. To put it another way, be the best you can be of who you are, and let the chips fall where they may.

Fear is not God's will for those of us who teach and preach any more than it is God's will for those to whom we are called to communicate. He has not given us a spirit of fear. Instead, He intends for us to live with His power, His love, and His self-control. This means that we are privileged to live with a "divine nonchalance." God's command is to courage. We are to live with the assurance that "God's payday is not always Friday." God understands His promises. He will fulfill them in His time, which is the best time.

I need to be constantly reminded that I may go all the way through this life without having fully realized the degree to which

God does complete what He has promised. It may be only when I stand before Him in heaven and He says, "Well done, thou good and faithful servant. Enter into your eternal reward," that I will fully realize His faithfulness on my behalf. I've discovered that there is never a moment in my ministry in which I have the feeling that I've "arrived." I'm only now beginning to realize that I will probably never have that feeling in this life.

Joshua was the lonely long-distance runner. In fact, I'm not certain that God trains sprinters. His promises are not just for a few moments, but for a lifetime. The potential He has invested in us is not short term. It's long term. The difficulties and defeats are not signs that we are failures. They are toughening processes that make us stronger servants of God.

This lifestyle of promise really reduces itself to a life of genuine trust in the Lord for forgiveness, for instruction, and for strength.

I've heard Donn Moomaw, pastor of Bel Air Presbyterian Church in California, talk about trust, distinguishing between intellectual belief and genuine leaning upon the Lord. He's held up a chair in front of a congregation, noting that it is one thing to believe that the piece of furniture is a chair capable of holding your weight. It's quite another thing to sit down in that chair, committing yourself to it, realizing in an existential way that it is a chair. We derive no benefit from a chair when we just think about it. It becomes a chair when we trust ourselves to it and find the support that it provides.

Joshua models a faith that is more than intellectual. He is willing to turn his back to the past, claim the promises, meet the conditions, and give all that it will take to complete the lifelong tasks entrusted to him.

NOTES

1. Trent C. Butler, *Joshua*, Word Biblical Commentary, vol. 7 (Waco, Tex.: Word Books, 1983), p. 10.

2. Charles Haddon Spurgeon, "Strengthening Medicine for God's Servants," in *The Treasury of the Bible*, 4 vols. (Grand Rapids, Mich.: Zondervan, 1968), 1:493.

Chapter Two—A People Mobilized for Action

Joshua 1:10–18

Scripture Outline

A Profile of a Leader (1:10–15)

A Profile of a People (1:16–18)

The initial verses of Joshua deal with his encounter as an individual with God. This lifestyle of promise is not fleshed out in an individualistic basis. God has spoken to a duly humbled Joshua, calling him to a lifestyle of promise. Moses is dead. God has gotten His point across that He needs new leadership that has a healthy self-esteem.

Joshua, fresh from his individual encounter with God, returns to the camp and faces the people. They need to be mobilized for action, to move out into the Promised Land. It's important that we as communicators make the point now that we are moving from talking about God's individual contact with us to the way God deals in the life of His people as a community. We know that God touches us as individuals. But He doesn't leave it there. God's interaction with us as individuals also has profound implications for the communities of faith with which we identify. Those of us who are preachers and teachers of God's Word know that a lifestyle of promise is not fleshed out in a "Lone Ranger" existence. It involves community. I'm not certain, however, that our congregations really hear that message. Joshua 1:10–18 gives us a unique opportunity to concentrate on life lived in a community.

When I originally set out to prepare my preaching outline of Joshua, I planned to preach one message on chapter 1. In fact, I announced a preaching schedule to my congregation to that effect. The couple dozen commentaries I have in my library give only passing notice to the technical dimensions of the last half of this chapter. For all practical purposes, the homiletical resources completely neglect this, concentrating on the first half of the chapter dealing with Joshua's call.

I see here a perfect bridge from the individual God/human interaction to the corporate responsibilities of both a leader and a people. We have an excellent model of Joshua and his interaction with God's people of the Old Covenant—Israel. The results of this study can be treated as archaeological remains put on museum display, reviewing the cognitive data surrounding the life and actions of an ancient people with their leader—Joshua. Or, we are privileged to use this narrative as a 3,300-year-old living narrative model directly applicable to our own individual lives and our interaction with others in our communities of faith. For us, this community of faith involves the people of the New Covenant—the church of Jesus Christ. Both communities, Israel and the church, are communities of hope, action, and promise. Joshua and Israel provide a model for our contemporary Christian community, showing us two primary pictures of a people mobilized for action. One is the picture of a leader. The other is the picture of a people.

A PROFILE OF A LEADER

10 Then Joshua commanded the officers of the people, saying, 11 "Pass through the camp and command the people, saying, 'Prepare provisions for yourselves, for within three days you will cross over this Jordan, to go in to possess the land which the LORD your God is giving you to possess.' "

12 And to the Reubenites, the Gadites, and half the tribe of Manasseh Joshua spoke, saying, 13 "Remember the word which Moses the servant of the LORD commanded you, saying, 'The LORD your God is giving you rest and is giving you this land.' 14 Your wives, your little ones, and your livestock shall remain in the land which Moses gave you on this side of the Jordan. But you shall pass before your brethren armed, all your mighty men of valor, and help them, 15 until the LORD has given your brethren rest, as He gave you, and they also have taken possession of the land which the LORD your God is giving them. Then you shall return to the land of your possession and enjoy it, which Moses the LORD's servant gave you on this side of the Jordan toward the sunrise."

—Joshua 1:10–15

A people mobilized for action has leadership that is qualified to lead. Something has happened to Joshua. This man, who had been so lacking in self-esteem, has encountered the living God. God has released within Joshua the leadership capabilities that He had been nurturing in him for several decades. Joshua returns to the camp and wastes no time in taking charge.

Four leadership qualities emerge, and Joshua possesses them. We need to examine our own lives to see what we can learn from the model given us by Joshua. We also have the privilege of communicating to others both the privilege and responsibility that are theirs in Christian leadership. Our teaching and preaching on this passage give us an opportunity to work at breaking down the laity and clergy distinctions. Joshua was not the only leader; he was also in charge. We would do well to avoid identifying ourselves too closely with Joshua, causing those with whom we are in communication to identify with his followers.

It will help to list some of the important leadership positions God has entrusted to each person. We can challenge our people to feel a sense of the romance in divine/human leadership as we take seriously our roles in both the home and the church. There are lessons here for fathers and mothers, as well as Sunday school teachers, elders, deacons, trustees, ushers, youth sponsors, and every other conceivable leadership position in which a believer finds himself or herself.

The first leadership quality is that a qualified leader *is in tune with God.* People have a right to expect godly leadership. This leadership must have a word from the Lord, and it must be obedient to that word. There's no room for double standards. Every religious leader must have a life that reflects a humbled dependence on the Lord and live in humble relationship with other leaders. He or she is not to be jealous of others whom God has chosen, for we are all part of God's community.

Too much leadership is managerial in style. It has read the latest books on administration. Knowledge of management theory is important, and this must never be minimized; however, it is no substitute for a growing, developing, daily relationship with the living God.

Joshua had been with God. He had listened to what God had to say and had dealt with his own internal fears and self-doubt. God had touched him. God had commissioned him and had told him to arise. As long as Joshua would be faithful to Him, God had promised to be faithful to Joshua.

This chapter of Joshua centers on the identity of God's people in relationship to its human leader. The leadership has passed from Moses to Joshua, and, as centuries go by, this leadership has continued to be passed on. Jesus becomes the new Joshua, embodying as no other leader in human history what it means to lead. People must have a strong identity with leaders who are loyal to that incomparable pioneer of the faith—Jesus Christ Himself. Such leadership must face the tasks given by God with a strong conviction and courage. Only with such leadership can people be expected to follow in positive ways. We cannot stress enough the importance of daily conversation with God, Bible reading, meditation, and prayer.

Richard C. Halverson, who has had a distinguished ministry as pastor of the Fourth Presbyterian Church in Washington, D.C., and as chaplain of the United States Senate, has for years emphasized the importance of leadership that lives in tune with God. He stresses the fact that no matter how large or small the leadership task may be, this contact must be there. He goes on to develop the concept that the larger the leadership task the more important it is that the leader be in tune with God. In his newsletter for men, *Perspective,* he writes these words:

> The *larger the rock* you drop in a quiet pool—the greater the ripples that radiate out from the splash washing across everything in their way as they circle toward the edge of the water.
>
> This is obvious when it comes to dropping pebbles in puddles . . . but what is *equally obvious*—yet too often overlooked by men—is the same identical principle in life! A man's impact moves out from him in concentric waves *touching everyone* within the sphere of his influence with greater or less force . . . depending on the man!
>
> The *bigger the man*—the greater his impact! *Good or bad,* it influences those around him. His sin moves out to cover the crowd—just as much as his righteousness. The little man can get away with things a big man *ought never do.* Because the little man isn't noticed like a big man, his actions and attitudes don't register the same force. The very fact a man has risen to a place of power and prestige *doubles or triples or quadruples* his responsibility. His life is continually influencing others—consciously or unconsciously. The greater the

heights he has reached . . . the more important his position . . . the *more eagerly people follow him.* He becomes an *example:* the standard—the norm. . . right or wrong. . . by virtue of his position. His life becomes a goal toward which other men strive. Either they *deliberately copy* the big man—thinking they are finding his secret of success. . . or else the fact that he does a thing—or does not—means *approval* or *disapproval* to them. If the big man does it—it's okay! In either case it's dangerous. Because often men who imitate actually imitate the *superficial*—the secondary—the idiosyncrasy . . . or the thing that's safe for the big man may destroy those who follow him.

Whether a man likes it or not—if he's in a place of leadership—he will be influencing others. He has no right just to consider himself. He must think in terms of his influence. This is *part of the price* of leadership! Not just the man himself—but what happens to those who follow in his footsteps—is the serious responsibility of the leader—the big man! This is *inescapable!*

"*To whom much is given—much shall surely be required!*"—*Jesus.*[1]

Though Halverson's letter was written for men, his point is clear for both women and men in leadership positions: it is crucial that a leader be in tune with God. The communicator must convey the fact that each of us has an impact on someone. We must take our role seriously. Each man and woman who follows Jesus is called to some sphere of leadership that requires time spent with God.

Second, a leader who is qualified to lead *is willing to take tough stands.* Joshua was not ambivalent nor did he delay. He recognized the moment of truth. He could no longer equivocate. The people must move into the Promised Land then or never. He issued the commands.

This need to take a firm position does not imply aggressive behavior that comes out of insecurity. This does not imply a cosmetic self-assurance or a manipulation of people into carrying out a partially prepared plan.

Forty years had passed, and much planning had already been done. Joshua's leadership had a continuity with what had gone before. Either the spies had already gone into Jericho and had come back with their reports or were now in the process of doing their reconnaissance and would soon be back with final information. There is no substitute for good preparation.

There is a moment, however, in which a leader must move from the preparation stage into the action stage. This is the moment of no return. It is at this moment that the leader is most vulnerable.

For many years, Ted W. Engstrom has given creative leadership to World Vision International, a Christian humanitarian organization. He's also made a lifelong study of leadership. He states:

> True leadership, even when it is practiced by the most mature and emotionally stable person, always exacts a toll on the individual. In our world it seems to be axiomatic that the greater the achievement, the higher the price to be paid. The same is true of leadership. Jesus Himself seemed to have this thought in mind when He said, "If you really want to find your life, you must lose it" (Luke 9:24).[2]

Engstrom notes that any worthwhile accomplishment has a price tag. The question is, How much is a person willing to pay in hard work and sweat? He lists some of the painful aspects of leadership. Every leader must expect *criticism*. It's part of the territory. *Fatigue* is to be expected. A good leader must learn how to handle stress without "burnout." *Loneliness* will be experienced. A leader lives in that no-man's land between identifying with his people and being isolated from them. A leader will be forced to make *unpleasant decisions*. Every decision, by the very nature of what a decision is, has a degree of finality to it that excludes the possibility of continuing to consider other options. *Rejection* comes every leader's way. Every normal, well-adjusted person wants to be liked; but a leader will not always be liked.

This passage gives a perfect opportunity to share one's own personal struggles in leadership. I have never yet had the luxury of making decisions that are free from controversy. Occasionally, an issue is clear-cut wherein the Bible speaks with clarity. Most of my struggles in leadership have come when decisions had to be made on which there was a difference of opinion. To do nothing indefinitely would have ended up being a negative course of action. A leader needs to bring his people to a decision. Not everyone reaches a decision at the same time.

We all know the feeling. Let's let our people know how we sometimes feel—lonely, criticized, rejected—when we've had to take the responsibility of mobilizing them to action. It will take some pressure off them. They, too, know these feelings, but they may not be as quick as we are to recognize them as the normal results of being a leader.

I have yet to serve a church in which everyone had the same view of me. Some see me as a knee-jerk conservative, while others see me as dangerously liberal in my leanings. Some view me as vacillating and indecisive. Others see me as too decisive and overly opinionated. For some, I'm too evangelistic; others say I don't really preach the gospel. To some, my mention of social concern is disturbing. Others pray that I will be more prophetic.

This text gives a wonderful opportunity for the leader to share these feelings, identifying with both Joshua and Moses. Having observed Moses and his struggles, Joshua could have rationalized indecision and lack of activity for another decade or two. Instead, he knew that the time for action had come. He was willing to mobilize the people, building on the past successes and failures of Moses.

The third quality of leadership is for a leader to be *able to delegate responsibility.* Joshua did this by working through the administrative structure that was already in place. He commanded the *"officers of the people"* to carry the word through the camp that, within three days, they would be passing over the Jordan River. The word *"officers"* literally means "scribes." This is hardly what they were. They were subordinate officers of some sort with both a military function and a responsibility in civilian government. Reference is made to them in Deuteronomy 16:18 and 25:9. In Exodus 5:6–10, they appear as "foremen" and as "taskmasters."

Nothing ruins a community faster than leadership that either ✗ doesn't know how to delegate or refuses to delegate responsibility. Moses learned this the hard way, as Exodus 18 records. He began his leadership career with a charismatic style. God had chosen him to be the leader, and Moses took the task seriously. By the sheer magnetism of his personality and God-given gifts, he led the people out of Egypt. He gave everything in those early months of the Exodus to the point of emotional and spiritual burnout. His father-in-law, Jethro, who happened to be visiting, observed the horrendous administrative bind in which Moses found himself and suggested that Moses delegate responsibility. Moses showed both his humility as a son-in-law and a willingness to learn as a leader. He accepted Jethro's advice that Moses consider himself as the personal liaison between God and the people, and instead of listening to every complaint and trying to solve every problem, delegate that responsibility to others. He also chose others of integrity—people who hated a bribe—to rule over a thousand, over a hundred, over fifty, over ten. Only the most difficult cases would come to Moses. The smaller matters would be decided through this delegated chain of command.

Joshua observed this and learned the lesson that he didn't have to control everything. He was willing to delegate.

The person who delegates has to trust those to whom he gives responsibility. The ideal community mobilized for action has a "network" of persons who faithfully carry out their responsibilities. They know that the leader trusts them to do their work. They are trained for their responsibility. They're given responsibility. They carry out their responsibility.

Fourth, a leader who is qualified to lead *has a plan of action.* This person deals in more than slogans. This leadership is not cosmetic.

Joshua commanded the people to do three things. The self-contained lesson in this plan of action could be a three-point message: prepare, pass over, and possess.

First, the Israelites were to prepare their provisions because manna would no longer be provided. They were coming into a land where there was food. They were to get ready for the conquest in a way that used their own natural resources. God only provides supernatural resources when natural provisions are not sufficient.

Some religions emphasize myths and fables. Although the Bible specifies that God occasionally functions in supernatural ways, this is not the primary stress of the Scriptures, and there is no reveling in the supernatural. For example, when Peter was in prison, his chains were loosed by an angel, and he was led out of his incarceration. God intervened supernaturally at the point of specific need. God did not then transport Peter on a magic carpet to the house where the believers were. Peter had to make his own way through the city of Jerusalem. Divine energy always stimulates activity. It never lulls one to sleep.

Second, the Israelites were to pass over the Jordan. That was Joshua's plan of action.

Third, they were to possess the land that God had prepared for them. He had given the promise. The action was to go and do the job.

A PROFILE OF A PEOPLE

¹⁶ So they answered Joshua, saying, "All that you com-
mand us we will do, and wherever you send us we will go.
¹⁷ Just as we heeded Moses in all things, so we will heed you.
Only the LORD your God be with you, as He was with Moses.
¹⁸ Whoever rebels against your command and does not heed
your words, in all that you command him, shall be put to
death. Only be strong and of good courage."

—*Joshua 1:16–18*

Now we see the profile of a people mobilized for action. Two
primary characteristics stand out.

First, a people mobilized for action *is willing to subordinate personal, vested interest for the community good.* Verses 12–15 tell the story
of the Reubenites, the Gadites, and the half-tribe of Manasseh. They
had already been given their land on the east side of the Jordan
River (Deuteronomy 3 and Numbers 32), and they were already
beginning to settle into a more sedentary lifestyle. They must
have had good reasons for not crossing the Jordan. They could
have declared that the other nine-and-a-half tribes had enough
manpower to conquer the land. Or their wives and children could
have been an excuse to stay at home. As it was, the tribes did leave
a sizable number behind to take care of their families. But they
kept their promise and were enthusiastically willing to support
the conquest. Fidelity to engagements is a noble quality, just as
laxity is a miserable shortcoming. Those provided for did not forget the others who were not yet settled. They assisted those in
need at great personal sacrifice.

This little historical vignette is a testimony against selfishness.
It's a statement of brotherhood and sisterhood. It speaks of loyalty
and attests to the public spirit that is to be ours as believers in
Jesus Christ. And it shows the importance of being obedient to the
commands of God, as were these tribes to the Mosaic commands.

Nothing destroys Christian community faster than petty, individual vested interests. This is seen in our nation. There are one-
cause groups dedicated to disrupting whatever general welfare stands
in the way of their particular concern. There's nothing wrong with
working hard for a cause, especially if it is a God-ordained cause.
We can thank God for those who dedicated themselves to the
abolishment of slavery. They crusaded with a single-minded purpose. Those who were most successful, however, saw their cause as
one among other causes. They approached it in a healing manner.

Anarchy was not their goal. Theodore White has noted in his writings how vested-interest groups at times have taken over the American political parties. Narrow, sectarian goals become primary concerns while the general good of the nation is minimized.

The same kind of thing happens in the church. Some advocate world missions to the neglect of home missions. Others will give only to what they can control at home and attack the concept of giving beyond the local community. Some emphasize evangelism to the neglect of Christian nurture. Others stress nurture to the neglect of evangelism. Some see the gospel in terms of spiritual salvation; others see it in terms of transformation of society. Some are priestly in their orientation while others are prophetic. Some want a stress on cognitive doctrine and technical Bible teaching. Others want the stress to be on relationships. Some see success measured in bricks and mortar. Others stress program. There is nothing wrong with any one of these emphases I've mentioned; each is correct in its place. What rips at the fabric of a church is when any one vested-interest group defines ministry in its own terms without seeing the gospel in all of its wholeness. We have individual gifts and interests that enrich the whole community when we subordinate ourselves to the community welfare.

I am excited to discover this New Testament principle so beautifully fleshed out in Joshua. This historical experience in the life of Israel gives us the perfect opportunity to stress the fact that there is no room for selfishness. We are a family. Within the ideal family, those who are rich share with those who are poor. We are called to be sensitive to the needs of the widow and the orphan. Those of us who are older don't retire from spiritual effort because our children are raised. We invest ourselves continually in the lives of future generations. How often have we seen persons who helped in one building program thirty years ago unwilling to help today? They feel that they have already fulfilled their responsibility. Instead, this biblical model alerts us to the importance of subordinating our own personal vested interest to the welfare of the entire community.

As preachers, we are privileged to model this lifestyle for our congregations. With one hand, we reach into our pockets to support the ongoing work of Christ's church. With the other hand, we reach into another pocket—that equity pocket, that capital God has given us—to help support a special project in a sacrificial way. We need make no apology as preachers in sharing with our people what tasks God has assigned to us. Ours is a radical commitment to the entire enterprise. We are to discourage the designation of time, talent, and money to only that part in which one is particularly interested, especially when that self-centered focus can detract from the area of broader need.

Second, a people mobilized for action *is willing to be united in a common task, following its God-given leadership.*

Verse 16 reads, *"So they answered Joshua, saying, 'All that you command us we will do, and wherever you send us we will go.'"*

This passage in Joshua emphasizes very clearly the importance of unity. As communicators, we are given an excellent example of how God's enterprise is much more effectively accomplished when God's people, in all of their diversity, are bound together by a common purpose. Moses was dealing with a huge company of mavericks during those forty years in the wilderness. Only at this point in the story is there a unity that enables the people to receive God's promises. I don't think we can emphasize this point too strongly.

The church must have unity if it is to be used. Thank God for the varieties in style and temperament in its people. But there must be a common task, and there must be a passion that motivates this common task.

This Joshua passage enabled me once again to remind the congregation I serve that we are not here at St. Andrew's in Newport Beach simply to keep a mainline, denominational church open and funded. Our session has worked hard to establish its goal for ministry. Again and again, we must remind ourselves of who we are. We are a Christ-centered, Presbyterian church committed to leading men, women, and children to personal faith in Jesus Christ; committed to nurturing and growing in our knowledge and love of Christ; and committed to deploying our resources, both personal and financial, in servant ministries for others. This must be our unified goal.

Perhaps your Christian community has expressed its goals in a slightly different fashion. Whatever those goals are, they must be kept in clear focus. The sense of common task must be felt with such deep conviction that we are willing to die for it. We must be open to God's leadership and how He expresses His will through those who are our installed leaders. In the case of Israel, it was Joshua and the various officers who would lead in the conquest. In the church today, we must be open to the leadership that God has given and remind ourselves that God expresses His will through those who are our installed leaders.

I've observed one church that not long ago had a powerful ministry for Christ. But in the last six years, it has paid a terrible price for violating this biblical concept. Instead of being united in a common task, willing to follow its God-given leadership, this congregation has become splintered as the creative methods for ministry, which worked so well for the better part of two decades, have needed to be adapted to a new set of circumstances. There has been disagreement among the laity as to whether or not this adaptation is appropriate. This church had sought out a pastoral leadership that could lead it into the future, only to divide into carping, critical, self-centered evaluations of the pastoral leadership's qualifications to lead. I've watched a six-year period in which four highly capable pastors, with superb track records elsewhere, have been forced to resign. Any one of these had the capabilities to provide leadership that could creatively have led this congregation into the future.

From our own experiences, we can tell story after story to parallel this case study. We need to level with the people we're called to lead. We can show them from this somewhat unusual moment in the life of Israel what can happen when God's people are united in a common task and willing to follow their God-given leadership. Put this into juxtaposition with those times when Israel was unwilling. Consider illustrating judiciously from churches you've observed that have been blessed by God when they have been responsive to their installed leaders but have paid a severe price when they have splintered into personal, vested-interest groups.

This was a new day for Israel. They were prepared to give to Joshua what they never gave to Moses—uncomplaining loyalty. It was only in the last days of Moses' life that the people became united around him. It's amazing how quickly they forget. They pledge to Joshua, *"Just as we heeded Moses in all things, so we will heed you. Only the LORD your God be with you, as He was with Moses"* (v. 17).

Yes, their memory was short; but in a way, it was a healthy sign that they were maturing. There was a continuity in this growth experience. Moses' story is one of unrequited affection. He loved the people, but they murmured and grumbled against him. Now they'd learned their lesson. Forty years of wandering in the wilderness had taken its inevitable toll in attrition. They knew that the only way they could accomplish anything for God was to be a united people, willing to follow their leadership. So they pledged their loyalty in a united way to Joshua and, in turn, expected him and the rest of their leadership to be loyal to God.

The world laughs at a divided church. It admires a people that differs in ages, temperaments, dress, economics, and political ideology but that has a oneness rooted in the person and work of Jesus Christ.

There are two kinds of Christian communities that I've observed. One is like sea gulls, made up of loners. You are only safe if you, as an individual, have got it together. If you're wounded, you are left to take care of yourself. The other is like Canadian geese. They help each other as they fly. They take turns in the lead position, cutting through the air interference, creating a draft that makes it easier for the others to fly. No one ever drops out alone. If one is injured, another stands by nursing it to health. It's a unified community that does not encourage superstar status.

The story is told of a man who died and stepped into the presence of Saint Peter. He asked if he could take a look at both heaven and hell. Saint Peter showed him a large banquet room of people eating magnificently prepared food. Then Peter took him to another large banquet room. Again, the man saw people eating magnificently prepared food. Somewhat confused, he asked Saint Peter, "Which of these rooms is heaven? Which is hell? They look the same to me."

Saint Peter said, "Let's go back and look more carefully at the persons in each of these rooms." The man did look and then noted that the only eating utensil assigned to each person in the two rooms was a long, sharp sword. In one room, the people were selfishly stabbing at their food and were slashing their faces and bodies in their endeavor to feed themselves. In the other room, the people had learned to pierce the food with the sword and then to ever so tenderly and sensitively feed each other.

Hell was the room filled with people so determined to do things their way that it was ending up a place of mangled, bloody bodies. Heaven was the room of unity, love, and joy.

A people mobilized for action involves the interaction of qualified leadership and unselfish persons with unified, common goals.

NOTES

1. Richard C. Halverson, *Perspective* 22 (November 4, 1970): 1.

2. Ted W. Engstrom, "The Price of Leadership," *Christian Leadership Letter*, January 1977, p. 1.

CHAPTER THREE—SO GOD CAN USE ANYONE

JOSHUA 2:1–24

Scripture Outline

God Working through the Ordinary and the Unlikely (2:1–7)

Rahab—A Worthwhile Model (2:8–24)

Israel is camped at Shittim several miles across the Jordan River from Jericho. Joshua has received his leadership credentials from God to become Moses' successor and has taken his position as commander in chief. His leadership is consolidated as this huge, migrating nation has put behind it forty years of murmuring and squabbling. They are ready to claim God's promise of the Promised Land.

Tucked into this history of the conquest is the fascinating story of two spies and a prostitute named Rahab.

Joshua, needing some final military intelligence about Jericho, sent two young men disguised as foreign travelers to the ancient fortress stronghold so critical to the Israelite entrance into the land. It was not surprising that these two spies found refuge in the house of a harlot, who was also most likely an innkeeper. Authorities were used to seeing strange characters go in and out of such a place—a place as good as any to maintain some kind of anonymity. They might have been able to gather intelligence of a military nature there, even though it may not have been the best place for a person of God to frequent for normal social relationships.

The king of Jericho, most likely a typical Canaanite kinglet, had his operatives at work, and the presence of the spies was reported to him. Suspecting that the two men were spies come to search out all the land, his officers demanded that Rahab produce them. But she had already hidden the men under stalks of flax that were laid out on the roof of her house to dry. Pointing toward the Jordan River, she told the authorities that the men had left the city under the cover of night. Why did Rahab lie to the king's messengers? Most likely she had overheard conversations that had taken place in her house. The soldiers and the citizens of Jericho couldn't help but be alarmed by that huge, migrating nation camped on the other side of the Jordan. As soon as the pursuers went out looking for the two spies, the gate to Jericho was shut.

Fascinated by the two Israelites, Rahab went up to the roof and expressed her own fear of the future and the fear that was beginning to grip the inhabitants of Canaan. She acknowledged her conviction that the God of Israel was determined to give the land over to the Hebrews. Rumors had come of how the Red Sea had dried up before the Israelites some forty years ago as they fled out of Egypt (Exodus 14). Rahab was also aware of Israelite victories over the Amorite kings, Sihon and Og, who had been utterly destroyed (Deut. 2:24—3:11; Num. 21:21–35). "And as soon as we heard these things, our hearts melted; neither did there remain any more courage in anyone because of you, for the LORD your God, He is God in heaven above and on earth beneath" (2:11).

Not only was Rahab gripped by fear; but also deep within her, there was a feminine intuitive sense that there were larger forces at work. It is amazing to find the sensitivities and insights of some people who make no profession of faith in Jesus Christ. In the most confused and evil people, there can be a spark of spiritual sensitivity that when fanned by the breath of the Holy Spirit can burst into hot flames. But I also find myself sadly disillusioned by the lack of wisdom and perception of some of my friends who profess a faith in Jesus Christ but have chosen to block themselves off from reflective observation.

In a self-protective plea, Rahab begged the men to offer a promise of safety for her and her family as repayment for having hidden them from the authorities: "Now therefore, I beg you, swear to me by the LORD, since I have shown you kindness, that you also will show kindness to my father's house, and give me a true token, and spare my father, my mother, my brothers, my sisters, and all that they have, and deliver our lives from death" (vv. 12–13). And the spies agreed to this reciprocity.

The location of Rahab's house made it easy for her to help them escape. Some scholars have surmised that Jericho was surrounded by two walls with a space of twelve to fifteen feet between them, with the inner wall being the strongest. Houses were built over the gap between the two walls, supported by timbers laid from one wall to the other and supported by small crosswalls of bricks. Because of this, Rahab's window probably faced out over the outer wall. She lowered the men by a rope through the window, pointed them toward the hills, urged them to hide in the hills for three days until the pursuers returned, and then cross over the Jordan back toward Shittim.

The spies promised to respect her request to protect her family if she promised to keep secret their visit. They pointed to a scarlet rope and told her to hang it in the window. Any of her family who remained in her house during the conquest would be safe. However, they warned her that if she told anyone about their business, they would not be bound any longer by this oath.

Then the men departed, doing precisely what she had said, finally returning to the camp giving the assurance to Joshua: "Truly the LORD has delivered all the land into our hands, for indeed all the inhabitants of the country are fainthearted because of us" (v. 24).

After Jericho was captured, the first item on the agenda of the two young spies was to rescue Rahab and her entire family prior to destroying the city by fire (6:22–25).

What a fascinating story! Most of us who are preachers and teachers of the Word are quite familiar with it. However, the people with whom we are communicating might not have a ready memory of this story. The name Rahab probably triggers some popular, stereotyped reactions from people, but they usually eclipse the historical narrative. I found that the reading of this entire chapter to the congregation, followed by a fast-moving recapitulation of the story with some additional archaeological insights added to it, provided a helpful setting for the theological grappling and the practical application that would follow.

The communicator can build on this fascinating story, with its potential excitement of an undercover intelligence operation, to capture the attention of those to whom we are communicating, providing a natural bridge to discover specific deep theological and spiritual truths in the story.

I'm convinced that God can use Rahab's story to show *what He can work through anyone who is available to Him.* Trent C. Butler states it in these words:

> The present OT context uses the narrative to give identity and courage to Israel, particularly to Israel without

land and power. That Israelite identity includes the ironic fact that God uses not only his own prophets and leaders to bring faith and courage to disconsolate Israel. God uses the most unexpected and immoral persons to further his purposes in the world. The leadership of Joshua dependent upon Moses is one side of the picture. The power of God to convince even the enemy is the other side. People of God must be open to learn from all sources which God would use. They must always be aware of their own prejudiced tendencies to look to powerful leaders for direction and to fear powerful enemy leaders. Throughout the Bible and church history, God has opened new doors and new opportunities for his people through the most unlikely people. Through it all, God has shown himself able to fulfill the promises he made. He has indeed proved to be the God of heaven above and earth below without competition.[1]

GOD WORKING THROUGH THE ORDINARY AND THE UNLIKELY

2:1 Now Joshua the son of Nun sent out two men from Acacia Grove to spy secretly, saying, "Go, view the land, especially Jericho."

So they went, and came to the house of a harlot named Rahab, and lodged there. ² And it was told the king of Jericho, saying, "Behold, men have come here tonight from the children of Israel to search out the country."

³ So the king of Jericho sent to Rahab, saying, "Bring out the men who have come to you, who have entered your house, for they have come to search out all the country."

⁴ Then the woman took the two men and hid them. So she said, "Yes, the men came to me, but I did not know where they were from. ⁵ And it happened as the gate was being shut, when it was dark, that the men went out. Where the men went I do not know; pursue them quickly, for you may overtake them." ⁶ (But she had brought them up to the roof and hidden them with the stalks of flax, which she had laid in order on the roof.) ⁷ Then the men pursued them by the road to the Jordan, to the fords. And as soon as those who pursued them had gone out, they shut the gate.

—Joshua 2:1–7

Our first major observation is this: God has a way of working through very ordinary and very unlikely people. I take tremendous encouragement from this fact. God does not depend on *Time, Newsweek,* or *U.S. News and World Report* analyses of the most influential men and women in America, in the English-speaking Western society, or even in the world. We are privileged to underline the fact that it's seldom that God makes His primary movement through those people whom you and I would be inclined to call the great "movers and shakers" of the world.

It's a fascinating paradox. On the one hand, God is the sovereign Creator and Sustainer of all that is; on the other hand, God is limited. Whatever our theological orientation may be in the ongoing debate between divine determinism and human initiative, this paradox does exist. God is sovereign; but at the same time, He has, at least to some degree, limited His power by giving free will to all humankind. Some of the most gifted, talented, and prominent people use those resources selfishly for themselves and actually become debilitated by their gifts. Then God has to look elsewhere for help and ends up using people of more modest talents and even questionable reputations. This is reassuring. And I've discovered that the people with whom I share in ministry are especially impressed with this biblical teaching.

This truth can be illustrated in the events following Moses' sending out of the twelve spies. Ten had come back with a negative report. Two had come back with a positive report, but they weren't given the time of day by the Israelites. The people scoffed at their optimism, thus minimizing God's capacity. Forty years later, the ten prominent spies who had carried the majority were dead, leaving only Joshua and Caleb. God had honored the faithfulness of those who had refused to decide with the majority, blessing their lives and ministries.

Now, forty years later, Joshua sends only two men to spy out Jericho. These two were *young* men, and they remain *anonymous.* Our people need to be constantly reminded that God works this way—through ordinary people of no special renown.

I found it helpful to illustrate this idea using my own experience. Nate Babcock is one of these whom God has used in my life. He was a young man in the church where I was raised in Cambridge, Massachusetts. He was one of the few men in the church who was willing to teach Sunday school at the elementary level, because, in the late 1940s and early 1950s, this was mostly viewed as a woman's job. But Nate faithfully taught me and my little group of buddies. He'd take us on special outings and would even bribe us to memorize Bible verses. I can still quote Psalm 103 over three decades later, although the brand-new major league baseball that he gave me as motivation is long lost. Not many people have heard of Nate Babcock. I'm sure there were more charismatic personalities, more knowledgeable men and women, people more mature in their grasp of theology and more inspirational in their potential impact upon youngsters. There were those with greater reputations. But these people were not available; quiet, modest, unassuming Nate was. His impact on my life has been profound.

The same was true of Tom Askew, my high school history teacher. He also loved Jesus Christ, and he challenged me to believe that my interest in politics and my love of the Lord were not incompatible. He encouraged me not only to read my Bible every day but also to read the entire newspaper daily and one major weekly news magazine as part of my Christian responsibility. I'll be indebted to Tom Askew for the rest of my life, as will scores of other high school students who studied under this young, somewhat anonymous, underpaid, struggling Ph.D. candidate who took me and my fellow students seriously.

These two men, in their youth, inexperience, and anonymity, made more of an impact on my life than any well-known preacher or charismatic youth minister I've ever met.

God works through very ordinary and unlikely people, such as the spies. And, there's Rahab, who had four strikes against her.

Strike one: Rahab was a *Canaanite*, not a Jew. Because of her bold act of befriending the spies, she and her extended family became part of Israel. All the Canaanites were not to be labeled "wicked." E. John Hamlin in his book *Inheriting the Land* states, "The Rahab group is a reminder of the fact that there were large bodies of potential allies in that decadent and corrupt city-state society. The 'wickedness' lay in the system in which some oppressed others. Many, however, could find freedom by crossing over to join the kingdom movement."[2]

Strike two: Rahab was a *woman*. An old daily Jewish prayer went like this, "I thank my God that I was not born a woman." This attitude has been demonstrated in patriarchal societies in various ways throughout the centuries. Women have been forced to become militant in Western society to achieve their equal rights. Many do not yet have the opportunity that should be theirs for personal advancement; much less do they receive equal pay for equal work. In many parts of the world, they still live as second-class citizens without the right to vote and, in some cultures, are even considered as objects to be owned. There are still cultures where female babies are subject to infanticide. God worked through this most fascinating person named Rahab, who happened to be a woman. God celebrates femaleness just as much as He does maleness, as both were created equal. This note must sound throughout all of our teaching and preaching in a way that does not patronize women but acknowledges God's affirmation of both female and male in His original creation.

Strike three: Rahab was a *prostitute.* Let's assume it doesn't bother us that God was working through a Canaanite. Not everyone could be an Israelite. Let's even imagine that in the chauvinistic culture of that time (or today) God could work through a woman. But the idea of God working through a prostitute? That may present problems— if not for us, for some of those with whom we are endeavoring to communicate. We need to stress that God sees potential in every single one of us, and He wants to make the most of that potential. As much as some will resist this truth, others, struggling with guilt and broken dreams, will find enormous relief and renewed hope as we develop this reassuring principle.

Some writers try to portray Rahab as a cultic prostitute, tied into the Canaanite fertility goddess worship. This seems unlikely as there was another Hebrew word to describe a religious prostitute. Most likely, Rahab and her family came from the poor segment of Jericho's society. The flax on the roof of her house gives the impression that her family lived by agriculture outside the city. The flax bundles were probably hauled up on the roof through the window, perhaps by the same rope by which the spies were lowered. Her family might have worked the land of some noble who supplied the flax for the linen workers, such as those mentioned in 1 Chronicles 4:21, who would in turn produce linen for the garments of the priests and the upper-class people of Jericho (Is. 3:16, 23). Rahab's house on the wall would serve as a place for her family to stay when they were in the city.

Rahab had, probably out of economic necessity, earned a living as a prostitute. Like most prostitutes, she lived on the edge of society. In ancient cities, as today, Rahab's occupational group was tolerated, but they went entirely without recognition, unless it was in the highly honored, self-lived prominence of cultic religious prostitution.

God has a way of working through the most ordinary and unlikely people who live very much on the edge of social respectability. Jesus attracted these to His inner circle.

Strike four: Rahab was *dishonest.* Some people excuse lying in some situations. I struggle with this as an ethical dilemma. Are there occasions when dishonesty is the highest ethic, such as times of war when one's own loved ones are threatened with illegal arrest and punishment? At what point is a "situational ethic" part of the biblical witness? I read passages in which I am instructed to let my "yea be yea and my nay be nay." If I had to lean any one direction, it would be toward a strict interpretation of the biblical admonitions toward honesty. I believe that God calls us to be people of integrity.

Yet here we have a strange combination. Rahab is a harlot and a liar who at the same time is a person of faith. Perhaps this is because the light often comes gradually and slowly to people like Rahab and, frankly, like a lot of us. The conscience is slowly enlightened. How many people were slaveholders after they became Christians? John Newton continued for some time in the slave trade, exporting his cargoes of fellow human beings, stolen from their homes, before he awoke to sense his sin and crime. No wonder he later wrote the words: "Amazing grace! How sweet the sound that saved a wretch like me! I once was lost, but now am found, was blind but now I see."

I have no question that Rahab changed both her profession and her ethics as she threw in her lot with God's people. But there can be no doubt as to how she was living when she first came into contact with the Israelites. Rahab was on the outermost circle of faith, just touching the boundaries. But the nearer she would come to the Lord, the more she would recoil from her previous lifestyle. Nonetheless, God is able to use the most unlikely of us— and, in the process, transform us.

Rahab was *a most unusual mother.* She came through quite a pilgrimage. She married, settled down, and raised a family and actually became one of the ancestors of Jesus Christ on Joseph's side. We need to emphasize the fact that she is listed in Christ's genealogy in Matthew 1:5–6: "Salmon begot Boaz by Rahab, Boaz begot Obed by Ruth, Obed begot Jesse, and Jesse begot David the king."

Rahab was a most unusual woman. Not only is she included in the lineage of Jesus, but she is also lauded as an *example of living faith* in Hebrews 11:31 and is *affirmed for her good works* in James 2:25.

What outstanding evidence of God's capacity to work through very ordinary and unlikely people. This could be restated in the words of E. John Hamlin:

Rahab was a paradigm of hope, showing that the old idols, the old corrupt ways of the past, could be given up. What Rahab did just before the fall of Jericho, Israel could do before [or after] the fall of Jerusalem. The contrast between Rahab at the bottom of the social scale and the king and nobles of Jericho at the top illustrates well what Jesus said: "Harlots go into the kingdom of God before you" (Matt. 21:31).[3]

RAHAB—A WORTHWHILE MODEL

[8] Now before they lay down, she came up to them on the roof, [9] and said to the men: "I know that the LORD has given you the land, that the terror of you has fallen on us, and that all the inhabitants of the land are fainthearted because of you. [10] For we have heard how the LORD dried up the water of the Red Sea for you when you came out of Egypt, and what you did to the two kings of the Amorites who were on the other side of the Jordan, Sihon and Og, whom you utterly destroyed. [11] And as soon as we heard these things, our hearts melted; neither did there remain any more courage in anyone because of you, for the LORD your God, He is God in heaven above and on earth beneath. [12] Now therefore, I beg you, swear to me by the LORD, since I have shown you kindness, that you also will show kindness to my father's house, and give me a true token, [13] and spare my father, my mother, my brothers, my sisters, and all that they have, and deliver our lives from death."

[14] So the men answered her, "Our lives for yours, if none of you tell this business of ours. And it shall be, when the LORD has given us the land, that we will deal kindly and truly with you."

[15] Then she let them down by a rope through the window, for her house was on the city wall; she dwelt on the wall. [16] And she said to them, "Get to the mountain, lest the pursuers meet you. Hide there three days, until the pursuers have returned. Afterward you may go your way."

[17] So the men said to her: "We will be blameless of this oath of yours which you have made us swear, [18] unless, when we come into the land, you bind this line of scarlet cord in the window through which you let us down, and unless you bring your father, your mother, your brothers, and all your father's household to your own home. [19] So it shall be that whoever

goes outside the doors of your house into the street, his blood shall be on his own head, and we will be guiltless. And whoever is with you in the house, his blood shall be on our head if a hand is laid on him. [20] And if you tell this business of ours, then we will be free from your oath which you made us swear."

[21] Then she said, "According to your words, so be it." And she sent them away, and they departed. And she bound the scarlet cord in the window.

[22] They departed and went to the mountain, and stayed there three days until the pursuers returned. The pursuers sought them all along the way, but did not find them. [23] So the two men returned, descended from the mountain, and crossed over; and they came to Joshua the son of Nun, and told him all that had befallen them. [24] And they said to Joshua, "Truly the LORD has delivered all the land into our hands, for indeed all the inhabitants of the country are faint-hearted because of us."

—*Joshua 2:8–24*

Not only does this chapter of Joshua emphasize our first major observation that God works through very ordinary and very unlikely people. It also brings us to a second observation. Rahab is worth having as a model. There are five particular qualities in Rahab's life that can be very instructive in practical ways.

First, Rahab had a *street-smart openness to truth* from wherever it came. She was faithful to what little light she did have. I need to learn from her because I have an inclination to live with a closed mind. I like to have everything neatly packaged. I don't want my security shaken. My desire for order and symmetry can cause me to live my life boxed in—and boxes are limiting.

Rahab and her fellow citizens of Jericho had heard about the Jews, whom we see as the underdogs. This isn't necessarily always true. It is true that the citizens of Jericho would have been alarmed by that huge encampment across the river. Rumors have a way of getting to the enemy side also. Rahab had heard about the Red Sea drying up and how the Israelites had defeated the two Amorite kings. But she was unwilling to be paralyzed by fear. In her own embryonic way, she was prepared to think theologically. Who are these people? Their God must be powerful. Rahab's questions were a great starting point for her faith. She was open to truth. As communicators, we need to expand our own parameters of thought. And part of our prophetic ministry is to challenge our people to a lifestyle of growth, as threatening as that lifestyle can be.

We need to challenge ourselves, and those with whom we communicate, to be willing to be surprised by God. Perhaps it was because she was a prostitute that Rahab was looking for something better.

Rahab might simply have been an open person who saw a need for change in her life. Perhaps things were not functional the way they were. Perhaps she was a very religious person seeking true spiritual reality or a cause more worthy than any she had experienced before. She could have been just fascinated by these two young men—Hebrew foreigners who weren't interested in using her body. She'd never met men like these before. Their God must not only be a God of great power, victorious in battle, He might also be a God who could bring to her a new beginning, a new ethic, a new self-esteem.

It's exciting to talk to an open-minded person. One day, I was watching the workmen erect the structural steel for our new church sanctuary. One of the neighbors walked up. He peppered me with one question after another—first about the building program and then about the church. Then he asked me why I was in the ministry. Then he had questions about Jesus Christ. He also asked me about people he knew at work and in the neighborhood who also claimed to be Christians, and he reflected on their struggles and their affirmations. No, he wasn't yet a Christian. Yes, he did accept my invitation to sometime attend St. Andrew's. Yes, he was a seeker for truth. That's what's important. We are reassured in Scripture that if with all our heart we seek the Lord we will find Him. Jesus said, "Seek and ye shall find. Knock and it will be opened."

Second, Rahab had the *courage to make a tough decision*. She didn't have a lot of time to think things through. She'd heard about the Jews, and now there were two in her house. She was available immediately to do the job of hiding them.

Our availability to God can change the whole future of our lives and perhaps the lives of others. Our availability to God involves a decision on our part. Are we going to be available to Him? Are we willing to take action? Are we willing to pledge ourselves to Him without all the answers? I know people who are immobilized for a lifetime by indecision. They are masters of the "do-nothing decision." They muse and philosophize forever. Once we have settled some of these basic decisions, we have God's prophetic mandate to challenge those to whom we preach and teach to make clear-cut decisions for Christ. We are to point out the fallacy that the apostle Paul referred to as "always learning and never able to come to the knowledge of the truth" (2 Tim. 3:7).

Third, Rahab was *willing to join a new family*—the family of God. She probably didn't fully understand the significance of the scarlet rope that the spies told her to hang from her window any more than did all the Jews who were saved out of Egypt understand the significance of the blood splashed over their doorways. They came to understand in the years ahead the significance of the blood sacrifice in the ordinance of the Passover. Perhaps the scarlet cord had in its color a significance that reached forward in history to the blood atonement of Jesus Christ. It might have been simply her way of "tying a yellow ribbon on the old oak tree," signifying her identity, love, and trust for a people and a God she was only beginning to know.

For Rahab, the scarlet rope was sacramental. It was an outward sign of an inner work of grace which God was bringing to pass in her life. It was a sign that she believed God to be God. She wasn't just going to add one more god to her pantheon of Canaanite gods. Rahab was willing to put aside all these gods for the one true God whom she would grow to know much more intimately in the future. How surprised she would be at first to realize that someday this God would enable her to get her whole life together in such a way that she and her loved ones would become an integral part of the Jewish family. Her name would go down in history not only as a harlot but also as a prostitute saved by the grace of God and one of the world's most unusual mothers—the mother of Boaz— which made her the great-great-grandmother of King David, one of the direct ancestors of Joseph, the husband of Mary to whom Jesus was born.

Fourth, Rahab had a *loyalty to her own human family.* What a virtue! She was willing to persuade them to trust her and her newfound God, and she assumed responsibility not just for herself but for her loved ones. Rahab ran a risk of their exposing of her as a traitor, as an enemy within the gates of her own native city.

Our loved ones need to know what we believe. They deserve the right to see the seriousness of our love for Christ and to know that this love makes us all the more loyal to them. What an alternative is Christian motherhood to the secular approach.

I've been fascinated by the actress Shirley MacLaine, obviously a very gifted woman. How brilliant she is, yet how confused. In a

Time magazine interview, she characterized her daughter Sachi's birth as "an accident." She said she "never" considered having another child. She added, "I never really embraced the label motherhood. I chose to call it personhood . . . Sachi and I are very close persons to each other. I let her grow up: she knows that anything she does is O.K. with me."[4]

What we see in the confused family loyalties of the secular entertainment world is also reflected at the other end of the economic spectrum in the black community. The NAACP and the National Urban League are deeply concerned about the breakdown of the American black family. It's of crisis proportion.

Those of us who do not relate either to the upper strata of the entertainment world or the lowest level of the black ghetto have our own malady. The absent, white, upper middle-class parent is so intent on professional advancement, economic gain, and career recognition that the home is emptied of both father and mother. This means the home is without any viable substitute for intimacy, nurture, worship, and ultimate concern conveying a sense of the solidarity of the family and the specialness and importance to that family unit of each individual.

Rahab loved her family. The scarlet cord was not appropriated just for herself but for all those who were willing to join her in faith.

Fifth, Rahab had a *lasting faith in the Lord.* Perseverance! She had met the conditions of faith and was willing to follow through. Now she had to conform her ways to God's ways, not just in the initial salvation of her life but in her whole new identity. No longer a prostitute or a Canaanite, Rahab was now a proselyte, one who became part of the Hebrew community, a believer in the Lord. There was a new moral, spiritual, and social framework within her for living. Rahab fleshed out what it is for a person to "become a new creature in Christ."

We are privileged to communicate the story of Rahab, one who became the ultimate example of what the apostle Paul described as happening time after time when he wrote to the Corinthians:

> Do you not know that the unrighteous will not inherit the kingdom of God? Do not be deceived. Neither fornicators, nor idolaters, nor adulterers, nor homosexuals, nor sodomites, nor thieves, nor covetous, nor drunkards, nor revilers, nor extortioners will inherit the kingdom of

God. And such were some of you. But you were washed, but you were sanctified, but you were justified in the name of the Lord Jesus and by the Spirit of our God (1 Cor. 6:9–11).

What a privilege it is to convey in our preaching and teaching that God is in the business of working through very ordinary and unlikely people, producing in each one of us qualities of His new creation, starting with us right where we are.

NOTES

1. Trent Butler, *Joshua*, Word Biblical Commentary (Waco, TX: Word Books, 1983), 7:35.

2. E. John Hamlin, *Inheriting the Land* (Grand Rapids, Mich.: Wm. B. Eerdmans, 1983), pp. 16–17.

3. Ibid., p. 18.

4. Elaine Dutka and Denise Worrell, "The Best Year of Her Lives," *Time*, May 14, 1984, pp. 60–70.

CHAPTER FOUR—THE CROSSOVER PEOPLE
JOSHUA 3:1–17

Scripture Outline

Those Crossover Times (3:1–4)

An Action Pattern for a Crossover People (3:5–17)

The spies have returned from Jericho, and their favorable report has been received. Joshua orders the Israelites to set out from Shittim to the edge of the Jordan River and wait for further instructions. After the people arrive at the Jordan, his instructions are given over a three-day period.

Some commentators make a major point of this three-day waiting period on the east bank of the Jordan. They identify this time mentioned in Joshua 3:2 with the three-day period mentioned in chapter 1, verse 11. The story of the spies and Rahab (2:1–24) is viewed as having happened during the same three-day interval as Joshua's interaction with the people written in Joshua 1:10–18 happened chronologically after the Israelites' move to the Jordan's edge (3:1–2). Most of the commentators do not even try to harmonize these two references to a three-day period. They may be identical periods of time or two different three-day periods.

Several commentators emphasize the significance of this apparent delay in crossing the Jordan. They see it not only as a period of time during which the spies made their reconnaissance and Joshua briefed the people. They also see it as having some significance in terms of the events related in chapter 5, which deals with certain sacramental rights that were carried out after the crossing at Gilgal which involved the celebration of Passover. I will discuss this view in more detail in chapter 6.

At the end of this three-day period, the twelve Levitical priests carry the ark of the covenant down into the Jordan River. They stand still in the middle of the river where the waters have stopped, leaving the river bed dry. After the people sanctify themselves in preparation to cross the Jordan, they follow the priests into the river at a distance, not getting too near the ark. God restates His promise to be with His people and to give them the land.

While the twelve priests hold the ark high in the middle of the Jordan, the waters piled up on the north side, the Israelites pass over into Canaan. Twelve ceremonial rocks are then piled in the middle of the Jordan before the waters return, while twelve more rocks are carried to the west bank for a memorial ceremony at Gilgal. Now that the Israelites are safe on the west bank, the priests carry the ark forward to join the rest of the nation. The waters sweep back into the river bed flooding their way several miles southward into the Dead Sea.

Within this story, there are two very significant theological observations that must be made and applied to our Christian lives as lived today. One of these observations deals with the memorial stones and the subject of memories. I will develop this further in chapter 5. The other observation deals with the kind of people that God wanted the Israelites to be and also yearns for us to be.

This sovereign God, who can part the waters, is a God who called Israel then, and us today, to be a "crossover people."

THOSE CROSSOVER TIMES

3:1 Then Joshua rose early in the morning; and they set out from Acacia Grove and came to the Jordan, he and all the children of Israel, and lodged there before they crossed over. ² So it was, after three days, that the officers went through the camp; ³ and they commanded the people, saying, "When you see the ark of the covenant of the LORD your God, and the priests, the Levites, bearing it, then you shall set out from your place and go after it. ⁴ Yet there shall be a space between you and it, about two thousand cubits by measure. Do not come near it, that you may know the way by which you must go, for you have not passed this way before."

—Joshua 3:1–4

Every life has its *crossover* times. Some people call them the "peak" experiences, but they are times of transition—often fraught with potential disaster. They are the times in life so familiar to those of the people of Israel capsuled in the phrase *"for you have not passed this way before"* (v. 4).

This was a traumatic time for Israel. The Israelites had spent forty years wandering in the wilderness. They were accustomed to that way of life. It must have been unpleasant, for the few days I've spent in the Sinai Peninsula and in the Negev have convinced me that just about any place on earth would be a better place to live. One of the astronauts, who has both walked on the moon and been to the Sinai Peninsula, has observed that the most comparable place on earth to the lunar terrain is the Sinai Peninsula.

Not everyone would agree with this somewhat negative appraisal. The nomads who live in that desolate land, for example, know where the springs are and how to find those places of oasis. They would panic if they had to move to a more lush, habitable place. The human inclination is to get used to one's natural and familiar habitat. Change doesn't come easy to anyone. There's always the resistance factor.

But the Israelites moved around frequently. Their journey began in Goshen near Rameses in Egypt and continued from the shore of the Red Sea, where the Hebrews were commanded to "go forward." The verb *nāsaʿ*—the Hebrew word for "journeyed"—is used (Ex. 14:15). Another translation of this word is "set out." There was this constant "going onward" with the Israelites. The word *nāsaʿ* is used eighty-nine times in the Book of Numbers. In the Book of Joshua, however, this word occurs only three times— once when Joshua and the people "set out" from Shittim (3:1) and twice when they "set out" from the east bank to cross the Jordan (vv. 3, 14). Crossing the Jordan meant the *arrival*, toward which the Exodus *departure* and the wilderness experience of covenant and training had been the preparation. The crossing was the fulfillment of God's promise to the patriarchs at the very beginning.

Now the word *ʿābar*—meaning to "cross over" or to "pass over"—is used twenty-one times in the story of the crossing (3:1— 5:1). This verb emphasizes the decisive nature of this moment in the history of the Hebrew people and distinguishes it from everything that had gone before. The word was never used to describe the passage through the waters of the Red Sea. Other Hebrew words were used that meant "enter" or "walk."

The word *ʿābar* connotes something with tremendous epic significance. To put it in the words of E. John Hamlin in his book *Inheriting the Land*:

> The reason for this is that the verb *ʿābar* implies crossing over a boundary, whether physical like a river valley

(Deut. 2:13–14), political like a nation's border (Deut. 2:18) or moral, as to enter a covenant (Deut. 29:12) or transgress a commandment (Deut. 26:13; Joshua 7:11, 15).

While walking through the waters of the Red Sea was both an escape and a liberation, crossing over Jordan meant entering a new kind of life in the Promised Land. The physical boundary formed by the deep rift of the Jordan Valley and River had to be crossed. More than that, the crossing marked a decisive transition which involved inheriting (acquiring tenancy rights) and finding "rest."

The land of Canaan was not an earthly paradise or a transcendent existence in which there would be no problems but a place where the whole nature of what it is to be God's people would have to be worked out. There would be the pain of failure and the joy of success. Canaan represented a great improvement over the past four hundred years, but it was not utopia.

Our lives, along with those of the people with whom we are endeavoring to communicate, have those occasional ʿābar times—those crossover experiences which can be frightening. This biblical narrative gives us a magnificent opportunity to identify with these crisis moments that we share with others. One of the most exciting experiences I've ever had as a pastor was to preach on this text, challenging my congregation as a community and as individuals to be an ʿābar people—a crossover people. I challenged them to be willing not just to "set out" each day in a regular routine, but instead to face those dangerous moments of a new beginning, willing to "cross over" into whatever new faith experiences and faith "land" God has in store.

The crossing over to Canaan was a brand-new experience for all the Israelites, except Caleb and Joshua—the only ones who had experienced the escape from Egypt through the Red Sea. The rest of the Israelites stood at the banks of the Jordan River during the flood season. This was a terrifying experience. Most of us are familiar with long wilderness experiences to which we've become accustomed. There are moments in which we stand shuddering at the edge of the Jordan, knowing that before us are rushing waters, the fortress city of Jericho, chariots of iron, and even giants in the land. As leaders, we tend to be conservative, as do our people. We don't have the natural openness that marked the life of Rahab.

The nature of her business caused her to take risks. This doesn't tend to be the nature of very many clergy and the majority of comfortable people who sit in comfortable pews. We are determined to hold on to the familiar. God wants to break through our constitutional conservatism and to help us become the *ʿābar* people—people who are willing to grow and expand, claiming new territory, inheriting the future He has in store.

List the *ʿābar* times, the crossover times in your life. Birth would be one. Some crisis in childhood may be another. Those important decisions we make in our teenage years have that quality. What college should I go to? What career should be mine? Should I marry? Whom should I marry? What job should I accept? Then we tend to settle down, don't we? A crisis may come. A painful divorce. A financial failure that seriously alters our lifestyle. Or perhaps a financial success that thrusts us into a potentially altered lifestyle. How do we handle a crossover experience and the fear of the unknown that it brings?

Some of us create an artificial crossover time. It may be at age forty or perhaps at fifty. We begin to think of old age. Frankly, there is no such thing. Try to tell that to the majority of the people in our culture, and they'll laugh at you. The Bible has no theology of retirement. You and I have the privilege of looking into the mirror every morning and seeing not a young face or an old face but a human being created in the image of God who was never more alive and never will be more alive in this life than we are at the present moment. Live every day to the fullest. Don't get locked in by your age. You are never too young. Don't let anyone despise your youth. You are never too old. And you as a preacher have the privilege of challenging your people with some of these thoughts. Why not tell them some stories out of your own life and out of the lives of those close to you?

Disease is one of these very significant crossover times. At this moment, several of my dear friends are struggling with cancer. One man is in his thirties; another is in his forties. Another friend is in his fifties. It's a frightening new pathway for them. Fear will not diminish the danger. But we are privileged to remind the people we serve that every pathway that is new for us is not new to our God. As we stand on the bank of that Jordan River in our lives, we all need to remember that our God is capable of making a way through that Jordan. He will walk through it with us, keeping our feet on dry ground. Even in the darkest hour of sickness, there can be a joy that is unspeakable. I love the way Charles Haddon

Spurgeon stated it: "What if I must weep to-morrow, yet will I sing to-day, and mayhap my song will gather such force, that some of its stanzas will overleap tomorrow, and I may sweeten my sighs with my psalms."[2]

Death itself is another one of these ʿābar moments. Christ has assured us that He has taken the sting out of death. The victory is His. Christ walks through that Jordan with us.

Another crossover time is that moment of spiritual decision when we open our lives to Jesus Christ in repentance and receive His forgiveness and grace. It's the moment in which we rededicate our lives to Him after days, months, or perhaps even years of wandering in our own spiritual wilderness. Once again, we're crossing over into the Promised Land, inheriting the promises God has given to us. Our people need to be reminded of the importance of spiritual decisions, of the willingness to take risks, of new commitments to Jesus Christ, as threatening and even frightening as some of these may be.

This crossover lifestyle also has implications for a community. I am convinced that too much of our talk about the Christian life is individualistic. Not only Joshua claimed the peak moment, but also the people, the nation of Israel, claimed it. They had been a ragtag people in Egypt, growing in numbers but slipping deeper and deeper into slavery. They had maintained some limited tribal identity which was deepened during the Exodus and the wilderness experience.

Many congregations are at the bank of the Jordan River. We are privileged to confront and challenge our people with the frightening but thrilling opportunities available at such moments. It is fascinating to discover that the crossover times—the ʿābar times—are ones fraught with tremendous potential difficulties. But this makes it all the more possible for God to show His power.

Actually, the Jordan River is not too difficult to cross most of the year. Many picture the "mighty Jordan" to be something like the Mississippi or the Columbia Rivers. It's actually a modest stream compared to those rivers. But it was a huge barrier to the Israelites camped along the east bank. For four hundred years, the Hebrew people had dreamed of the Promised Land. For forty years, they had fantasized about what lay beyond the river but also cultivated deep fears of the giants in the land. In addition to their fears, God brought them to the Jordan intentionally at the time of year when the river was swollen by the spring rains and the melting snows from the Lebanon mountains. The river could not be forded by the normal means, which for the boatless Hebrews would have been difficult yet possible. To cross during this floodtide was unthinkable with their resources.

It is in moments such as these that we are privileged to be the crossover people.

AN ACTION PATTERN FOR A CROSSOVER PEOPLE

[5] And Joshua said to the people, "Sanctify yourselves, for tomorrow the LORD will do wonders among you." [6] Then Joshua spoke to the priests, saying, "Take up the ark of the covenant and cross over before the people."

So they took up the ark of the covenant and went before the people.

[7] And the LORD said to Joshua, "This day I will begin to exalt you in the sight of all Israel, that they may know that, as I was with Moses, so I will be with you. [8] You shall command the priests who bear the ark of the covenant, saying, 'When you have come to the edge of the water of the Jordan, you shall stand in the Jordan.' "

[9] So Joshua said to the children of Israel, "Come here, and hear the words of the LORD your God." [10] And Joshua said, "By this you shall know that the living God is among you, and that He will without fail drive out from before you the Canaanites and the Hittites and the Hivites and the Perizzites and the Girgashites and the Amorites and the Jebusites: [11] Behold, the ark of the covenant of the Lord of all the earth is crossing over before you into the Jordan. [12] Now therefore, take for yourselves twelve men from the tribes of Israel, one man from every tribe. [13] And it shall come to pass, as soon as the soles of the feet of the priests who bear the ark of the LORD, the Lord of all the earth, shall rest in the waters of the Jordan, that the waters of the Jordan shall be cut off, the waters that come down from upstream, and they shall stand as a heap."

[14] So it was, when the people set out from their camp to cross over the Jordan, with the priests bearing the ark of the covenant before the people, [15] and as those who bore the ark came to the Jordan, and the feet of the priests who bore the ark dipped in the edge of the water (for the Jordan overflows all its banks during the whole time of harvest), [16] that the waters which came down from upstream stood still, and rose in a heap very far away at Adam, the city that is beside Zaretan. So the waters that went down into the Sea of the

Arabah, the Salt Sea, failed, and were cut off; and the people crossed over opposite Jericho. ¹⁷ Then the priests who bore the ark of the covenant of the LORD stood firm on dry ground in the midst of the Jordan; and all Israel crossed over on dry ground, until all the people had crossed completely over the Jordan.

—Joshua 3:5–17

Three specific instructions are given to the Israelites waiting at the edge of the Jordan River. We could call these action-pattern orders which marked the lives of a crossover people who were open to God's leading.

The first action-pattern order is: *Follow the Lord.* This is stated in a strange sort of way. Up until now, during their time in the wilderness, the people of Israel followed the cloud by day and the pillar of fire by night. Now these two divinely instituted symbols have been removed. The ark of the covenant takes their place: "When you see the ark of the covenant of the LORD your God, and the priests, the Levites, bearing it, then you shall set out from your place and go after it. Yet there shall be a space between you and it, about two thousand cubits by measure. Do not come near it, that you may know the way by which you must go, for you have not passed this way before" (vv. 3–4).

The ark is mentioned fifteen times in chapters 3 and 4. This religious object has fascinated many people through the last three thousand plus years, even inspiring movies such as *Raiders of the Lost Ark.* A large box containing sacred objects, the ark was seen as the portable throne of the invisible God. The ark of the covenant contained the Ten Commandments given to Moses on Mount Sinai (Deut. 10:1–5) or even the whole book of the covenant teaching (Deut. 31:24–26). In this way, the ark symbolized the commands of the covenant that God had established with the people of Israel. This whole covenant relationship—an entire way of life—went with them as they crossed over the Jordan. Inside the ark was also a jar of manna, reminding the people of how God had taken care of them during the wilderness experience.

The ark symbolized the presence of the Lord with His people. They had to be certain of divine leadership, and the ark was the sign that God was leading them. They were not just a migratory people optimistically yet futilely thinking they could go into the land of Canaan. They were God's people being led by God.

The ark also symbolized the specific teachings and direction that God had given to His people. They had the assurance of His direction over the untrodden and unfamiliar way ahead of them. God would teach them what they needed to know as they traveled into Canaan.

It's also fascinating to note that the people were ordered to keep a specific distance of two thousand cubits (approximately one thousand yards) from the ark. Some would say that this was to keep a separateness between the people and the holy God. There is some precedence for this in the Scriptures for one was not to touch the ark, treating lightly the things of God. More significant, at this moment, was the importance of staying far enough away from the ark so that it could be seen as it was held up during the crossing of the Jordan. The ark was to lead the way into these untrodden paths. Then as the people crossed over the Jordan onto dry ground, they were able to look into the piled-up waters, trusting God to keep the path dry until all of them were across. It was by the power of God that they were able to cross into the land.

If we are to be a crossover people, we need to keep our eyes fixed on Jesus Christ. Every time new members join the church I serve, I remind them that the pastors and elders of the church are given responsibilities to set a godly example. But the church does not belong to the pastors and the elders; it belongs to Jesus Christ. Our feet are clay, and He is the only One who will not let them down. Only Christ is capable of leading us across the difficult waters, providing the ultimate direction. This is why we need to know His Word and why obedience is so critical. We are claiming the Promised Land. We are following the Leader. We are obedient to His Word. We live in relationship with Him, but we must not let the distinction blur between the creature and the Creator.

The second action-pattern order is: *Sanctify yourselves.*

God gave specific directions for ceremonial cleanliness in the Old Testament times. Building on this, Joshua said to the people, *"Sanctify yourselves, for tomorrow the LORD will do wonders among you"* (v. 5).

Whenever we face new opportunities, God's voice tells us to "sanctify yourselves." Then and now God calls His people to holiness, purity, and separation. For the Israelites on the edge of the Jordan, I imagine this meant that they would wash themselves with water and practice the ceremonial rites that would make them clean. For us today, this means that we should come afresh to claim the cleansing of the precious blood of Jesus Christ which washes away all sin, all uncleanness. It also means opening ourselves increasingly as the Holy Spirit enables us to be used by God.

It is so special to see men and women opening themselves increasingly to God's presence in their lives. A number have sought me out individually as their pastor, confessing particular sins that have held them in tight clutches over a period of years, asking for prayers of release from that bondage, praying for God's cleansing from that uncleanliness. God has chosen not to work in all His fullness in the lives of people who are unwilling to open their hearts to His cleansing and to His leadership. I'm struck by the phrase in the opening prayer in the Presbyterian wedding ceremony that reads, "Sanctify them, making them fit for their new estate." This simply describes an *'ābar* moment, a crossover time of marriage, in which two people need a special cleansing as they inherit God's promises.

The third action-pattern order is: *Follow courageous leadership.* Our leaders are to be the first ones to place their feet in the water.

> *"Now therefore, take for yourselves twelve men from the tribes of Israel, one man from every tribe. And it shall come to pass, as soon as the soles of the feet of the priests who bear the ark of the LORD, the Lord of all the earth, shall rest in the waters of the Jordan, that the waters of the Jordan shall be cut off, the waters that come down from upstream, and they shall stand as a heap"* (vv. 12–13).

This is not the traditional custom of priests. We clergy do not usually lead the people in hazardous undertakings. Most of us are often more content with the status quo. But God instructs us to be in the vanguard of change. God will ask nothing of our people that He does not first ask of us. We must urge our people to hold us accountable to this principle.

We are to stay with the enterprise, to continue holding up the ark so that others can see it. They should look for and expect spiritual qualities in those who have been called to serve them. The clergy will never be perfect in this life, but we must hold each other accountable to disallow ambition, greed, and a desire for fame. These temptations are natural to those in positions of leadership. God calls us to faithfulness, though. We are to symbolize the bringing together of the divergent component parts of the community as did the twelve priests who held up the ark, symbolic of the twelve tribes who had become fused together as one nation. Don't stay back on the east side of the Jordan. Be one of the crossover people, urging those with whom you communicate to also be crossover persons.

I love the final words of this chapter, which really do present the basic text for a sermon or lesson: *"Then the priests who bore the ark of the covenant of the LORD stood firm on dry ground in the midst of the Jordan; and all Israel crossed over on dry ground, until all the people had crossed completely over the Jordan"* (v. 17).

God's promises are now being fleshed out not only in the life of Israel but also in the life of each one of us who is willing to follow Him, to be sanctified, and to follow courageous human leadership. As I think of this text, the words of William Williams in his great hymn, "Guide Me, O Thou Great Jehovah," keep throbbing through my heart and mind:

> When I tread the verge of Jordan,
> Bid my anxious fears subside;
> Death of death, and hell's destruction,
> Land me safe on Canaan's side;
> Songs of praises, songs of praises
> I will ever give to Thee,
> I will ever give to Thee.

NOTES

1. Hamlin, *Inheriting the Land*, p. 23.

2. Spurgeon, *The Treasury of the Bible*, 1:516.

CHAPTER FIVE—THE IMPORTANCE OF MEMORIES

JOSHUA 4:1–24

Scripture Outline

Memory Stones (4:1–14)

What Do These Stones Mean? (4:15–24)

We will never be more alive in this life than we are right now. One of the great biblical affirmations with which we begin many a worship service is the statement "This is the day which the Lord hath made. Let us rejoice and be glad in it." A Christian is a "now" person.

I know many people who refuse to live in the present. Several of them are *past oriented* and are ultraconservative. Their lives are fueled by nostalgia. They yearn for a return to the "good old days" (which I can't believe were as good as they remember them to be).

Other people are *future oriented.* They are radicals who are discontent with the present and are planning to change everything. It makes little difference what gets destroyed for they see very little value in the present order. They are dedicated to breaking down social conventions; nothing is sacrosanct. If they have their way, human society will be radicalized.

The problem with the ultraconservative and the ultraradical is that both are escaping from the present into a fantasy world. The present isn't perfect, but neither was the past nor will the future be on this earth. I'm convinced that both the ultraconservative and the ultraradical are hungrily searching for meaning—a meaning that tends to elude them.

A major biblical theme is that we are privileged to live in the present—one day at a time—claiming the Lord's meaning and strength for the immediate day.

This fourth chapter of Joshua, however, grapples with the fact that a basic component of life is a hope for the future that is based on the memories of the past—which help bring meaning to the present. *Memories are important!* They are the soil of our present experiences into which our roots sink deeply and from which we receive nourishment. The superstructures of our lives are built upon the foundation of our memories. We are instructed by our memories as to the most creative way to live in the present, and they help equip us with a positive hope for the future.

Most people are somewhat familiar with Murphy's Law: If anything can possibly go wrong, it will go wrong. There's a corollary to this—Harvey Klotz's Law, which says, "Murphy was an optimist!"

Professor Leonard J. Bowman developed or "discovered" what he calls Murphy's Decalogue while teaching at Marycrest College in Davenport, Iowa. Although written with some of the whimsy of Murphy's Law, it has a degree of theological depth. I first ran across it in Martin Marty's commentary on the interaction of religion and culture titled *Context.* The list reads:

1. If anything can be misunderstood or misinterpreted, it will be, and in the most grotesque possible manner.

2. The person with the most serious of intentions is liable to make the most serious of misinterpretations.

3. The more grotesque the misinterpretation, the more tenaciously it will be defended.

4. If anything is essential to the meaning of a religious tradition, that is what will be forgotten.

5. The religious leaders of a tradition are liable to be among the first to forget and the last to remember. (5.1. Eventually someone will remember. 5.1.1. But only partially.)

6. Given a key word in an authoritative tradition, the word will remain constant and its meaning variable.

7. Given a new religious expression, its wisdom will tend to be overlooked by later generations and its folly perpetuated.

8. The clearer and more sensible the expression, the less trustworthy the insight.

9. For any religious tradition, what is obvious to the scholar will be incomprehensible to the believer and vice versa.

10. The inner thoughts of simple believers contain more wisdom than the tomes of theologians. (10.1. No one knows the inner thoughts of simple believers.)[1]

Underneath the whimsy of Bowman's observations is a fairly deep truth. If there is anything essential to the meaning of a religious tradition, that is what will be forgotten, and the religious leaders are likely to be among the first to forget and the last to remember. The more seriously we take the faith and endeavor to protect the religious institution, the easier it is to lose touch with the basic elementary principles of the faith.

For example, we can be such defenders of theological truth that we lose the spirit of love. Smoothly running an institutional structure can be so important that we forget the people whom that structure is to serve. We may concentrate so much on maintaining a sense of kindness and acceptance that we lose sight of basic truths that must not be forgotten. We can become so involved in the building of buildings that we forget the mission that is to be carried out within those buildings. Statistical dynamics of budgets and membership enrollments and attendances can so preoccupy us that we forget that God does not evaluate success on the basis of numbers.

Christian life is to be lived in the present, not to be a captive of the past or the future. However, I'm pressured by the pragmatic demands of my contemporary ministry to produce verifiable results in the present in such a way that the very truth of living one day at a time can become the heresy of a rootless existence. I see other pastors who have apparently cut themselves free from an accountability to the historic dimension of their faith and/or from an accountability to what results their pragmatic actions in the future will bring. The part of me that wants to succeed craves to accommodate the *now mentality* so as to produce measurable success, to impress significant others who view my ministry.

I am convinced that the same struggle that is mine, and perhaps yours, is the struggle of the people whom we serve and with whom we desire to communicate. They, too, in their way, can get caught up in this confusion of values. They, too, want to live creatively, successfully in the present, avoiding that ultraconservatism of a past orientation and that radicalism of a future orientation. In the process, they, too, can lose their moorings.

MEMORY STONES

4:1 And it came to pass, when all the people had completely crossed over the Jordan, that the LORD spoke to Joshua, saying: [2] "Take for yourselves twelve men from the people, one man from every tribe, [3] and command them, saying, 'Take for yourselves twelve stones from here, out of the midst of the Jordan, from the place where the priests' feet stood firm. You shall carry them over with you and leave them in the lodging place where you lodge tonight.' "

[4] Then Joshua called the twelve men whom he had appointed from the children of Israel, one man from every tribe; [5] and Joshua said to them: "Cross over before the ark of the LORD your God into the midst of the Jordan, and each one of you take up a stone on his shoulder, according to the number of the tribes of the children of Israel, [6] that this may be a sign among you when your children ask in time to come, saying, 'What do these stones mean to you?' [7] Then you shall answer them that the waters of the Jordan were cut off before the ark of the covenant of the LORD; when it crossed over the Jordan, the waters of the Jordan were cut off. And these stones shall be for a memorial to the children of Israel forever."

[8] And the children of Israel did so, just as Joshua commanded, and took up twelve stones from the midst of the Jordan, as the LORD had spoken to Joshua, according to the number of the tribes of the children of Israel, and carried them over with them to the place where they lodged, and laid them down there. [9] Then Joshua set up twelve stones in the midst of the Jordan, in the place where the feet of the priests who bore the ark of the covenant stood; and they are there to this day.

[10] So the priests who bore the ark stood in the midst of the Jordan until everything was finished that the LORD had commanded Joshua to speak to the people, according to all that Moses had commanded Joshua; and the people hurried and crossed over. [11] Then it came to pass, when all the people had completely crossed over, that the ark of the LORD and the priests crossed over in the presence of the people. [12] And the men of Reuben, the men of Gad, and half the tribe of Manasseh crossed over armed before the children of Israel, as Moses had spoken to them. [13] About forty thousand prepared for war crossed over before the LORD for battle, to the plains of Jericho. [14] On that day the LORD exalted Joshua in the sight of

all Israel; and they feared him, as they had feared Moses, all the days of his life.

—Joshua 4:1–14

In this chapter of Joshua, I rediscover that the God who has offered us promises for the future, which sustain us in the present, understands our tendency to lose touch with matters of ultimate concern in our preoccupation with the unrelenting demands of the present. Therefore, He creates for us memorials, reminders that help keep our focus on our roots. This chapter dramatically reveals the importance of remembering. Israel has finally passed over the Jordan River. The priests had, all this time, kept high the ark of the covenant so that all those passing over could see it. God had held back the southward flow of the Jordan River, enabling the people to cross over on dry ground.

At this point, God instructed Joshua to create a memorial. Twelve men, one from each tribe, were to take a stone from the riverbed, hoist it upon their shoulders, and carry it to Gilgal, the place of encampment on the west bank. These twelve stones were to be arranged as a memorial of how God had led His people across the Jordan River at floodtime—a miraculous act never to be forgotten. So Joshua chose and instructed the twelve men, saying:

> ✝ *"Cross over before the ark of the LORD your God into the midst of the Jordan, and each one of you take up a stone on his shoulder, according to the number of the tribes of the children of Israel, that this may be a sign among you when your children ask in time to come, saying, 'What do these stones mean to you?' Then you shall answer them that the waters of the Jordan were cut off before the ark of the covenant of the LORD; when it crossed over the Jordan, the waters of the Jordan were cut off. And these stones shall be for a memorial to the children of Israel forever."* (vv. 5–7) ✝

Then Joshua himself set up twelve stones in the very middle of the Jordan, at the place where the priests, bearing the ark of the covenant, had stood. Apparently, this was his own moment of memorial. Then Joshua commanded the priests to carry the ark forward up the west bank of the Jordan. As the priests' feet were lifted up on dry ground, the waters of the Jordan returned to their place, flooding their way down to the Dead Sea. The priests and

Joshua joined the people encamped at Gilgal. He gave a speech to the entire encampment, telling the people about the importance of these stones as a memorial.

And the Scripture says, *"On that day the LORD exalted Joshua in the sight of all Israel; and they feared him, as they had feared Moses, all the days of his life"* (v. 14).

There is a place for memorials. We dare never forget this, and we must keep this thought before our people. These stones were to be an enduring sermon, directed not for the ears but for the eyes. They were to stand as a reminder to future generations that Israel crossed the Jordan not because of its own ability, its own strength, or its own cleverness, but because of God.

We know that God has, through the centuries, given us signs, symbols, and memorials. We need to be reminded of the importance of these and occasionally to review them, both for ourselves and for the sake of our people. God gave Noah the rainbow as a perpetual reminder of His love, as He also gave Abraham and the Jews circumcision as a sign of the covenant. God gave Miriam's poetry to commemorate the crossing of the Red Sea. He gave the ark, holding the law, and the manna as symbols of His continuing provision. The temple in Jerusalem reminded all of His dwelling. Worship is so basic to our faith. It reminds us of who God is and what He has done. He gave us the Cross and the empty tomb as historic statements of His love and grace.

God gave us Himself, in human form, in the miracle of the Incarnation. And our crucified and risen Lord gave us baptism as a symbol of His death, burial, and Resurrection which frees us from any condemnation. The Lord's Supper enables us to look back to the Cross and forward to the marriage supper of the Lamb as we handle the bread and the cup.

I'm convinced that God has chosen the foolishness of "preaching" to bring together a divine intersection of His Truth as it is most fully revealed in Jesus Christ and in the Scriptures. The human personality of the preacher articulates that Word under the influence of the Holy Spirit in a way that speaks as nothing else speaks to contemporary men and women. The great Episcopal preacher Phillips Brooks referred to preaching as the way in which God conveys His Word through a person to other persons. God's Word is not just doctrinal truth or the record of some of the historical events that happened in biblical history. It involves also the individual memories that we are given that help validate in a contemporary way what God has done in past history.

80

I trust you are free to share yourself in your preaching and teaching. If you've not yet come to that point, please consider it. There are dangers, of course. A few of the members in each of the churches I've served have criticized me for occasionally talking about my own experiences or about what God has done in my life. At times, I am tempted to pull back from this relational sharing. Then I realize it's in the very vulnerability of that personal sharing that God has chosen to speak, so long as I'm faithful to the Scriptures and point to the person and work of Jesus Christ.

What memories do you caress in prayerful gratitude? Concentrate on particular memories that enable you to live more productively in the present with the assurance of the future hope that is yours in Jesus Christ. I urge you to share these memories in your preaching, perhaps in the very sermon or Bible lesson that is based on this chapter in Joshua.

There are the memories of *places,* places for us that are every bit as spiritually significant as the pile of stones at Gilgal.

In my memory, I return to a place—my father and mother's room. The date is Labor Day morning, 1945. I knelt at a chair as a five-year-old tyke, praying for Christ to come into my life.

There's a football practice field outside Wheaton, Illinois, where one crisp, early spring night in 1955, I paced back and forth, wrestling as to whether or not I would allow Jesus Christ to become the Lord of my life—spiritually, physically, emotionally, and intellectually.

The eighth green of Princeton's Springdale golf course was where I would walk late at night during my seminary days as I struggled with theological questions, and I anguished over them and whether or not to go into the ministry. It was there late one night in 1963 that that prolonged decision process finally came into focus.

There are *people.* For me, there are a wife, three daughters, a wonderful father and mother, a sister, in-laws, friends of the past, friends of the present, a Sunday school teacher, a high school teacher, a few college and seminary professors, two or three mentors in ministry, colleagues with whom I've worked, and congregations with whom I've served. How often do you sit down and muse on those memories, thanking God for those people He's used in your life?

There are *experiences.* How important it is to remember them. Do you keep any record of your experiences in written form so that you can go back to them again and again to be renewed?

Some I've written down, but not enough. My wife, Anne, has done a better job of this in keeping her spiritual journal. I commend the practice to those in my congregation. What a privilege to keep in a private place a notebook in which one writes out those private thoughts about oneself, about God, and about the difficult and joyous circumstances of life. Date your journal and write in it frequently. Urge your people to do this. Then, periodically, go back and read what you were experiencing a year ago today, or five years ago today, or ten years ago today. There is, in the review of past experiences (some very painful), a reminder of God's faithfulness which gives a spiritual energy for the present.

There are *physical gestures* that have great significance. Emotionalism and evangelism can turn people off. At the same time, a spiritual life that is strictly cerebral is devoid of the richness of emotional expression that God has invested to one degree or another in each of us. This is why evangelists and pastors through the years have given an invitation to kneel down, stand up, come forward, raise a hand, a physical gesture that puts an exclamation mark at the end of the spiritual decision. I am as determined as you are not to manipulate people emotionally. At the same time, I know the importance of a physical gesture. So, I, too, have run the risk of using some of the above methods, but I acknowledge that they're not for everyone. On some occasions, I have, at the end of a sermon, invited the entire congregation to stand with heads bowed in seconds of silent prayer, praying whatever prayer is appropriate to them and then quietly, with their toe, to make the sign of the cross on the floor and to stand on that cross as a symbol of what Christ has done for them. This symbolized a decision that they were then making, a gesture of commitment that they could remember at a future moment in time.

Recently, a dear friend of mine, who has been struggling for years with whether or not to receive Jesus Christ, told me of a friend who reached out to him and said, "If you return this handshake, it's a symbol that you now have committed your life to Christ." My friend will never forget that handshake, that gesture.

There are *mementos*. Look around your house and your study. I have carvings, books, pictures, scrapbooks, furniture, and many miscellaneous objects scattered all through my study at the church and in the various rooms of my home. As I stop and look at them, they flood my heart with memories of life, of God, of people, and of experiences. God knows how we think. He knows that our memories are triggered by objects. This is why He told

Joshua to take those stones, stones out of the Jordan River, and have them carried to a place of remembrance. Look around your home, your study, and the other special places of your life with gratitude, thanking God for the memories those objects stimulate within you.

There's the *Bible*. What a book of memories this is. But it's not to be worshiped as a book. Granted, it may serve its purpose on a coffee table in the home of some of those to whom we minister as a reminder that this family claims to be Christian. Occasionally, they may dust it off and read it. Some are doing it more often these days; others are doing it a little less frequently. Before I'm too critical of others, I'd better look at myself. Do I only open it when there's a sermon or a Bible lesson to prepare? Or, do I dust it off daily, seeing it as the history of what God has done in my behalf?

There are the *sacraments*. Now, I don't believe that the water guarantees salvation for little ones who aren't old enough to know what it's all about. But it does jog our memories as parents to our responsibility to dedicate and rededicate our little ones to the love of Jesus Christ. It reminds us as a congregation of the responsibility we have to tell the old, old story of Jesus and His love. It does give the opportunity for the adult who has recently come to faith in Jesus Christ to make a public profession of an inner work of grace. And what a privilege it is to celebrate the Lord's Supper. We take the bread and give thanks for it, breaking it as a representation of Christ's body broken for us some two thousand years ago in human history. We drink of the cup in memory of His blood shed for the remission of our sins.

WHAT DO THESE STONES MEAN?

15 Then the LORD spoke to Joshua, saying, 16 "Command the priests who bear the ark of the Testimony to come up from the Jordan." 17 Joshua therefore commanded the priests, saying, "Come up from the Jordan." 18 And it came to pass, when the priests who bore the ark of the covenant of the LORD had come from the midst of the Jordan, and the soles of the priests' feet touched the dry land, that the waters of the Jordan returned to their place and overflowed all its banks as before.

19 Now the people came up from the Jordan on the tenth day of the first month, and they camped in Gilgal on the east border of Jericho. 20 And those twelve stones which they took out of the Jordan, Joshua set up in Gilgal. 21 Then he spoke to the children of Israel, saying: "When your children ask their

fathers in time to come, saying, 'What are these stones?' 22 then you shall let your children know, saying, 'Israel crossed over this Jordan on dry land'; 23 for the LORD your God dried up the waters of the Jordan before you until you had crossed over, as the LORD your God did to the Red Sea, which He dried up before us until we had crossed over, 24 that all the peoples of the earth may know the hand of the LORD, that it is mighty, that you may fear the LORD your God forever."

—*Joshua 4:15–24*

What a powerful privilege we have to expose ourselves and our people to the memorial stones, whatever they may be. Look at what Joshua said to the people at Gilgal in the last four verses of the passage just above.

It's important that we not make fetishes of the places, the people, the experiences, the physical gestures, the mementos, the Bible, or even the sacraments. The power resides not in the objects but in the crucified and risen Lord. It's easy to get so caught up that we forget the *essence* of our faith. Becoming so preoccupied in our religious life, we can forget what it's all about in its very basis. We can get so busy trying to get God to do what we want done that we lose sight of our responsibility to do what He wants done. We want Him to be what we want Him to be instead of asking Him to help us be what He wants us to be.

Our tendency with religious faith is to do to it what many museums have done to the sundial. We take this historical object and build a museum over it, admiring it for what it was in history, never letting the sun get near it so that it can show us the time of day.

What do the stones at Gilgal and our own personal stones mean? What do we say to our people about the significance of these memorial stones?

One: We alert them to the importance of *remembering the wonderful works of God.* There is a continuity. We are never more alive than we are right now. The present aliveness, however, is connected to an aliveness we experienced a few days ago or a few years ago. And that aliveness today is connected to an aliveness that we will experience a few days or a few years from now and in eternity, which we will experience in the presence of Jesus Christ. Remembering enables us to see this continuity.

Two: We alert our people to our mutual *tendency to forget what God has done.* I can become so preoccupied with the immediate moment and my apparent lack of resources for it that I forget my present has a history. The past is a prelude to this moment. It is a setting that makes the solitaire of the present stand out in all of its brilliance. We need to remember our tendency to forget.

Three: We alert them to the *importance of thanksgiving*, even in difficult times. When was the last time you said, "Thank you, Lord," in the midst of an impossible situation? I am facing two or three impossible situations right now. I can become so preoccupied with them that I forget God's provisions in the past. How much better to sit down and just listen in a litany of praise and thanksgiving for how faithful God has been in the past. By caressing these memories, my heart lifts in present thanksgiving to the God who is capable of bringing me through these difficulties even as He has in the past.

Four: We alert our people to the fact that these stones remind us not only of what God has done for us but *also what He has done for others*. I have a disease called myopia—a spiritual myopia. I am spiritually nearsighted. I get so preoccupied with my problems that I don't see the world beyond. This God is not just my God. He's not just the God of the people to whom I preach. Both my congregation and I have to remember this. He is the God of the entire universe. He's the God who reminds me of what He has done for others and what He wants me to do for others.

We minister in an era and a culture in which many are caught up in or are just coming out of the "me-centeredness" cult. So many books, lectures, and sermons are geared to how "I can be happy." Is this our chief end on this earth? Is my whole reason for being here that of personal happiness and success? Or are we here to glorify God and enjoy Him forever? If that's the case, an enjoyment of Him involves obedience in which we reach out and touch others. In the process, we see God at work in others. We need to put on the spectacles that correct our nearsightedness and share this prescription with others.

Five: We alert our people to the privilege of *making provision for future generations*. God didn't put those stones there just for Joshua's generation. He knew that this generation would have children and that they would have children and then there would be grandchildren and great-grandchildren who would come by Gilgal. They would see the Jordan River, yawn as they went their way, forgetting the miracle in which God held back the floodwaters and enabled the people to come across on dry ground. The stones would be there as a reminder for future generations—a way of passing on the faith.

Six: We alert them to the fact that *memorials can be simple.* They are not necessarily elaborate—simple stones out of the riverbed, drops of water in baptism, bread and grape juice in the Lord's Supper. Memorials need not be elaborate to be significant.

Seven: We alert them to the *corporate unity that is ours* as the people of God.

God told Joshua, "I want a man from each of the twelve tribes. I want a stone representing each of the twelve tribes." And God has continued that way all through history. When He became a man in Jesus He picked twelve disciples, a cross section of humanity with varying temperaments, backgrounds, and personalities. He treated women with varying temperaments and personalities with respect. God warns us in this way against the danger of provincialism. It wasn't just a series of individuals that passed over the Jordan. Scripture says, "And it came to pass, when all the people had completely crossed over the Jordan" (4:1).

This is important—when it says *all the people.* The Hebrew word used here for the people or nation is *gôy.* The emphasis here is clearly on the concept of the entry of the entire nation. Even representatives of the sons of Reuben, Gad, and the half-tribe of Manasseh, whose families were already ensconced on the east bank, were fully armed. They led the ranks across the Jordan in a declaration of national unity and oneness. There's a corporate unity demonstrated in these stones. This shatters that rugged individualism, that "Lone Ranger" approach to the Christian faith that marks so much of today's piety. We're a family, a people, a nation. We can't go it alone in the Christian faith. We need each other. We have a solidarity that is of ultimate significance.

Take some time to look at these stones—your stones—and let the memories flood within yourself and into the lives of your people, reminding them of who God is, who you are, who they are, from whence we've come, why we're here, and where we're going.

NOTE

1. "Murphy's Decalogue," *Context*, November 1, 1983.

CHAPTER SIX—A TIME FOR RENEWED COMMITMENT

JOSHUA 5:1–15

Scripture Outline

When God Acts, People Take Notice (5:1)

Reconsecration Precedes Forward Action (5:2–10)

Alert to Change (5:11–12)

Every Leader Needs to Be Led (5:13–15)

I srael has come to a most significant moment. A national history that had begun with Abraham some eight hundred years before was entering a new stage. The people have crossed over the Jordan as the floodwaters were held back by the Lord. And the memorial stones have been placed as a reminder of God's goodness. Now these Israelite nomads are encamped at Gilgal preparing to attack Jericho. Ironically, God has something else in mind.

This fifth chapter of Joshua presents some unique opportunities for preaching and teaching. It's not a difficult chapter for exegesis. There's a lot of technical material available in the commentaries that elaborates on the reestablishment of the rite of circumcision, the renewed observance of the Passover, the cessation of the daily manna, and Joshua's encounter with the Commander of the Lord's army.

However, there is a dearth of homiletical material that uses a direct connection between the biblical text and a contemporary application. The average, modern congregation might not be particularly interested in all of the intricate details surrounding the rite of circumcision and the observance of the Passover—at least in this particular setting. As communicators, we need to dig more deeply into this passage to discover the connecting point to where our people live today. I don't know that I've ever studied harder or struggled more with a passage as I've sought to discover the ageless message contained in this review of historical events. The results made the work worthwhile.

At the beginning of our fall church program on "Friendship/ Loyalty" Sunday, I preached a sermon with four major points. One could very well preach a mini-series with each of these four points being the central thrust of a different message. Although this did not end up being one of my more dramatic pulpit presentations, I was amazed to discover that the people were very attentive as the message, bathed in prayer, seemed to chart a course for a kind of new beginning in the life of our congregation.

WHEN GOD ACTS, PEOPLE TAKE NOTICE

> **5:1** So it was, when all the kings of the Amorites who were on the west side of the Jordan, and all the kings of the Canaanites who were by the sea, heard that the LORD had dried up the waters of the Jordan from before the children of Israel until we had crossed over, that their heart melted; and there was no spirit in them any longer because of the children of Israel.
>
> —*Joshua 5:1*

Now we come to another moment of truth. The Israelites are actually in the land, camped at Gilgal not too far from Jericho, which is a fortified city. They're probably quite anxious, wondering if they can succeed in the conquest. There's that tendency toward a "minority complex" which causes us to become preoccupied with our own problems, causing us to forget that nonbelievers, too, have their fears.

From the standpoint of the Amorites and the Canaanites, they, too, are human and also have their fears. When the kings of the Amorites and the kings of the Canaanites heard how the Lord had dried up the Jordan River before the Israelites, enabling them to cross over, *"their heart melted; and there was no spirit in them any longer because of the children of Israel"* (v. 1).

Rumors have a way of traveling, but people react differently to the rumors of what God has done. Pharaoh, for example, had hardened his heart. He had been determined not to capitulate to this Jewish God who had worked such great wonders in the plagues. Pharaoh should have been impressed with God's miracles, but he refused to be.

It was a different story for the kings of the Amorites and the Canaanites. They had heard rumors about these people whose God had parted the Red Sea. Then they had heard of other kings who had been defeated in battle. Even Rahab the harlot had heard those rumors. This was the moment of truth. The Israelite nation had crossed the Jordan in a supernatural act. This action couldn't help but impress the local inhabitants; Jericho was terrified. Its citizens wondered when Joshua would strike and what Israel would do next.

There's an important insight hidden in this observation: fear can go two ways. Our tendency is to know our own fears but not to acknowledge the fears of others. I've met a number of Christians who suffer from inferiority complexes, seeing themselves as inferior because they are Christians. They, too, have this minority mentality and are inclined to believe that by being Christians they've given up something and somehow the nonbelievers have things a little better.

How important it is to stop and realize that this just isn't the case. A true pagan doesn't have the slightest idea of where he's come from, why he's here, or where he's going, so he or she has to create a sense of self-purpose. Neither does he have any appreciation of the grace of our Lord Jesus Christ and the forgiveness that is ours as we confront our sins and allow them to be blotted out forever by His blood. A true pagan has heard rumors that there may be a God; and in quiet, introspective moments, he or she may even begin to wonder, begin to doubt his or her lack of faith, and begin to yearn for something better. The nonbeliever is all alone and either doesn't acknowledge that there is a God or doesn't take the time to be touched by that God. As a result, the nonbeliever is either consciously or unconsciously on the lookout for some reality.

The citizens of Jericho could actually handle their gods, which were made of clay and stone. But the Canaanite fertility gods and goddesses had no reputation for parting waters, providing manna and quail, or leading with pillars of fire by night and a cloud by day. Spies from Jericho had been on the lookout and had seen those hundreds of thousands of Israelites cross over the Jordan and camp on the west bank. And, now, the full citizenry could see them preparing for battle on the plains of Jericho. They compared gods, and their hearts melted in fear. When the true God acts, people take notice.

There is an awe and curiosity the nonbeliever has about a person who is alive in Jesus Christ. My first pastorate was the Key Biscayne Presbyterian Church in Florida with 280 members. Key Biscayne had a population of six thousand, with a seven-mile-long causeway connecting the island to Miami. It was noted for its lovely beaches. On this particular occasion, Billy Graham had come down to Key Biscayne for a few days of relaxation before his New York crusade. He invited my wife, Anne, and me and my associate, Jim Stout, and his wife to have breakfast with him at the Key Biscayne Hotel. What a special experience it was for two young pastors and their wives.

We talked about a lot of things. But what impressed me most was one particular statement he made: "The world will come with fascination to watch a person who is willing to burn himself out for Jesus Christ." I've never forgotten that because it twisted around my whole way of thinking about myself and my ministry. I had bought into a kind of cultural accommodation and felt that I could minister best if I looked as much as possible like the nonbelievers around me. I had not intentionally compromised any biblically taught convictions, but some believers are so heavenly minded that they appear to have little relevance to this world. In my endeavor to avoid alienating nonbelievers, I tried to be as much like them as possible. In the process, I could walk into or out of some situations without being distinguished from anybody else.

Graham wasn't urging the four of us to be religious oddballs. What he was saying was that we shouldn't be afraid to be who we are. The world is dying to see people who are different, to observe someone who has an alternative. As much as we need to build bridges of communication and adapt ourselves on nonessentials to our culture, there does need to be a separation between a believer and a nonbeliever that is apparent.

The Canaanites had heard that the Israelites were different and were watching them. The God who could hold back the Jordan River would be a dangerous God with which to tangle in battle. People today are watching us; they hear our words and want to know whether or not our actions back them. Wherein they see us faithful, they cannot fail but be impressed. Some will respond, as Rahab did, trusting this God. Others will recoil in fear and fight Him with everything they have. If we take our Lord seriously, we shouldn't be surprised that others are constantly taking notice of us. We need to encourage ourselves and the people we serve to remember this.

RECONSECRATION PRECEDES FORWARD ACTION

2 At that time the LORD said to Joshua, "Make flint knives for yourself, and circumcise the sons of Israel again the second

time." [3] So Joshua made flint knives for himself, and circumcised the sons of Israel at the hill of the foreskins. [4] And this is the reason why Joshua circumcised them: All the people who came out of Egypt who were males, all the men of war, had died in the wilderness on the way, after they had come out of Egypt. [5] For all the people who came out had been circumcised, but all the people born in the wilderness, on the way as they came out of Egypt, had not been circumcised. [6] For the children of Israel walked forty years in the wilderness, till all the people who were men of war, who came out of Egypt, were consumed, because they did not obey the voice of the LORD—to whom the LORD swore that He would not show them the land which the LORD had sworn to their fathers that He would give us, "a land flowing with milk and honey." [7] Then Joshua circumcised their sons whom He raised up in their place; for they were uncircumcised, because they had not been circumcised on the way.

[8] So it was, when they had finished circumcising all the people, that they stayed in their places in the camp till they were healed. [9] Then the LORD said to Joshua, "This day I have rolled away the reproach of Egypt from you." Therefore the name of the place is called Gilgal to this day.

[10] Now the children of Israel camped in Gilgal, and kept the Passover on the fourteenth day of the month at twilight on the plains of Jericho.

—Joshua 5:2–10

From a military standpoint, the perfect moment to attack Jericho would have been immediately upon crossing the Jordan River. The inhabitants of that great crossroad city couldn't help but tremble at the thought of such a powerful God. Joshua had intuitive military skills, and his intelligence reports had already alerted him that the people of Jericho were afraid. Instead of allowing the people to attack at the moment in which Jericho was most fearful, God wanted them to stop and get their priorities straight—because they'd been disobedient.

God doesn't function on our timetables; He has a way of making us bide our time. He's more patient than we are. God had some work to do with the Israelites before He was prepared to lead them into battle. During the wilderness wanderings, they had neglected at least two very important aspects of the Mosaic law.

One of these was circumcision, the initiatory rite into the covenant privilege of God's family which marked the Jewish nation. On the eighth day after birth, male babies were circumcised. This was not exclusively a custom of the Jews. Others of the Semitic people practiced the same rite. God had commanded that this would be a sign that would mark the male flesh of His covenant people. The rite had been instituted by Abraham (Genesis 17) and was required of those who would eat the Passover (Ex. 12:43–51). The strange story of Moses' firstborn son's circumcision is told in Exodus 4:25–26. Somehow while wandering in the wilderness, the people had neglected this rite. Instead of allowing them to go into battle at the time Jericho must have been most fearful, God instructed the Israelites to be circumcised. This was done at a place that came to be known as Gibeath-Haaraloth, the "hill of the foreskins."

Only Joshua and Caleb were spared. The reason is outlined in verses 4 and 5: "*All the people who came out of Egypt who were males, all the men of war, had died in the wilderness on the way, after they had come out of Egypt. For all the people who came out had been circumcised, but all the people born in the wilderness on the way, as they came out of Egypt, had not been circumcised.*" Joshua and Caleb were the only two male-warrior survivors of the Egyptian experience.

There's a strange humor to this. The citizens of Jericho are frightened at the very moment when the citizens of Israel are most vulnerable, when all of the Jewish males are helpless, having just been circumcised.

There are two particular reflections we can make on the meaning of circumcision here.

One involves healing. Verse 8 reads, "*So it was, when they had finished circumcising all the people, that they stayed in their places in the camp till they were healed.*" The Hebrew has a sense of double meaning. There was the literal healing from the wounds of the operation and also a spiritual healing. It was the kind of healing the Israelites had experienced in the wilderness. When punished by God by the plague of the serpents, they were restored to life as they looked to the bronze serpent (Num. 21:8–9). Circumcision in this sense can be seen as the wounding and recovery, a kind of death and resurrection.

The second reflection on circumcision comes in God's words: "*This day I have rolled away the reproach of Egypt from you*" (v. 9). Most likely, the "*reproach of Egypt*" was the humiliation of slavery in Egypt which made the Israelites subject to insult and disgrace from all the nations. Now this humiliation was coming to an end as the Israelites have become a free people, entering the Promised Land. Circumcision is a sign of their freedom. It is a token of the dignity that was being exchanged for years of servitude. The word *gilgal,* "wheel" in Hebrew, can also mean "circle." This etymology is suggested in Joshua 4:20 when the memorial stones are set in place. This is a wordplay. The rite of circumcision symbolically rolls away the reproach of the Egyptian slavery.

God had a second expectation of the people. Not only were they to be circumcised, they were also to celebrate the Passover. Passover was the thanksgiving festival to commemorate the escape from the bondage of Egypt. This same generation that was uncircumcised also had not celebrated the Passover since receiving the law at Mount Sinai. The Passover celebration provided a bonding experience and tied them to other times in their past and in their future. According to Exodus 12, the sacrificial lamb was selected on the tenth day of the first month, and the Passover meal was held on the evening of the fourteenth day. Some scholars note how God's timing was precise. The Israelites came out of the Jordan on the tenth day of the month. According to Joshua 4:19, the first Passover in Canaan was a memorial of that first Passover some forty years earlier when God began to deliver the slaves (Ex. 12:14).

This Passover observance has been continued on a regular basis to the present time. It's important to know that it was one of the six major Passover events highlighted in the Old Testament. E. John Hamlin notes that the first Passover commemorated the end of the slavery and the beginning of the long march from Goshen to Gilgal. Exactly a year later, the second Passover was held at the end of the sojourn in Sinai where the covenant bond had been completed by the giving of the covenant teaching. The third Passover was celebrated as the Hebrew people were ready to inherit the Promised Land. Reported in 2 Chronicles, the fourth Passover feast was held by Hezekiah and marked the end of the period of disobedience and the beginning of his reform movement (ch. 30). The fifth Passover was held in 622 B.C. as King Josiah continued Hezekiah's reform, following the dark age of King Manasseh. And in 515 B.C., when Zerubbabel and the high priest Joshua were in Jerusalem, the sixth Passover marked the completion of the second temple.

These were moments of reconsecration that Israel needed. God was not content to let them charge into the Promised Land because they had neglected to obey the Mosaic law. Now they paused and regrouped, finding an even greater sense of identity in their circumcision and in the observance of the Passover.

Obviously, these two events in one way have very little significance for us today. What is there here for us to communicate to people for whom circumcision and the Passover are ancient rites?

As for circumcision, both the Old and New Testaments contain a much deeper meaning for what would appear to be a simple physical surgery carried out for hygienic or religious reasons. The apostle Paul, on occasion, referred to circumcisers as "mutilators of the flesh" (Phil 3:2, NIV). What is fascinating to notice is that, even in the Old Testament times, the physical act of circumcision was minimized. It was much more important to be a person who had a "circumcised heart." Moses said, "Therefore circumcise the foreskin of your heart, and be stiffnecked no longer" (Deut. 10:16). Jeremiah 4:4 reads,

> "Circumcise yourselves to the LORD,
> And take away the foreskins of your hearts,
> You men of Judah and inhabitants of Jerusalem,
> Lest My fury come forth like fire,
> And burn so that no one can quench it,
> Because of the evil of your doings."

This is a call to repentance, whether it be thirty-two hundred years ago or now. God is prescribing for His people a radical spiritual surgery. He is tired of our stiff-necked ways, our forgetfulness of Him and His teachings. He calls His people of all generations to a circumcision of the heart, to a spirit of brokenness and openness before Him which provides the true identity for His people.

As for the Passover, we can build on the great Old Testament observances, reminding ourselves of that evening on which Jesus took bread and wine. He was celebrating the Passover on the night of His betrayal, and He applied a new significance to those ancient symbols. Christ is now our Passover. The remembrance of what He has done in the past is one of our best preparations for the future. In my loneliest times, I think of God's faithfulness and His ministry through all of His people. Jesus is the Lamb of God who takes away all the sins of the world.

We are privileged to ask ourselves and our people some very basic questions. Have we neglected the things of God? Have we been wandering in the wilderness, doing our own thing independent of Him? Although over three millennia separate us from Israel camped at Gilgal, spiritually there's very little difference. We can become preoccupied with our careers, eking out our own existence and giving the best we can to our children. In the process, we can lose our identity. Christianity is only one generation from extinction. We need to challenge ourselves and our people anew to that circumcision of the heart and the observance of those means of grace that remind us of who we are.

Have we neglected a serious observance of the sacraments? Are ✶ baptism and the Lord's Supper central in our worship? Are we encouraging a family-oriented worship in which our children are exposed to the great hymns of the faith, the preaching of the Word, and the fellowship of other believers in a way that gives them a sense of corporate identity? Or are we simply trying to amuse them, teasing them along, appealing to our mutual narcissism? Do our children observe us in activities that let them know that we love Jesus and want to serve Him? Do they observe a humility in us that admits when we are wrong, confessing our sins both to God and to each other? They need to see that our hearts are circumcised and that we daily observe our Passover in Christ. ✶

ALERT TO CHANGE

[11] And they ate of the produce of the land on the day after the Passover, unleavened bread and parched grain, on the very same day. [12] Then the manna ceased on the day after they had eaten the produce of the land; and the children of Israel no longer had manna, but they ate the food of the land of Canaan that year.

—Joshua 5:11–12

Something dramatic happened as soon as Israel had celebrated the Passover. The next morning, the manna ceased after they had eaten of the fruit of the land of Canaan.

This must have been startling. A whole generation of people had become dependent on the miraculous daily appearance of the manna that God had provided. Now that it was no longer available, they had to work to provide their own food. They must have been frightened as their circumstances changed.

As shocking as these moments of change are, this Old Testament story reminds us that God's provision is suitable to our present circumstances. For God to have continued to provide manna would have made the people dependent in an unhealthy way.

I'm increasingly convinced that God's method of provision moves from the supernatural to the natural. He is more likely to intervene in a supernatural way when there is no natural source of supply. He is the Lord of both the supernatural and the natural. Nothing good exists that He did not originate. This doesn't mean that He is always going to provide the same good in the same way. Our needs change, and we grow beyond one kind of provision to another. It's imperative that we keep ourselves open to this growth process.

Local churches tend to be some of the most conservative of all human institutions. Part of what makes our churches dull to many people is that we have accommodated ourselves to the status quo. Change is upsetting, so we learn to not rock the boat. This particular passage in Joshua gives us a perfect opportunity to show how God allows circumstances to change and how He shifts His methodologies to match the needs of the people because of those changed circumstances.

These two verses give us an exciting opportunity to remind our people that change is a fact of life. There is a time for change. And God's resources are sufficient to help us live creatively with any change.

EVERY LEADER NEEDS TO BE LED

13 And it came to pass, when Joshua was by Jericho, that he lifted his eyes and looked, and behold, a Man stood opposite him with His sword drawn in His hand. And Joshua went to Him and said to Him, "Are You for us or for our adversaries?"

14 So He said, "No, but as Commander of the army of the LORD I have now come."

And Joshua fell on his face to the earth and worshiped, and said to Him, "What does my Lord say to His servant?"

15 Then the Commander of the LORD's army said to Joshua, "Take your sandal off your foot, for the place where you stand is holy." And Joshua did so.

—Joshua 5:13–15

As Joshua walks alone near the city of Jericho, he tries to figure out how his people can win the battle. It appears to be an impregnable city. Then he becomes aware that there is a Man standing before him with His sword drawn. Joshua addresses the Man asking whether or not He is friend or foe. The Man answers, *"No, but as Commander of the army of the LORD, I have now come"* (v. 14). Joshua immediately falls on his face and worships this Person. He asks, *"What does my Lord say to His servant?"* (v. 14). Before this Man, who refers to himself as the Commander of the army of the Lord, Joshua falls on his face, asking for orders. This Commander asks Joshua to remove his sandal from his foot, for he is on holy ground. Joshua obeys.

What impresses me most about this fifth chapter of Joshua is that, for once, the people of Israel, the leadership of Israel, and the God of Israel seem to be functioning in harmony. The people are no longer getting ahead of God or lagging too far behind Him. So often, the prophets, the priests, or the kings were either ahead of the people or behind the people or ahead of God or behind God. There was a kind of zig-zag going on in the spiritual history of Israel. But not now. The promises God made to Joshua, as recorded in the first chapter, seem now to be coming to fruition.

Joshua realized that the Lord is right here with us if we are open to Him. We can talk to Him. He has promised never to leave us or forsake us. Our extremity is God's opportunity. He is the Captain, the Commander in Chief, the One who gives the orders and then gives us enough strength to live one day at a time.

The question is, Are we willing to fall down on holy ground and worship Him? This action has had good precedent. It's precisely what Moses did when he encountered the living God. Now Joshua, years later, follows the same example. He falls down and worships his Commander.

Scholars have questioned who this Commander actually is. Some have referred to him as an angel. Others say that this is an Old Testament theophany, that God Himself appeared, perhaps in the very person of Jesus Christ. This is my belief. Joshua understood his need of divine guidance. He had tremendous capabilities, but he knew his limitations. When the Lord appeared, Joshua was prepared to fall down and worship. He was prepared to humbly listen and then to stand up and obediently implement the instructions given him by his Commander.

At the turn of the last century, biblical scholar George Adam Smith wrote about this encounter:

> It is a noble illustration of the truth, that, in the great causes of God upon the earth, the leaders, however, supreme and solitary they seem, are themselves led. There is a rock higher than they; their shoulders, however broad, have not to bear alone the awful burden of responsibility. The sense of supernatural conduct and protection, the consequent reverence and humility which form the spirit of all Israel's history, have nowhere in the OT received a more beautiful expression than in this early fragment.[2]

How important it is to be commissioned by God to whatever leadership tasks we are committed. Some of the greatest military leaders of all human history became pathetic characters because pride had taken over. They had become their own leader and had not humbled themselves, falling on their faces, claiming the strength of the Lord.

How true this also is for those of us in Christian ministry. Pride can so quickly take over. When God is at work in us people will take notice. It's all the more important that we reconsecrate ourselves individually and corporately, allowing Him to work those changes in us that are necessary and to offer His provision. God is our leader, and He goes with us into battle.

Every believer in Jesus Christ is called to some leadership function. Each leader needs to be led, and the ultimate leader is the Commander of the army of the Lord, before whom we are privileged daily to fall on our faces, acknowledging His holiness, His supreme leadership, and His promise to provide the energy we need for the tasks that are ours.

NOTES

1. Hamlin, *Inheriting the Land*, pp. 36–37.

2. Nolan B. Harmon, ed., *The Interpreter's Bible*, 12 vols. (Nashville: Abingdon Press, 1953), 2:576.

CHAPTER SEVEN—JERICHO—A MODEL FOR VICTORY

JOSHUA 6:1–20

Scripture Outline

Our God Is a God of Strange Strategies (6:1–5)

The Result of True Worship Is Obedience (6:6–19)

God Gives Victory to His Obedient People (6:20)

Few Bible stories do more to capture one's imagination than the story about Joshua and the battle of Jericho. It's the stuff of Hebrew liturgy that has brought enormous encouragement to devout Jews down through the centuries.

Giving this story a beyond-Sunday, second look, though, raises practical questions about miracles. Are we going to rationalize away what happened? Or are we going to take it at face value—that God did, in a supernatural way, cause the walls to tumble? The sooner we state our belief in God's sovereignty and our conviction that God did, in a miraculous way, give Jericho into the hands of the Israelites, the more quickly prepared we are to make practical applications of a contemporary nature.

A second look at this story also raises reflective questions about ethics. It makes us take a good hard look at ourselves, at others, and at God. Is this God who commanded the wholesale slaughter of the entire population of Jericho—with the exception of Rahab and her household—the same God who reveals Himself with such tenderness and compassion in the person of Jesus Christ?

Again, I would assume that the evangelical teacher and preacher would say a ready yes. That's not enough. My original intention was to preach one sermon on the entire sixth chapter, delaying the tough questions raised by God's unequivocal slaughter of certain Amorite and Canaanite populations. Instead, my study and my endeavor to listen to the kinds of questions my people raised demanded that I break Joshua 6 into two sections, preaching two sermons. I announced to my congregation right from the start that I would not be avoiding the painful questions the next few chapters of Joshua raise for today's society. This way, I was free to dig into the major insights that can be received from a study of the Jericho victory while promising to tackle the tough questions in the next sermon or, in this case, in the next chapter of this commentary.

In one way, this is a strange story about an ancient battle. In another way, it is the model for victorious Christian living. One could become preoccupied endeavoring to analyze the isolated, important traditional elements of this story—Joshua, the holy war scheme, Rahab, the use of the number seven, the place of the ram's horn, God's treasury house, and the priestly celebration. The serious student can pursue each of these themes in great detail with the help of the numerous technical commentaries.

Three primary insights are derived from this text that are as applicable to today as they were to the ancient Hebrews.

OUR GOD IS A GOD OF STRANGE STRATEGIES

6:1 Now Jericho was securely shut up because of the children of Israel; none went out, and none came in. 2 And the LORD said to Joshua: "See! I have given Jericho into your hand, its king, and the mighty men of valor. 3 You shall march around the city, all you men of war; you shall go all around the city once. This you shall do six days. 4 And seven priests shall bear seven trumpets of rams' horns before the ark. But the seventh day you shall march around the city seven times, and the priests shall blow the trumpets. 5 It shall come to pass, when they make a long blast with the ram's horn, and when you hear the sound of the trumpet, that all the people shall shout with a great shout; then the wall of the city will fall down flat. And the people shall go up every man straight before him."

—*Joshua 6:1–5*

God actually goes out of His way to choose absurd means to do His will.

Any tactical plans Joshua had in mind aren't known. We can imagine some of the strategic conversations he must have had with his top military advisors. The spies had brought back their intelligence which, combined with other available knowledge, had given Joshua insights into the military and psychological preparedness of

Jericho. We don't know how elaborate his plans were, but they were abruptly disrupted when he met the Commander of the army of the Lord. God had other plans.

Note that the people of Jericho were expecting a siege and were hiding behind double walls, which they hoped would prove impregnable. God promises Joshua the victory and then outlines a most curious strategy. He orders Joshua to march around the city once every day for six days with armed men in the front of the procession. They were to be followed by seven priests, each blowing a ram's horn signal trumpet as he marched, followed by those carrying the ark of the covenant, who were then followed by a rear guard of armed men. Specific instructions were given that the people of Israel were to march silently. On the seventh day, they were to rise at dawn and march around the city in the same manner seven times. On the seventh time, when the priests had blown the trumpets, the people were to shout with a great shout, and the walls of the city were to fall down flat.

Have you ever heard of a crazier military strategy? Could you imagine a general who had graduated from the United States Military Academy sketching such a war plan? It doesn't make any sense—and that's probably the very reason God came up with the plan.

I believe that the deepest theological message of this story is that God is teaching us to trust Him instead of using our own cleverness. It's not inconceivable that the Israelites could have made a swift attack on the frightened inhabitants of Jericho, scaled the walls, and perhaps, with a fairly substantial loss of life, ultimately won the battle. But God had another plan.

This is not the first occasion upon which God has come up with a strange strategy. He did it generations earlier when He observed intense human rebellion against Himself. He singled out Noah to build an ark, which was God's strategy for bringing judgment upon sin and yet preserving an ongoing human race.

God also used a different strategy in the story of Gideon. By Gideon's time, the Israelites had conquered the land but weren't too secure. Those in the northern part were being periodically invaded by the Midianites. So God appeared to a reluctant young man named Gideon, urging him to sound a call to arms. Thirty-two thousand volunteers responded to Gideon's call. He must have been impressed with this response, but God's reaction was "Too many soldiers! Reduce the number."

The apostle Paul shared a theological reflection on God's strange strategy: "For Jews request a sign, and Greeks seek after wisdom; but we preach Christ crucified, to the Jews a stumbling block and to the Greeks foolishness, but to those who are called, both Jews and Greeks, Christ the power of God and the wisdom of God. Because the foolishness of God is wiser than men, and the weakness of God is stronger than men" (1 Cor. 1:22–25).

The writer of Hebrews reemphasized the same theme: "For the word of God is living and powerful, and sharper than any two-edged sword, piercing even to the division of soul and spirit, and of joints and marrow, and is a discerner of the thoughts and intents of the heart" (4:12).

God urged Gideon to pare the number lest Israel become cocky, believing it had victory over the Midianites by its own power. God's whole modus operandi is to minimize human, prideful self-confidence. It comes in a poor second best with the transcendent equipment the Lord offers. Finally, Gideon reduced the number to a disciplined three hundred. God could do more with three hundred through His strange strategy than Gideon could do with thirty-two thousand in their own human strength.

The Scottish theologian-preacher James S. Stewart has written a powerful sermon about Gideon titled "The Strange Strategy of God." It's a very helpful sermon for one endeavoring to preach about Joshua. Stewart builds on the historical precedent of Gideon, making this broader, powerful observation about God's ongoing work:

> How in point of historical fact did Christ's church, in the great days after Pentecost, sweep the Mediterranean world? Not because they were mighty and many and influential, not because they numbered their legions by scores of thousands—nothing of the kind—but simply because the few that there were of them were dead sure of Christ, believing in his passion and resurrection and eternal Lordship, and believing not vaguely and conventionally, as we so often do today, but believing with intensity and passion, for they were experiencing his living presence with them every day and recognized it as literally the most important fact in all the world.
>
> This was the miracle of Pentecost. And we are needing nothing short of a new Pentecost to recreate that attitude within us. May God grant it to us soon![1]

God's ultimate strange strategy is revealed in the miracle of the Cross of Jesus Christ. This doesn't appear to be the way to conquer the world. The Romans couldn't possibly have been impressed. They were used to the circus, military parades, and spectacular events. They admired generals who returned from great battles. In fact, the Romans developed the military siege to a fine art. When they wanted to capture a city, they would encircle it and cut off its water and food supply. The Romans were prepared to maintain a siege year upon year if they really wanted to capture a particular city.

It seems unlikely that the Israelites could conquer Jericho by walking around the city silently once a day with the exception of seven priests blowing seven trumpets. Increasing the number of encirclements to seven on the seventh day and then breaking the silence with the trumpet sound and loud shouting could hardly cause the walls of Jericho to crumble. There must have been a better strategy to bring about a more glorious victory.

The ultimate impossibility is that God became a man who went to the Cross bearing the sins of the world, rising from the dead, offering forgiveness and new beginnings. It doesn't make sense. Why should we be forgiven? Why should we have a fresh start? Why shouldn't we work really hard and somehow earn our salvation in more conventional ways? God hasn't chosen to work that way. Our own cleverness and human power is insufficient. "For the weapons of our warfare are not carnal but mighty in God for pulling down strongholds" (2 Cor. 10:4).

God has a way of turning everything upside down. The inhabitants of Jericho are paralyzed with fear. They've heard of a God who has led the Israelites through the Red Sea, maintained them in their forty years of wandering in the wilderness, and has now held back the Jordan River so that they can cross over on dry ground. Then the Israelites, in their moment of greatest strength, are instructed to circumcise all of the males, rendering them militarily helpless. Now, healed from that bloody ritual, they end up making what appears to be a benign religious pilgrimage around the impregnable walls of Jericho. The inhabitants, once fearful, begin to feel safe behind their military fortifications. Now perhaps, they're venturing up onto the walls, looking down, sneering at those foolish Israelites whose ultimate armament is only their faith in Jehovah. The Hebrews are beginning to learn what God had time and time again tried to teach them: "'Not by might nor by power, but by My Spirit,' Says the LORD of hosts" (Zech. 4:6).

More than twelve hundred years later, the writer of Hebrews penned these powerful words of history:

By faith they passed through the Red Sea as by dry land; whereas the Egyptians, attempting to do so, were drowned. By faith the walls of Jericho fell down after they were encircled for seven days. By faith the harlot Rahab did not perish with those who did not believe, when she had received the spies with peace. And what more shall I say? For the time would fail me to tell of Gideon and Barak and Samson and Jephthah, also of David and Samuel and the prophets: who through faith subdued kingdoms, worked righteousness, obtained promises, stopped the mouths of lions, quenched the violence of fire, escaped the edge of the sword, out of weakness were made strong, became valiant in battle, turned to flight the armies of the aliens (11:29–34).

THE RESULT OF TRUE WORSHIP IS OBEDIENCE

6 Then Joshua the son of Nun called the priests and said to them, "Take up the ark of the covenant, and let seven priests bear seven trumpets of rams' horns before the ark of the LORD." 7 And he said to the people, "Proceed, and march around the city, and let him who is armed advance before the ark of the LORD."

8 So it was, when Joshua had spoken to the people, that the seven priests bearing the seven trumpets of rams' horns before the LORD advanced and blew the trumpets, and the ark of the covenant of the LORD followed them. 9 The armed men went before the priests who blew the trumpets, and the rear guard came after the ark, while the priests continued blowing the trumpets. 10 Now Joshua had commanded the people, saying, "You shall not shout or make any noise with your voice, nor shall a word proceed out of your mouth, until the day I say to you, 'Shout!' Then you shall shout." 11 So he had the ark of the LORD circle the city, going around it once. Then they came into the camp and lodged in the camp.

12 And Joshua rose early in the morning, and the priests took up the ark of the LORD. 13 Then seven priests bearing seven trumpets of rams' horns before the ark of the LORD went on continually and blew with the trumpets. And the armed men went before them. But the rear guard came after the ark of the LORD, while the priests continued blowing the trumpets. 14 And the second day they marched around the city once and returned to the camp. So they did six days.

[15] But it came to pass on the seventh day that they rose early, about the dawning of the day, and marched around the city seven times in the same manner. On that day only they marched around the city seven times. [16] And the seventh time it happened, when the priests blew the trumpets, that Joshua said to the people: "Shout, for the LORD has given you the city! [17] Now the city shall be doomed by the LORD to destruction, it and all who are in it. Only Rahab the harlot shall live, she and all who are with her in the house, because she hid the messengers that we sent. [18] And you, by all means abstain from the accursed things, lest you become accursed when you take of the accursed things, and make the camp of Israel a curse, and trouble it. [19] But all the silver and gold, and vessels of bronze and iron, are consecrated to the LORD; they shall come into the treasury of the LORD."

—Joshua 6:6–19

When Joshua encountered the Commander of the army of the Lord, he fell on his face and worshiped. And when the Commander of the Lord's army said to him, "Take your sandal off your foot, for the place where you stand is holy" (5:15), the Scripture says, "And Joshua did so."

Joshua had learned to move beyond worship to obedience. He had learned that obedience becomes the sign of whether or not one's worship is authentic. The rhythm of his life was to fall down, worship, listen, and then obey. The guiding principle for Joshua was that once the mind of God was indicated, there was nothing more for him to do than to obey. When we come to that point in life, we have made a spiritual breakthrough.

My tendency is to argue with God. There is some precedence for this in the Scriptures. We are free to express any concern we have to the Lord. Abraham pled on behalf of Lot when God's judgment was about to come down on Sodom and Gomorrah. God listened and was prepared to discuss the matter. God encourages our honest prayers. In the final analysis, God knows what is best.

I have a tough time learning this lesson. But the sooner I do, the sooner I will benefit from the time and energy no longer spent in fighting Him, trying to convince Him that I know better than He does. I've got to realize I'm creature, He is Creator, and it is not for me to criticize the plans of the omniscient One.

Can I improve on His ways of doing things because I think I know better? I'm afraid I need a lesson in humility. In fact, at those moments, I need a lesson in what true worship is. False worship is for me to step into the presence of God in an endeavor to manipulate Him to do my will. I need to be reminded that men and women throughout all human history have tried to purchase God. True worship is for me to step into His presence and allow Him to bring my will into conformity with His will. True worship is for me to obey Him wherein I understand why He has a particular will for my life. And it's also to obey Him when I don't understand why He has a particular plan for my life.

This incident of Joshua's falling on his face in worship, listening to what God has to say, and going back to the camp obedient to God's strategy gives us an exciting opportunity to share our own struggles in faith with our people and to inspire both them and ourselves with Joshua's example.

I wish I could have heard the reaction of Joshua's military advisors when he came back to the camp with God's strategy. He had to be a pretty believing man to try to sell it to them. Bill Cosby has a routine that a witty colleague or two might have played around with: "Okay, Joshua, let me be sure that I've got this straight. You say that for six days we'll walk around the city of Jericho carrying the ark of the covenant, saying absolutely nothing, with seven of our priests blowing the ram's horn trumpets? Then on the seventh day we walk around seven times silently? Then all at once, when the trumpets start blowing, we all start shouting, and those double walls are going to fall down? Come on, Joshua, that doesn't really make a whole lot of sense."

We don't know how much Joshua told them, but he had to have at least given them the strategy. He might not have told them that God had promised that the walls would come tumbling down. The fact is that Joshua didn't play religious games. He worshiped sincerely. He believed God and was willing to act on God's instructions. No matter how foolish he would look, he was prepared to do what God wanted him to do. It's straightforward trust and obedience that has enabled God's people through all human history to make a difference. When that quality of trust and obedience is gone, we people of God so tragically mess up our own lives, the lives of our children, our colleagues, and ultimately, the very life of our nation.

One person said to me, "Well, God hasn't been telling me anything recently. Sure, if God came to me like He did to Joshua, I'd obey Him." It's difficult for some to realize that God has come in the person of Jesus Christ. My friend forgets that if he has trust in Christ as his Savior, he has His very indwelling presence in the person and work of the Holy Spirit. He has what God has outlined as a strategy for living—the world's finest strategy. When he obeys that strategy, his life will go well. If he disobeys it and tries to live a "smarter way," his life will end up in tragedy.

Our people need to hear this word. They need to observe us as we illustrate from our own lives and from the lives of others what we've observed. We need to say bluntly that they are only flirting with disaster if they claim to be one of Christ's and are willing to live in disobedience. What happens to a soldier who refuses to obey the order of his commander? He's court-martialed and pays the price for that disobedience.

Our Commander, Jesus Christ, is not as severe as a military commander. He gives us every opportunity to obey—so much so that we begin to take Him for granted. I'm convinced that we need to toughen up in terms of our own personal Christian lives as preachers. And we need to have the courage to share honestly this frank word of challenge with our people.

Christ commands us to go into the world and share our faith with others. But we often disobey because we are frightened, too busy, or afraid of being laughed at.

God sketches for us an economic lifestyle in which we are privileged to use the 90 percent He's given us to meet our own personal needs. Then we are to return to Him a minimum of the first fruits—the 10 percent off the top before taxes. Tithing is His minimum standard. We are to do this not grudgingly or of necessity but cheerfully. Jesus reaffirmed this, alerting us that we should do this and more also. But we disobey and kid ourselves into thinking that 90 percent is not "enough." We nibble away at the tithes and offerings that are God's.

He tells us to be concerned for the widow, the orphan, the prisoner, the poor. We are threatened by this and pretend that it's not really a part of the gospel, so we disobey.

He tells us that our sexual relationships are to be reserved to the covenant that is ours in marriage. No premarital or extramarital sexual intercourse is appropriate for the believer. So even some of us theologians, as well as Christian laymen, come up with clever rationalizations, trying to prove that God's teachings are out of date and that He doesn't really know what is best.

We forget that ours is a spiritual warfare. All too often we try to live our lives on human terms. We forget that a personal Satan is out to destroy us. We allow him to trip us up in our marriages and in our work lives. We allow him to trip us up in our social relationships because we are not staying in close contact with the Lord. Our worship is empty because we fail to flesh it out in obedience.

The sad thing is that we so often forget the Good News that this same Word of God invites us at any moment to come and claim God's forgiveness, a new beginning, and urges us to invite our people to that.

On the seventh day, when the trumpets sounded, the people shouted, and the walls of Jericho fell down, Joshua obeyed not only the strategy for battle but also the instructions the Lord gave in the moment of victory. He gave safety to Rahab, honoring the promise of the two spies. He ordered the people to keep themselves from particular objects that were to be destroyed so as to avoid trouble that would come upon them. He gathered all the silver, gold, and vessels of bronze and iron, which would be sacred to the Lord and which were to go into His treasury. Joshua obeyed, and he led the people in obedience.

GOD GIVES VICTORY TO HIS OBEDIENT PEOPLE

20 So the people shouted when the priests blew the trumpets. And it happened when the people heard the sound of the trumpet, and the people shouted with a great shout, that the wall fell down flat. Then the people went up into the city, every man straight before him, and they took the city.
—*Joshua 6:20*

For me, this verse is the key verse of the whole passage we have been considering in this chapter.

In telling this Old Testament story dealing with an event that happened over three thousand years ago, there's a danger of getting stuck in the historical past. Jericho has been a heap of ruins during all these years. The Romans built a new city a modest distance away. Today there's a city referred to as modern Jericho. It, too, is some distance from these ruins. The intent of addressing this text is not to spend all of our time talking about the Israelites, the Amorites, and the Canaanites. The purpose is to point out that our life is a struggle. We, today, are engaged in a spiritual battle. There is a Jericho or several Jerichos in each of our lives.

So I put two questions to my congregation.

Question 1: "What is the Jericho or what are the Jerichos in your life?" I urged them to make a list of those points at which they are most vulnerable. What are the temptations? What are the points of spiritual warfare? Is it a struggle with doubt? Is it a hard time taking

God and His Word at face value? Is it a struggle with an unforgiving spirit? Is it resentment and bitterness toward someone who has betrayed your trust? Is it a struggle with illness that is getting the upper hand? Is it the loss of a loved one? Is it a struggle with an addiction to alcohol or drugs? Is it a struggle relationally with a partner or child? Is it a struggle with emotions that are confusing? Is it a struggle with the overbearing power of someone who is trying to control you?

Question 2: "Are you letting God conquer your Jerichos for you?" Is He being allowed to wage the battle or are you doing it in your own power? Is the strategy His or yours?

This story of Jericho reminds us that God is in the business of giving victory to His obedient people when we move beyond our own clever plans to a straightforward trust and obedience. This is where the litany of Hebrews 11 makes so much sense. It's "by faith" that the walls of Jericho fell down. It was the ark of the covenant, representing the presence of the Lord, not human energy, that carried the day. It's when we admit our own vulnerability and let go of it, turning it over to the Lord, that we have the spiritual empowerment sufficient for the greatest Jericho, the most impregnable stronghold of Satan. We need to be honest; we need to admit our area of weakness and relinquish it, allowing God to work in our lives, doing what He wills. This will take patience. He works in unseen and unheralded ways; and sometimes that victory takes a little longer than we desire. So we are privileged both in words and in deeds to model to those who listen to and watch this Jericho story of victory.

NOTE

1. James S. Stewart, *King Forever* (Nashville: Abingdon, 1975), pp. 91–92.

CHAPTER EIGHT—TWO DIFFERENT GODS?
JOSHUA 6:21–27

^{21} And they utterly destroyed all that was in the city, both man and woman, young and old, ox and sheep and donkey, with the edge of the sword. ^{22} But Joshua had said to the two men who had spied out the country, "Go into the harlot's house, and from there bring out the woman and all that she has, as you swore to her." ^{23} And the young men who had been spies went in and brought out Rahab, her father, her mother, her brothers, and all that she had. So they brought out all her relatives and left them outside the camp of Israel. ^{24} But they burned the city and all that was in it with fire. Only the silver and gold, and the vessels of bronze and iron, they put into the treasury of the house of the LORD. ^{25} And Joshua spared Rahab the harlot, her father's household, and all that she had. So she dwells in Israel to this day, because she hid the messengers whom Joshua sent to spy out Jericho.

^{26} Then Joshua charged them at that time, saying, "Cursed be the man before the LORD who rises up and builds this city Jericho; he shall lay its foundation with his firstborn, and with his youngest he shall set up its gates."

^{27} So the LORD was with Joshua, and his fame spread throughout all the country.

—Joshua 6:21–27

Years ago, I spent some time with Madalyn Murray O'Hair, the outspoken representative of atheism in the United States. As a young girl, she had occasionally attended the First Presbyterian Church of Pittsburgh, Pennsylvania, which at the time of our interview I was pastoring. Although she was making one of her typical television appearances on a prime-time interview show that I hosted, I went out of my way to spend some time with her off camera. Under those circumstances, she was no longer the outrageous preacher-baiting character to whom I'd become so accustomed.

I asked her what turned her away from her childhood Presbyterianism to atheism. She described one long weekend as a teenager when she was determined to read the Bible from cover to cover and noted that most Christians have never done so. She said the stories of God-ordained cruelty and even genocide in the Old Testament, along with the hypocritical way many Christians live, turned her away from Christianity. Although Madalyn Murray O'Hair is an extreme example, her arguments must be addressed.

THE PROBLEM

Every so often someone says to me, "I can believe in the God of the New Testament, the God of Jesus, the God of love, but not that other God of the Old Testament, the One who kills innocent babies and women, that wrathful, vengeful God. There are two Gods. The One of the Old Testament, the God of law, and the One of the New Testament, the God of grace. I can accept the New Testament God but not that Old Testament God."

I preached on the Book of Joshua for my own congregation, while at the same time researching and writing each of the chapters of this commentary. Several days after I preached on the battle of Jericho, one of the more active members of my church approached me, saying, "As we study Joshua, I'm overwhelmed by the atrocities in which God demanded that all the people of Jericho be slaughtered. This troubles me. How can a good God act in such an arbitrary way?"

These comments must be taken seriously. As communicators, we must be listening to our people as well as speaking to them. They are puzzled by the "slaughters of people" that we read about in the Old Testament. We could try to sidestep the issue by not even addressing the specifics of such battles as Jericho. We could spiritualize passages such as Joshua 6:21–27. If we do this, however, we are picking and choosing what we want out of God's Word and not dealing responsibly with the text. I found that in all good conscience I had to address these questions raised by not only some in my congregation but also by myself. These comments and questions must be faced, and there are answers we need to have about God.

Not only are there answers in this text to the questions we ask about God, there are also implications for how we act. For example, the first Crusade culminated in the capture of Jerusalem and the defeat of Muslim defenders on July 15, A.D. 1099. This victory was achieved by terrible bloodshed and slaughter. The Christian historians of that event note that some ten thousand Muslims were beheaded in the Great Mosque. The vicinity of the Sacred Precinct was choked with blood and corpses. These chroniclers, mainly Christian clerics, accounted these facts with joy, applauding the "justice" that was done.[1] Roland Bainton, in his book *Christian Attitudes toward War and Peace,* notes that a favorite text of the Crusaders was drawn from the Old Testament: "Cursed is he who does the work of the LORD deceitfully, / And cursed is he who keeps back his sword from blood" (Jer. 48:10).[2]

Basic to this Jericho story and other significant messages in the Old Testament are specific commands of God that trouble our contemporary mindset and bring us to the kinds of questions already raised. These are the instructions God gave the people before the battle: "Now the city shall be doomed by the LORD to destruction, it and all who are in it. Only Rahab the harlot shall live, she and all who are with her in the house, because she hid the messengers that we sent" (v. 17). Then, obedient to prior instructions, the Israelites encircled the city in the prescribed way. They blew the trumpets, shouted, and the walls fell down. This troubling, historical record is included: *"And they utterly destroyed all that was in the city, both man and woman, young and old, ox and sheep and donkey, with the edge of the sword"* (v. 21).

There are real questions that can honestly be raised by sensitive Christians. If we, who take the Bible seriously, skirt these questions in our preaching and teaching, we run two major risks. One risk is losing to sad disbelief those who never get beyond these questions. They deserve to hear us acknowledge the problem and at least speak to it. Second, we risk losing the richness of theological and spiritual insight that is ours as we wrestle with the tough questions. There are some answers as to why God acted in the ways that trouble us.

As I did my research on this, I noticed that there are some writers and commentators who simply do not acknowledge a problem. They are faithful, daily readers and teachers of the Bible. For them, the issue of war, and God's apparent ruthless dealings, is not a problem. Perhaps they've never wrestled with this issue or maybe they have already dealt with it. It may be that they simply take this for granted and "spiritualize" these Old Testament passages. At various points in my preaching from Joshua, I, too, have spiritualized in an endeavor to allow the ancient message to be contemporary. I took literally the fact of this battle of Jericho having happened in history. Then I swept quickly over these apparent atrocities and, in a spiritual way, applied God's strategy and the importance of our obedience to our contemporary Christian life. I rejoiced in the victory that God gives to those totally committed to Him, while neglecting to emphasize that, as a historical record, this passage describes the literal slaughter of men and women, young and old, done in the name of obedience to God. In contemporary times, such activity could very well be followed by a war-crimes trial.

It is legitimate to spiritualize the text; however, we must also take the biblical text seriously as history. Then we confront three major problems, which Peter C. Craigie outlines in his book *The Problem of War in the Old Testament*.[3]

First, there is the *problem of God*, or the theological problem. This problem is that one of God's dominant representations in the Old Testament is as a warrior. It is difficult to reconcile this concept with the New Testament description of God as loving and self-giving.

Second, there is the *problem of revelation*, which is very complex. Granted, there will always be wars. But why was it necessary for so much of the Old Testament literature to include such graphic accounts of these wars? Could not God have papered over this earthy material and simply not have inspired the Scripture writers to include this factual but question-producing material?

Third, there is the *problem of ethics*. Are we to discount the Old Testament when it comes to learning ethics? Is Christianity based on New Testament ethical precepts alone? The Ten Commandments, one of the greatest, divinely revealed outlines of ethics, is in the Old Testament. But if we learn one kind of ethical standard from the Old Testament, are we to conclude that we are eagerly to involve ourselves in such unrelenting and totally warlike activities? Is this the model?

Our generation is not the first to raise these questions. They go all the way back to the first centuries of the Christian church. Marcion, the wealthy shipowner, came to Rome just before A.D. 140. He was active in the Orthodox Christian community but was then excommunicated. He raised these same questions and concluded that there was such a radical contrast between the New Testament gospel and the Old Testament law that he ultimately rejected the whole Old Testament. This God of law and righteousness he called a "demiurge," a secondary deity who made the world. To Marcion, the Old Testament and its morality became a document of an alien religion and its God a dangerous power. Marcion was declared a heretic.

This reasoning emerged again in the fourth century. Called Manichaeism, it was a dualistic system contrasting the God of the Old Testament with the God of the New Testament. The Old

Testament was viewed as an inferior and un-Christian book. In the twelfth century, the Catharists, "the pure ones," further developed this same line of thinking.

Today there are certain theological writers who hold to this same approach. The late Harry Emerson Fosdick, in his *Guide to Understanding the Bible*, outlined three offensive characteristics in Old Testament ethics. He observed that the Old Testament is exclusive and provincial, whereas the New Testament is universal and open to varying cultures. The Old Testament is inhumane, class conscious, chauvinistic, emphasizing slavery and polygamy, whereas the New Testament is humane. The Old Testament emphasizes external rites, rituals, bans, a religious calendar, whereas the New Testament emphasizes the inward spiritual qualities.[4]

Questions are raised. But are there any answers? Obviously, I cannot do justice to this matter in one chapter. Neither can I solve all these problems that have puzzled great theological ethicists throughout all the centuries of Christian thought. However, I am convinced that to avoid raising these questions is unwise. Let me make some observations that I trust will help clarify our understanding as communicators, push us into a deeper study, and enable us at least to acknowledge to those with whom we are sharing this study of Joshua the fact that we have reflected on these questions.

FOUR OBSERVATIONS

Four observations come to mind.

Observation 1: The God of the Old Testament and the New Testament is the same God. The Bible tells things realistically and states matters the way they are. God could have inspired a cosmetic document designed to make Him look good. Instead, His revelation states what actually happened, which should be encouraging to us.

Some have tried to work their way around the questions we've raised by attributing these apparent discrepancies between the Old and New Testament God to the evolution of our human thought about God. They think that this can be done without radically changing the nature of the Scriptures. The Old Testament is a major part of the Bible. It is the sacred writings of the Hebrews, the basic document on which the New Testament church built its faith, and the New Testament writers quoted it with frequency. Peter C. Craigie puts it in these words:

> To be faithful to our Christian legacy, it is necessary to
> keep the whole Bible; alternatively, one may reject the

whole Bible. It is very difficult, however, to settle in a half-way house, for the canonical Scriptures include both Testaments; while the relationship between those Testaments may be difficult to understand, nevertheless to question a part of the canon of Scripture is to question the whole. To oversimplify a very complex issue, the canon of Scripture places us in a "take it or leave it" situation; either alternative may be chosen in honesty, but the logic of a mid-way position is dangerous.[5]

This is one God, the God who is associated with the wars of ancient Israel and at the same time is the God who yearns for peace, who begs us to love one another, even our enemies. Simply to dismiss the Old Testament would be to dismiss a part of God and remove from Him a certain quality that actually enhances His holiness, His majesty, His sovereignty, and His grace.

Observation 2: This God has not chosen to remain aloof but has come incarnationally into this mixed-up world to involve Himself in our painful existence.

When we study history, what do we spend the most time studying? Is it the history of intellectual thought or the history of culture? Is it the history of science or the history of religion? All of these are major themes. However, I suggest that the greatest part of our history is devoted to the history of war. The annals of history are filled with the specific records of one war after another. Even the twentieth century, our own "enlightened era," is outlined by the history of the two great world wars with all of their horrible atrocities. And there are lesser wars that are major subpoints in this outline. They, too, have their terrible record of humankind's inhumanity to humankind. War is a sinful, human activity. It shows our inhumanity.

Now we come to what may very well be the most powerful discovery we will ever make. To see God as a God who involves Himself in our human wars, as sinful as they are, shows us that we have a God who has chosen to involve Himself in our lives, as sinful as they are. God could have functioned antiseptically, separately from us. After all, He is God—righteous, clean, and holy. He could have functioned in an entirely transcendent way over and above us. He could have miraculously wiped out the entire human race and started over. Or He could have simply turned His back on us and moved on out into some other place of His universe and let us rip ourselves apart with whatever pathologies are ours.

Instead, He chose, from the beginning, to enter into conversation with the part of His creation that bears His very image, fallen in rebellion and sin as we are. He walked in the garden with Adam and Eve, promising that One would come who would crush the head of the serpent. He entered into a covenant with Abraham. And God has kept His side of that covenant all through history to this present moment, even with humanity's sinful and rebellious nature. God's participation in human history, through our lives, does not primarily give us a glimpse of His moral being. Rather, it demonstrates His will and activity. He has offered us salvation by entering our lives. He participates in every aspect of human existence. He is involved with sinful persons and employs the very human beings who need salvation.

This does not mean that God likes war. We human beings are the ones who create wars. It is no surprise that there are wars among nations. Peter C. Craigie states it with such strength:

> The participation of God through evil human activity has a positive end in view; that is to say, the judgment of God, in the larger perspective, is the other face of the coin which is the mercy of God. Hence, on some occasions the reasons for God's exercise of sovereignty in war may be made evident (e.g., the punishment of evil men and nations by Israel, or the punishment of Israel by foreign nations), but they may remain as much a mystery as the initial mystery of God's creation of, and gift, of life.[6]

War is horrible, and people who have gone through war decide that they want peace. World War I was supposedly the "war to end all wars." Then came World War II, which made the First World War look like child's play. Now, in our enlightened twenty-first century, we have created an environment in which we have tiptoed to the edge of a nuclear precipice. Violence begets violence. God doesn't enjoy this. He is simply exercising His option of staying completely above it, turning His back on us, forgetting us, or loving us so much that He walks through this with us.

Our God is a God of "solidarity." He identifies with us as we are, not as He would like us to be. This is why the Bible is a story of people, ordinary people, good and bad. God acknowledges the fact of sin. He enters into a covenant with us, which He keeps even when we do not. The God of the Old and New Testaments is the same God. The only difference is that in the New Testament He actually fulfills what He promises in the Old Testament and becomes a man and goes to the Cross in that ultimate act of solidarity, identification, Incarnation.

Observation 3: God does judge, but He does it consistently.

God hates sin. He may be in constant contact with us, but this doesn't mean that He has compromised His holiness. When Joshua declares in the following words, "Now the city shall be doomed by the LORD to destruction, it and all who are in it" (v. 17), he is referring to objects or people that threaten to pollute the faith and the practices of Israel. These were banned from ordinary use or contact. The word in the Hebrew is *hērem*. The word applies to something separated or banned from ordinary use by a ritual act. In Deuteronomy 7:26, it is seen as the "accursed thing," and the polluted person is viewed as "cursed." A city that has turned away from God (Deut. 13:12–14) becomes *hērem*. It must be *hēremized*, utterly destroyed. This includes its inhabitants, its cult objects, its cattle, all of the spoil—a "whole burnt offering to the LORD."

The precedent for this is in Deuteronomy. Long before they actually came into the Promised Land, God outlined for the Israelites the importance of their remaining separate from the people of the land.

They were to be a holy people, maintaining the covenant:

> "When the LORD your God brings you into the land which you go to possess, and has cast out many nations before you, the Hittites and the Girgashites and the Amorites and the Canaanites and the Perizzites and the Hivites and the Jebusites, seven nations greater and mightier than you, and when the LORD your God delivers them over to you, you shall conquer them and utterly destroy them. You shall make no covenant with them nor show mercy to them. Nor shall you make marriages with them. You shall not give your daughter to their son, nor take their daughter for your son. For they will turn your sons away from following Me, to serve other gods; so the anger of the LORD will be aroused against you and destroy you suddenly. But thus you shall deal with them: you shall destroy their altars, and break down their sacred pillars, and cut down their wooden

images, and burn their carved images with fire" (Deut. 7:1–5).

Again, in Deuteronomy 18, God specifies certain practices that are an abomination to Him. It isn't that God arbitrarily hates these people; He hates their practices. He stands in judgment of what we do as human beings that destroys our humanness. He wants us to be a holy people, uncontaminated by those things that would destroy us. We have very strong teaching in the Mosaic Law that reads:

> "When you come into the land which the LORD your God is giving you, you shall not learn to follow the abominations of those nations. There shall not be found among you anyone who makes his son or his daughter pass through the fire, or one who practices witchcraft, or a soothsayer, or one who interprets omens, or a sorcerer, or one who conjures spells, or a medium, or a spiritist, or one who calls up the dead. For all who do these things are an abomination to the LORD, and because of these abominations the LORD your God drives them out from before you" (Deut. 18:9–12).

God is not functioning from whim. He is not an immoral God who arbitrarily devastates innocent people. As early as Genesis 15, hundreds of years before when He promised the land to Abraham, He referred to His people coming back into the land in the fourth generation: "For the iniquity of the Amorites is not yet complete" (v. 16). God is not going to bring His judgment upon an innocent people. God, in His foreknowledge, knows that several hundred years later Jericho, an Amorite city, will have to be severely judged. Jericho will join other doomed, sinning cities such as Babel (Gen. 11:4), Sodom (Gen. 19:4–29), Nineveh (Nah. 3:1), Tyre (Ezek. 26:17–19), Babylon (Jer. 50:23), and even Rome (Rev. 18:10).

God does judge, but He does it consistently. He judges not only the pagan people but also the Israelites. As they disobey God and accommodate themselves to these abominable practices, foreign powers—as insignificant as the city-state Ai and as overwhelming as Assyria and Babylonia—are the agents of His judgment upon His own chosen people. God cannot wink at sin.

Whatever contaminated the religion of His people, leading to inevitable compromise, was to be utterly destroyed. Sin is contagious and cannot go unpunished. A malignancy must be surgically removed.

Observation 4: God is also the God of grace, even in these Old Testament times.

The wilderness journey is over. The people of God—Israel, a stiff-necked, stubborn people—have now humbled themselves, reconsecrating themselves through circumcision and the observance of the Passover. God is ready to move in great spiritual power.

We see an amazing case study here of Rahab and her family. What more likely person would qualify for destruction than a Jericho prostitute? Yet we see here the fleshing out of the ongoing promise that God makes in His Word: "If with all your heart you truly seek me, you shall truly find me." The Jericho story is much more than just one of promiscuous massacre. This is the story of a sensitive, caring God who initiates His infinite grace. It is fascinating to observe how the writer mentions the destruction of Jericho and in the same written expression mentions the salvation of Rahab. We see this in Joshua 6:17, 22–23, and 24–25. Three times the destruction and redemption are mentioned almost in a kind of written/verbal refrain:

> But they burned the city and all that was in it with fire. Only the silver and gold, and the vessels of bronze and iron, they put into the treasury of the house of the LORD. And Joshua spared Rahab the harlot, her father's household, and all that she had. So she dwells in Israel to this day, because she hid the messengers whom Joshua sent to spy out Jericho (vv. 24–25).

Did Joshua send the spies into Jericho for intelligence alone? What great discoveries did they make that influenced the military strategy? God already knew His strategy. It appears that God knew that inside the walls of the doomed city was a sinful woman who hungered for righteousness, for a new life. Even as, hundreds of years later, Jesus must "needs go through Samaria" to bring spiritual deliverance to a similar woman sitting by Jacob's well, God sent those spies into Jericho as witnesses to His grace and deliverance to save this woman who was open to learn of Him. Rahab had truly sought the Lord. Now, faithful to the promise He made to her, God delivered her from Jericho and ultimately drafted her into the very genealogy of the promised Messiah. This is the same God who yearned for His people to be a holy people, a people uncontaminated by what would destroy their spiritual and personal vitality.

It is this same God who is no respecter of persons, whose judgment is severe upon sin and whose grace extends to all who trust Him. He is the God not of violence but of peace, the God who breathes His *shalom* into the lives of those who genuinely trust Him. He is the God who wants to convince us that violence only leads to more violence. Even in the Old Testament, God talks about the lion and the lamb lying down together.

We dare not tar and feather God with responsibility for violence that is done in His name or violence He would repudiate. God yearns for *shalom*. Peace is not just the absence of conflict; in its ultimate sense, it is "wholeness." It involves not only the cessation of war but also the absence of injustice and falsehood. God's grace and peace are not sentimental notions. They can only become operative where both His judgment and His love function in a strange and delicate tension. Even here, in this ethically puzzling story of Jericho, we see that out of the smoldering embers of a doomed city emerge a woman and her family who discover the liberating dynamic of God's peace that passes all understanding and His amazing grace.

This is not the final word. No human being has the final word on this topic. However, we as preachers dare not avoid recognizing the questions that come to mind as we read these complex Old Testament histories. Wherein we can shed some light, we must do it. Wherein we have no easy answers to these complex ethical and spiritual issues we must humbly acknowledge that fact, modeling what it is to bow in finite worship before the infinite God who has made provision for all humanity in the life, death, and Resurrection of Jesus Christ our Savior and Lord.

NOTES

1. John Gray, *A History of Jerusalem* (London: Robert Hale, 1969), pp. 236–37.

2. R. H. Bainton, *Christian Attitudes Toward War and Peace* (Nashville: Abingdon, 1960), p. 112.

3. Peter C. Craigie, *The Problem of War in the Old Testament* (Grand Rapids, Mich.: Wm. B. Eerdmans, 1978), p. 35.

4. Harry Emerson Fosdick, *Guide to Understanding the Bible* (New York: Harper, 1960), p. 8.

5. Craigie, *The Problem of War in the Old Testament*, p. 12.

6. Ibid., p. 42.

CHAPTER NINE—ACHAN AND AI—LEARNING HOW TO AVOID SPIRITUAL DEFEAT

JOSHUA 7:1—8:35

Scripture Outline

> Vulnerability at the Moment of Success (7:1–6)
>
> Turning Defeat into Victory (7:7–13)
>
> The Profound Effect of the Disobedience of One (7:14–18)
>
> A Scenario That Leads to Personal Defeat (7:19–23)
>
> The Severity of God's Judgment (7:24–26)
>
> A Hopeful Conclusion (8:1–35)

The story of Ai and Achan is really all about learning to avoid spiritual defeat. Israel is in the fresh flush of victory suffering a temporary defeat and being restored once again to victory. But it's more than ancient history. This story is one as ancient as the ages and as contemporary as today. It has particular relevance to those with whom we are endeavoring to communicate God's Word.

The whole matter of victory and defeat in the spiritual life of a nation and of an individual is the essence of this story. The two battles with Ai make interesting reading. One could make comparisons between Joshua's military strategy in the battle that led to defeat and the subsequent battle that led to victory. Such an approach would lend little light to believers today, though. Instead of dealing with the mechanical aspects of military strategy, I took the entire seventh and eighth chapters of Joshua as a case study. It is a superb model for the nation and the individual who desires to avoid spiritual defeat. I extracted six contemporary lessons from this experience of the man Achan and Israel's two battles with Ai.

VULNERABILITY AT THE MOMENT OF SUCCESS

7:1 But the children of Israel committed a trespass regarding the accursed things, for Achan the son of Carmi, the son of Zabdi, the son of Zerah, of the tribe of Judah, took of the accursed things; so the anger of the LORD burned against the children of Israel.

2 Now Joshua sent men from Jericho to Ai, which is beside Beth Aven, on the east side of Bethel, and spoke to them, saying, "Go up and spy out the country." So the men went up and spied out Ai. 3 And they returned to Joshua and said to him, "Do not let all the people go up, but let about two or three thousand men go up and attack Ai. Do not weary all the people there, for the people of Ai are few." 4 So about three thousand men went up there from the people, but they fled before the men of Ai. 5 And the men of Ai struck down about thirty-six men, for they chased them from before the gate as far as Shebarim, and struck them down on the descent; therefore the hearts of the people melted and became like water.

6 Then Joshua tore his clothes, and fell to the earth on his face before the ark of the LORD until evening, he and the elders of Israel; and they put dust on their heads.

—Joshua 7:1–6

Lesson 1: We are extremely vulnerable to temptation in moments of apparent success. Satan has a superb strategy. He goes for the kill when we are on a high. There is a danger in overconfidence.

When I am struggling, I am much more dependent upon the Lord. When my finances are low, I pray for help. When my body is broken by illness, I request enough strength to live with my pain one day at a time. If it's even more intense, I trust the Lord hour by hour and minute by minute. When I am released from the hospital and go home, my prayers are much less intense. When one of my children is going through some personal struggles, I pray a lot more. When there is a crisis in my career or a loved one is desperate, I turn more quickly to the Lord. Then I get the mistaken notion that I can handle things with my own strength when everything is going smoothly. It has been said, "The reason we Christians are in trouble so much is that this is the only time God hears from us."

Joshua illustrates this truth. Seldom has a military campaign been carried out with greater dependence upon the Lord than the battle at Jericho. It was a total faith effort—a miraculous, God-given victory. One of the strongest fortified cities of the Middle East crumbled before the onslaught of the Lord. Joshua is a hero. The last words dealing with Jericho are, "So the LORD was with Joshua, and his fame spread throughout all the country" (6:27). Joshua knew that the battle against Jericho was an impossibility in human terms. God gave the victory. Joshua and Israel were the beneficiaries.

Joshua, like any good military strategist, was determined to consolidate that victory with another. He sent his spies several miles up into the northern Judean hills to do reconnaissance on a small city named Ai. The report came back: *"Do not let all the people go up, but let about two or three thousand men go up and attack Ai. Do not weary all the people there, for the people of Ai are few"* (7:3).

So Joshua acted quickly, thinking it would be an easy battle. He didn't even think to pray. After all, any army that had defeated Jericho shouldn't have a problem with little Ai. Joshua was also aware that he was notorious for his military prowess. His fame had spread throughout all the country.

The Israelites, however, were defeated. The men of Ai chased them down those rugged hillsides and killed thirty-six troops. This is ironic when, in their potential vulnerability to the archers on the walls of Jericho, not one was killed.

This defeat can be transposed into the spiritual battles that we fight each day. We have to conclude that, apart from Jesus and the help of the Holy Spirit, the smallest temptation will be too powerful for us.

There is an insightful observation made by the historian in verse 5. He stated, *"Therefore the hearts of the people melted and became like water."* The last time that expression was used was when Rahab described the fear within Jericho of the reputation of the approaching Israelites. She told the spies that when the citizens of Jericho heard about God's deliverance through the Red Sea and how the Israelites had defeated the Amorite kings, Sihon and Og, "Our hearts melted; neither did there remain any more courage in anyone because of you, for the LORD your God, He is God in heaven above and on earth beneath" (2:11). How quickly the tables can turn.

Confidence in God, which produces success and victory, can very quickly turn to self-confidence. "Pride goes before destruction. A haughty spirit before a fall." This is an important lesson never to forget. Yesterday's victory will not bring victory today. Joshua's experience helps us get this point across to our people.

I am haunted by this spiritual reality. I've seen so many Christian leaders once powerful in their ministries fall by the wayside in embarrassing defeat. There are evangelists who once led hundreds and even thousands of people to personal faith in Jesus Christ whose lives ended up as hollow shells of what they once were spiritually. Pastors of energetic churches filled with people growing in their faith, at a moment of self-confidence, have stumbled in defeat, never to regain their former stride. Youth ministers, Christian musicians, founders of Christian parachurch organizations, all with God-given genius, have knocked down spiritual walls much larger and impenetrable than those physical walls of Jericho, only to be defeated by some little Ai. In pride, in self-confidence, at the very moment of victory, Satan caught them at the soft spot in which they were vulnerable to their specific kind of temptation. His poison arrow did its work.

I've been quite aware of my own vulnerability as I've wrestled with this biblical text. While working on this chapter, I spoke at a spiritual renewal weekend at the Webster Groves Presbyterian Church in St. Louis, Missouri. I was overwhelmed with my own inadequacy. The last large renewal retreat held at that church had three speakers teamed together in one dynamically explosive weekend—Keith Miller, Bruce Larson, and Lloyd Ogilvie. In my view, these are three of the most outstanding conveyors of Christ's new life to contemporary American Christians. I went into that conference more prayerful than I have ever been before and enlisted the prayers of other believers. I spoke not one sentence without a transparency of openness to the Lord. In dependence upon His power, God blessed in a remarkable way. I left St. Louis overwhelmed with what God had done in bringing some spiritual victories that went beyond my personal abilities and comprehension.

Then I caught a plane to Dallas, Texas, where I would be speaking twice the next day at the Highland Park Presbyterian Church. I checked into my hotel on a Sunday afternoon and decided to watch a few minutes of what proved to be the last game of the World Series. I flicked on the television set only to see a succession of quick previews of adult sex films that were available at a modest price, piped directly into the privacy of my room with a single fingertip touch of any of four buttons. By God's grace, I resisted. But, frankly, the struggle, the temptation, was there.

Every single rationalization went through my mind as to how I needed to be aware of the kinds of entertainment that traveling men were seeing if I were to have a valid ministry to such men. It wasn't just a passing temptation. Every single time I turned on the television during the next twenty-four hours to simply catch the early-evening, late-night, or early-morning news, those same titillating movie reviews came on. The TV was wired for the ads, so there was nothing I could do about it. Each time, whatever preparations I had been making for my messages, whatever prayers I had been praying, whatever Scripture I had been reading, whatever healthy thoughts about my wife, Anne, and my three daughters I had been having, they were all jeopardized until I claimed the strength of the Lord to press the local and network channels and avoid those others that would represent succumbing to defeat. I've been in other such hotels before. Never has the struggle been so intense and never had I been in that environment on the heels of such a spiritual blessing in ministry.

TURNING DEFEAT INTO VICTORY

7 And Joshua said, "Alas, Lord GOD, why have You brought this people over the Jordan at all—to deliver us into the hand of the Amorites, to destroy us? Oh, that we had been content, and dwelt on the other side of the Jordan! 8 O Lord, what shall I say when Israel turns its back before its enemies? 9 For the Canaanites and all the inhabitants of the land will hear it, and surround us, and cut off our name from the earth. Then what will You do for Your great name?"

10 So the LORD said to Joshua: "Get up! Why do you lie thus on your face? 11 Israel has sinned, and they have also transgressed My covenant which I commanded them. For they have even taken some of the accursed things, and have both stolen and deceived; and they have also put it among their own stuff. 12 Therefore the children of Israel could not stand before their enemies, but turned their backs before their enemies, because they have become doomed to destruction. Neither will I be with you anymore, unless you destroy the accursed from among you. 13 Get up, sanctify the people, and say, 'Sanctify yourselves for tomorrow, because thus says the LORD God of Israel: "There is an accursed thing in your midst, O Israel; you cannot stand before your enemies until you take away the accursed thing from among you.'"

—*Joshua 7:7–13*

Lesson 2: Defeat can be turned into victory if we take it to God. Joshua was devastated in the Ai defeat. Tearing his clothes, he fell on the earth before the ark of the Lord until evening. He and the elders of Israel put dust upon their heads. He cried out, arguing with God, asking why. We need to remind ourselves and our people of the importance of giving vent to our feelings as we talk to God, of throwing ourselves prostrate on the floor or a bed, or pounding our fists in anguish. When there's been some terrible reversal, some awful defeat, some life-threatening situation, God doesn't expect us to be stoic or to pretend it isn't there. We are privileged to learn from Joshua.

He could have denied reality. The loss of 36 men didn't seem so great when 2,964 men had returned home safely. They could always hit Ai again with more strength the next time.

But Joshua wasn't content to take this somewhat detached philosophical approach. The power that had been present at Jericho was no longer there. His leadership was empty, and he was going to wrestle this thing through with God and find out what was the cause. So he continues to cry out, "Why?" Joshua throws at the Lord his inner thoughts of how it would have been much better to have stayed on the other side of the Jordan. What gain was there to come over to Jericho, only to be destroyed by the Amorites?

> "Alas, Lord GOD, why have You brought this people over the Jordan at all—to deliver us into the hand of the Amorites, to destroy us? Oh, that we had been content, and dwelt on the other side of the Jordan! O Lord, what shall I say when Israel turns its back before its enemies? For the Canaanites and all the inhabitants of the land will hear it, and surround us, and cut off our name from the earth" (vv. 7–9).

We have the opportunity to identify with Joshua and to enable the people with whom we are communicating to relate similar feelings they have had. Sometimes we might have reached that depth of despair when we were in total honesty trying to serve God, trying to do the best we could, and something went wrong. Use the example of Joshua. We are privileged to validate our feelings and the ruggedly honest conversations with God that they can produce. We must encourage ourselves and our people to tell God when we feel foolish and when we feel like He's been allowing us to flounder on our own when we really were trying to serve Him.

Joshua takes this little monologue one step further into what almost sounds like blasphemy: "Then what will You do for Your great *name?"* (v. 9). He is quick to turn the tables on God, saying, "Not only do I look like a fool, but You might also look foolish. For You are the God who defeated Jericho. Right at the moment the Amorites and the Canaanites have come to stand in awe of Your power, You go down with us in ignominious defeat at the hands of little Ai. What are You going to do about this, God?"

God honors this kind of prayer that has a kind of transparency. We need to encourage it and to help our people feel free to talk this way to God. There is nothing that He desires more of us than an honest, open heart free to express our deepest concerns. God honors our prayers if we are willing to bring that additional dimension to conversation that Joshua brought—if we are willing to finally quit talking and start listening.

God has been a part of this conversation. He has heard every question that Joshua has raised, and He has some answers. There is a reason for the trouble and the defeat. Reality is often difficult to accept. It is easier to see life in our own illusionary ways.

God levels with Joshua:

> *So the Lord said to Joshua: "Get up! Why do you lie thus on your face? Israel has sinned, and they have also transgressed My covenant which I commanded them. For they have even taken some of the accursed things, and have both stolen and deceived; and they have also put it among their own stuff. Therefore the children of Israel could not stand before their enemies, but turned their backs before their enemies, because they have become doomed to destruction. Neither will I be with you anymore, unless you destroy the accursed from among you. Get up, sanctify the people, and say, 'Sanctify yourselves for tomorrow, because thus says the Lord God of Israel: "There is an accursed thing in your midst, O Israel; you cannot stand before your enemies until you take away the accursed thing from among you"'"* (vv. 10–13).

Joshua got his answer. Defeat can be turned to victory if we are prepared to throw ourselves prostrate before the Lord, to open up honestly with Him and to listen and to act upon what He says.

THE PROFOUND EFFECT OF THE DISOBEDIENCE OF ONE

14 'In the morning therefore you shall be brought according to your tribes. And it shall be that the tribe which the Lord takes shall come according to families; and the family which

the LORD takes shall come by households; and the household which the LORD takes shall come man by man.
¹⁵ Then it shall be that he who is taken with the accursed thing shall be burned with fire, he and all that he has, because he has transgressed the covenant of the LORD, and because he has done a disgraceful thing in Israel.' "
¹⁶ So Joshua rose early in the morning and brought Israel by their tribes, and the tribe of Judah was taken. ¹⁷ He brought the clan of Judah, and he took the family of the Zarhites; and he brought the family of the Zarhites man by man, and Zabdi was taken. ¹⁸ Then he brought his household man by man, and Achan the son of Carmi, the son of Zabdi, the son of Zerah, of the tribe of Judah, was taken.

—Joshua 7:14–18

Lesson 3: The disobedience of one individual can have a profound effect upon a whole community. God does not wink at sin. Sin corrupts, and what is done in private has a public effect. God is blunt with Joshua and tells him that someone else has caused Israel's troubles. Something had been done in private that had a public effect. Someone in disobedience had taken of the *"accursed"* ("devoted," RSV) things that were to have been destroyed in Jericho. The word for the "accursed" (or "devoted") thing, what was to be destroyed at Jericho, is mentioned seven times in this chapter. This is no meaningless act to God.

God tells Joshua to line up the people, tribe by tribe, family by family, household by household, man by man, and examine everyone until the one who has brought this evil upon Israel is uncovered and the abomination is destroyed. Sanctification and purification were needed.

Achan is the archetype of the dark side that marks every human individual and every human community. Joshua made the mistake of going into battle without having consulted the Lord. He was vulnerable in his moment of victory at Jericho. But Joshua was also sensitive to the Lord. He was open to learn, modeling for us what it is to keep close accounts with God.

Achan, however, represents that spiritual malignancy, that cancer, which, if allowed to grow, can choke the vitality of an individual, of a family, of a church, and even of a nation. He is determined to hide; and thus far, he has successfully pulled off his cover-up. But as Joshua works through from tribe to family to household to individuals, he finally comes to the family of Judah, to the household of the Zarhites, to the family of Zabdi, to Achan the son of Carmi. Joshua questions Achan. Achan finally acknowledges his sin and admits that he is the cause of the troubles of Israel.

A much deeper truth comes out, though, than just that of Achan's sin. Disobedience to God is a contagious disease that has serious effects on the broader community. My sin cannot be isolated from you, and your sin cannot be isolated from me. There are corporate implications for our sin. Those to whom we are communicating need also to be aware of this. We cannot make this point forcefully enough. The British Bible expositor, Alan Redpath, puts it in these words:

> Now mark well a lesson here for all time. What actually had happened? One man had stolen property which belonged to God, had taken of the spoils of victory that were to be set apart for the Lord. One individual in the camp had betrayed God's trust, and the verdict from heaven was not, "Achan hath sinned," but "Israel hath sinned." One man had failed, and the whole army was defeated. You see, the children of Israel were a nation—they were brought to redemption ground as one man, the weakest of them and the strongest of them. They were a complete entity; God was dealing with them as a corporate body through whom His purposes for men were to be fulfilled.[1]

Redpath goes on to say, "I trust that the Holy Spirit is going to write this lesson deeply on your hearts. Where one member of a local fellowship is guilty before God of sin, the verdict from heaven is, 'My people have sinned.' When one man steps out of blessing and does something contrary to God's will, the verdict of the all-searching eye of our Master is, 'My people have sinned.'"[2]

A church family can be defeated by the malignancy of an individual's unconfessed sin.

A SCENARIO THAT LEADS TO PERSONAL DEFEAT

[19] Now Joshua said to Achan, "My son, I beg you, give glory to the LORD God of Israel, and make confession to Him, and tell me now what you have done; do not hide it from me."

[20] And Achan answered Joshua and said, "Indeed I have sinned against the LORD God of Israel, and this is what I have

done: ²¹ When I saw among the spoils a beautiful Babylonian garment, two hundred shekels of silver, and a wedge of gold weighing fifty shekels, I coveted them and took them. And there they are, hidden in the earth in the midst of my tent, with the silver under it."

²² So Joshua sent messengers, and they ran to the tent; and there it was, hidden in his tent, with the silver under it. ²³ And they took them from the midst of the tent, brought them to Joshua and to all the children of Israel, and laid them out before the Lord.

—*Joshua 7:19–23*

Lesson 4: There is a scenario that leads to defeat. Confronted, Achan was devastatingly honest and admitted that during the battle of Jericho he had taken three things that were either to be destroyed or turned over to the Lord's treasury. He had stolen a beautiful Babylonian coat, two hundred shekels of silver, and a bar of gold weighing fifty shekels. Achan told Joshua:

> *"Indeed I have sinned against the Lord God of Israel, and this is what I have done: "When I saw among the spoils a beautiful Babylonian garment, two hundred shekels of silver, and a wedge of gold weighing fifty shekels, I coveted them and took them. And there they are, hidden in the earth in the midst of my tent, with the silver under it" (vv. 20–21).*

First Achan said, *"I saw."* He must have been mesmerized. Second, he said, *"I coveted."* There is no question as to whether or not he really needed the garment, the silver, and the gold. He couldn't use it. James said that "every good and perfect gift comes from above." What good is a treasure that you cannot use, that you have to keep hidden, that is not yours?

It's no accident that the final and most inward of all the Ten Commandments deals with covetousness. Part of the Old Testament law reads, "You shall burn the carved images of their gods with fire; you shall not covet the silver or gold that is on them, nor take it for yourselves, lest you be snared by it; for it is an abomination to the Lord your God" (Deut. 7:25). Jesus restated this in more contemporary words: "Take heed and beware of covetousness, for one's life does not consist in the abundance of the things he possesses" (Luke 12:15). Covetousness destroys joy in the Christian. The grass is always greener on the other side of the fence. When we spend our time looking across the fence at what we don't own, we miss seeing how gracious God has been in what is legitimately ours.

Achan said, "I saw, I coveted, I took, and I hid." Silver and gold are not bad in themselves, but how often they take over our minds and lead us away from God into an idolatry of things. This is a familiar story. Adam and Eve also wanted something that was forbidden. Achan's story is ours wherein we are unwilling to say with the apostle Paul, "I have learned in whatever state I am, to be content" (Phil. 4:11).

THE SEVERITY OF GOD'S JUDGMENT

24 Then Joshua, and all Israel with him, took Achan the son of Zerah, the silver, the garment, the wedge of gold, his sons, his daughters, his oxen, his donkeys, his sheep, his tent, and all that he had, and they brought them to the Valley of Achor. 25 And Joshua said, "Why have you troubled us? The LORD will trouble you this day." So all Israel stoned him with stones; and they burned them with fire after they had stoned them with stones.

26 Then they raised over him a great heap of stones, still there to this day. So the LORD turned from the fierceness of His anger. Therefore the name of that place has been called the Valley of Achor to this day.

—Joshua 7:24–26

Lesson 5: God's judgment is not to be taken lightly. Achan's tale is one of the saddest stories in the entire Bible. Achan, the mantle, the bar of gold, the silver, and his sons and daughters, and oxen and asses and sheep, and his tent and all he had were taken up to the Valley of Achor, which means the valley of trouble. Joshua asked Achan, *"'Why have you troubled us? The LORD will trouble you this day'"* (v. 25). And Israel stoned Achan and his family, then burned them with fire. There was raised over him a great heap of stones as a reminder of Achan's sin and the Lord's turning from His burning anger, restoring Israel to a right relationship with Himself.

I'd like to sugarcoat this whole story and say that when Achan admitted his sins, God forgave him and everything was all right. Terrible things happen in this world to which there are consequences. God dealt swiftly with Achan. He could not afford to let the malignancy of greed run rampant among His people as they came into the Promised Land.

What about Achan's innocent family? Perhaps they were not so innocent. Undoubtedly, they were accomplices to the crime, aiding and abetting in this cover-up. In Deuteronomy 24:16, God makes it clear that children are not to pay for the crimes of their parents, and parents are not to pay for the crimes of their children. We see then—as we see with the Mafia today—that unless we get to the heart of the problem and surgically remove the cancer, the malignancy will spread. There is no record here of repentance. Achan and his family had done their best to cover up their deed. The penalty was severe. "The wages of sin is death." Even as God's mercy deals graciously with the most unlikely people, such as Rahab, who seek after Him, His justice and wrath keep Him from winking sentimentally at what is wrong.

A HOPEFUL CONCLUSION

8:1 Now the LORD said to Joshua: "Do not be afraid, nor be dismayed; take all the people of war with you, and arise, go up to Ai. See, I have given into your hand the king of Ai, his people, his city, and his land. 2 And you shall do to Ai and its king as you did to Jericho and its king. Only its spoil and its cattle you shall take as booty for yourselves. Lay an ambush for the city behind it."

3 So Joshua arose, and all the people of war, to go up against Ai; and Joshua chose thirty thousand mighty men of valor and sent them away by night. 4 And he commanded them, saying: "Behold, you shall lie in ambush against the city, behind the city. Do not go very far from the city, but all of you be ready. 5 Then I and all the people who are with me will approach the city; and it will come about, when they come out against us as at the first, that we shall flee before them. 6 For they will come out after us till we have drawn them from the city, for they will say, 'They are fleeing before us as at the first.' Therefore we will flee before them. 7 Then you shall rise from the ambush and seize the city, for the LORD your God will deliver it into your hand. 8 And it will be, when you have taken the city, that you shall set the city on fire. According to the commandment of the LORD you shall do. See, I have commanded you."

9 Joshua therefore sent them out; and they went to lie in ambush, and stayed between Bethel and Ai, on the west side of Ai; but Joshua lodged that night among the people. 10 Then Joshua rose up early in the morning and mustered the people, and went up, he and the elders of Israel, before the people to

Ai. [11] And all the people of war who were with him went up and drew near; and they came before the city and camped on the north side of Ai. Now a valley lay between them and Ai. [12] So he took about five thousand men and set them in ambush between Bethel and Ai, on the west side of the city. [13] And when they had set the people, all the army that was on the north of the city, and its rear guard on the west of the city, Joshua went that night into the midst of the valley.

[14] Now it happened, when the king of Ai saw it, that the men of the city hurried and rose early and went out against Israel to battle, he and all his people, at an appointed place before the plain. But he did not know that there was an ambush against him behind the city. [15] And Joshua and all Israel made as if they were beaten before them, and fled by the way of the wilderness. [16] So all the people who were in Ai were called together to pursue them. And they pursued Joshua and were drawn away from the city. [17] There was not a man left in Ai or Bethel who did not go out after Israel. So they left the city open and pursued Israel.

[18] Then the LORD said to Joshua, "Stretch out the spear that is in your hand toward Ai, for I will give it into your hand." And Joshua stretched out the spear that was in his hand toward the city. [19] So those in ambush arose quickly out of their place; they ran as soon as he had stretched out his hand, and they entered the city and took it, and hurried to set the city on fire. [20] And when the men of Ai looked behind them, they saw, and behold, the smoke of the city ascended to heaven. So they had no power to flee this way or that way, and the people who had fled to the wilderness turned back on the pursuers.

[21] Now when Joshua and all Israel saw that the ambush had taken the city and that the smoke of the city ascended, they turned back and struck down the men of Ai. [22] Then the others came out of the city against them; so they were caught in the midst of Israel, some on this side and some on that side. And they struck them down, so that they let none of them remain or escape. [23] But the king of Ai they took alive, and brought him to Joshua.

[24] And it came to pass when Israel had made an end of slaying all the inhabitants of Ai in the field, in the wilderness where they pursued them, and when they all had fallen by the edge of the sword until they were consumed, that all the Israelites

returned to Ai and struck it with the edge of the sword. 25 So it was that all who fell that day, both men and women, were twelve thousand—all the people of Ai. 26 For Joshua did not draw back his hand, with which he stretched out the spear, until he had utterly destroyed all the inhabitants of Ai. 27 Only the livestock and the spoil of that city Israel took as booty for themselves, according to the word of the LORD which He had commanded Joshua. 28 So Joshua burned Ai and made it a heap forever, a desolation to this day. 29 And the king of Ai he hanged on a tree until evening. And as soon as the sun was down, Joshua commanded that they should take his corpse down from the tree, cast it at the entrance of the gate of the city, and raise over it a great heap of stones that remains to this day.

30 Now Joshua built an altar to the LORD God of Israel in Mount Ebal, 31 as Moses the servant of the LORD had commanded the children of Israel, as it is written in the Book of the Law of Moses: "an altar of whole stones over which no man has wielded an iron tool." And they offered on it burnt offerings to the LORD, and sacrificed peace offerings. 32 And there, in the presence of the children of Israel, he wrote on the stones a copy of the law of Moses, which he had written.

33 Then all Israel, with their elders and officers and judges, stood on either side of the ark before the priests, the Levites, who bore the ark of the covenant of the LORD, the stranger as well as he who was born among them. Half of them were in front of Mount Gerizim and half of them in front of Mount Ebal, as Moses the servant of the LORD had commanded before, that they should bless the people of Israel. 34 And afterward he read all the words of the law, the blessings and the cursings, according to all that is written in the Book of the Law. 35 There was not a word of all that Moses had commanded which Joshua did not read before all the assembly of Israel, with the women, the little ones, and the strangers who were living among them.

—*Joshua 8:1–35*

Lesson 6: The end of this scenario is hope. It's a short lesson but the most encouraging of all. Joshua did not procrastinate but came right to the Lord with his problem. He searched for the causes of his defeat, then dealt confessionally with the sin and took a cleansing action.

Joshua set up another memorial to God. Many years later, this valley of trouble, Achor, through God's strange capacities, becomes converted to newness of life when it is labeled by the prophet Hosea a valley of future hope. God is sovereign and wills not defeat but victory for His people who live in transparent repentance and openness to Him. This tragic story of warning moves in positive transition with this statement, "So the LORD turned from the fierceness of His anger" (7:26).

Achan's story tells how one man's sin brought a nation to defeat. But now, humble repentance and dependence upon the Lord have turned that temporary defeat into a victory against Ai. God commended Joshua for dealing decisively with Achan and assured him:

"'Do not be afraid, nor be dismayed; take all the people of war with you, and arise, go up to Ai. See, I have given into your hand the king of Ai, his people, his city, and his land'" (8:1).

This time, Israel is allowed to keep the booty, but it is God who gives the strategy. He instructs Joshua to carry out a carefully planned ambush, which succeeds. There is no necessity to go into the specific details of this military attack. What is important is that Israel is once again in right relationship with God. The victory is theirs because He is in charge and has given them the victory. The conquest of the Promised Land is now back on schedule.

Chapter 8 concludes with a most fascinating little vignette. Verses 30–35 describe how Joshua built an altar of unhewn stones at Mount Ebal. He presented a burnt offering and a peace offering to God. Then Joshua wrote upon the stones a copy of the law for others who passed by to read. He also read the entire law to the people, reminding them of their roots and the importance of being in right relationship with God.

There is some question as to the exact sequence of events that would have taken the people all the way from Ai and Gilgal to Mount Ebal and then back to Gilgal. Some scholars believe that this event happened at a later time but that it is included here by the author of Joshua to remind future readers of the Mosaic precedent for the conquest and the terms of the law which regulate all that has happened and will happen. Whether this appears in perfect chronological sequence or not, it is clear that a new era has begun. The Canaanites are beginning to join together. The once tragic events at Ai have now come to a hopeful conclusion. Joshua and the people are aware of their vulnerability and the importance of staying in right relationship with God.

NOTES

1. Alan Redpath, *Victorious Christian Living* (Westwood, N.J.: Fleming H. Revell Co., 1955), pp. 118–19.

2. Ibid., p. 119.

CHAPTER TEN—DECEPTION, GULLIBILITY, AND INTEGRITY

JOSHUA 9:1–27

Scripture Outline

  Deception (9:1–13)
  Gullibility (9:14–15)
  Integrity (9:16–27)

Anew era has begun as the Canaanites are beginning to join to-gether. The first verses of chapter 9 describe the kings, who were in the hill country of Judea and the lowland all along the Mediterranean Coast, entering into an alliance to fight against Joshua. There is much more about these people and others in chapters 10 and 11. In the meantime, a most fascinating story unfolds about the people of Israel and the Gibeonites.

Even as the different kings mentioned were making their alliance to fight against Israel, there were several cities a few miles north of Jerusalem that had heard about Joshua and what had happened to Jericho and Ai. These Hivite towns were coordinated by the leaders of Gibeon who, fearful of the Israelites, concluded that it was better to give in than to fight. Fearful of annihilation, either through defeat in battle or by straightforward surrender, they worked out a clever strategy. Pretending to be from a far country, they took worn-out sacks, torn and mended wineskins; dressed themselves up in worn-out clothes, patched sandals; packed dry and moldy food; and made their way to Joshua at the base camp in Gilgal. They stated, "'We have come from a far coun-try; now therefore, make a covenant with us'" (v. 6).

Initially, Joshua suspected that they might be trying to deceive him and questioned them further. They told of how they had heard about God's dealings with Israel in Egypt and about the Israelites' exploits in the wilderness. They described their town council meetings in which they had been instructed to travel the long distance so as to enter into peace negotiations. Joshua, touched by their appeal, entered into a covenant with them to let them live.

Within three days after the covenant was established, the Israelites discovered how they had been deceived. These people lived only three days away from Gilgal in their cities of Gibeon, Chephirah, Beeroth, and Kirjath Jearim. The Israelites murmured against their leaders, accusing them of being gullible. Joshua and the leadership, aware of how they had been tricked, acknowledged this. But they also acknowledged that a covenant was a covenant and could not be taken lightly. Joshua honored the covenant while making a curse against the Gibeonites for their dishonesty. They were cursed to be the servants of the Israelites. Yet for the generations to come, they were to be protected by the Israelites, even to the point that Joshua was prepared to go to battle to defend them from their enemies.

The question for us as preachers is, How can we treat this fascinating, historical vignette in a way that speaks with contemporary relevance? Is this simply a quaint story that provides an interesting change of pace in what is otherwise an extremely intense narrative of conquest? Or is there deep symbolism involved?

E. John Hamlin sees these historical events as a prime teaching tool in which the Joshua story is remembered, condensed, and structured by a nameless author whom he refers to as "the Teacher." Hamlin favors a much later dating of Joshua and sees the Teacher as a member of a reform group that worked for many decades from the time of King Hezekiah to the time of King Josiah and on into the exilic period. It was this group that inspired the great reform led by Josiah in 622 B.C. called the Deuteronomic Reform. Hamlin sees the Teacher as using already existing materials, including an earlier version of Joshua 2 through 12, contributed by a northern writer in the ninth century B.C. whom he calls the Narrator.[1]

Writing from this perspective, Hamlin then sees the life of Israel in Canaan as being like the life of Christians in every nation, a life characterized by a tension between faith and practices on one side and the demands of living in the world with different cultures and values on the other side. Therefore, he develops three models.

The first he calls the "Jericho model," which stresses the radical discontinuity between the revolutionary new society of Israel and the old corrupt society of Canaan. There was to be no coexistence.

Jericho, its inhabitants, and its culture were to be completely destroyed except for certain objects which were then incorporated into the worship structures of the Israelite community.

The second he calls the "Ai model." This is preceded by the solemn warning of the Achan story that leads to a modification. There can be a continuity of material things—such as the spoils of battle that were denied at Jericho but were allowed at Ai—as long as these material things are used fairly for the common good. Any relationship between the people and the culture, including religion, is still strictly forbidden.

The third he calls the "Gibeon model." In this, a revolutionary community meets a friendly group from a Canaanite society who seeks alliance with them and offers great strategic benefits to the newly arrived company. An outright rejection of this request and offer by the Gibeonites on the sole ground that they are Canaanites (the Jericho model) is ruled out. Acceptance of the benefits while rejecting the alliance (the Ai model) would be cynical opportunism. The Gibeon model finds a way of living side by side for mutual benefit.

There are times when an alliance between faith and culture may be mutually beneficial. The Israelite side of the alliance should constantly keep aware of the Canaanite "poison in the wine," with their eyes open to discern and readily reject the Canaanite gods. At the same time, a blind prejudice and hatred of the Canaanites and greed for their goods are likely to erupt in Israel and spoil the chance of a fruitful alliance. Only wise leadership can prevent this. Therefore, the true evaluation of the Canaanite culture comes in the context of Israelite worship, which must be ready to accept foreign values and customs in the service of God.[2]

As I wrestled with this passage, endeavoring to be conscious of the needs of the congregation to whom I would be preaching, I could not dismiss this lightly as an interesting footnote in the history of the conquest. Nor could I bring myself to accept uncritically Hamlin's conclusions. They provide stimulating ideas for further reflection in the context of cross-cultural ministry. If I were preparing a lecture on Christian missions, Hamlin's theory would provide three fascinating models for cross-cultural interaction. And, if I were convinced of his critical conclusions as to the date of authorship, I might be inclined to prepare a sermon incorporating some of these stimulating insights.

I decided to treat this at face value as a historical event, however, a fascinating story that triggers reflective thought on three themes that the average Christian deals with daily. These are the themes of deception, gullibility, and integrity.

DECEPTION

9:1 And it came to pass when all the kings who were on this side of the Jordan, in the hills and in the lowland and in all the coasts of the Great Sea toward Lebanon—the Hittite, the Amorite, the Canaanite, the Perizzite, the Hivite, and the Jebusite—heard about it, ² that they gathered together to fight with Joshua and Israel with one accord.

³ But when the inhabitants of Gibeon heard what Joshua had done to Jericho and Ai, ⁴ they worked craftily, and went and pretended to be ambassadors. And they took old sacks on their donkeys, old wineskins torn and mended, ⁵ old and patched sandals on their feet, and old garments on themselves; and all the bread of their provision was dry and moldy. ⁶ And they went to Joshua, to the camp at Gilgal, and said to him and to the men of Israel, "We have come from a far country; now therefore, make a covenant with us."

⁷ Then the men of Israel said to the Hivites, "Perhaps you dwell among us; so how can we make a covenant with you?"

⁸ But they said to Joshua, "We are your servants."

And Joshua said to them, "Who are you, and where do you come from?"

⁹ So they said to him: "From a very far country your servants have come, because of the name of the LORD your God; for we have heard of His fame, and all that He did in Egypt, ¹⁰ and all that He did to the two kings of the Amorites who were beyond the Jordan—to Sihon king of Heshbon, and Og king of Bashan, who was at Ashtaroth. ¹¹ Therefore our elders and all the inhabitants of our country spoke to us, saying, 'Take provisions with you for the journey, and go to meet them, and say to them, "We are your servants; now therefore, make a covenant with us." ' ¹² This bread of ours we took hot for our provision from our houses on the day we departed to come to you. But now look, it is dry and moldy. ¹³ And these wineskins which we filled were new, and see, they are torn; and these our garments and our sandals have become old because of the very long journey."

—Joshua 9:1–13

This story of deception says that dishonesty, for whatever reasons, may work temporarily but is never a permanent solution to whatever difficult situation arises. God recognized that the Gibeonites were not all bad. They were people concerned with their families' welfare. These men were being lobbied to join the alliance against Israel, which was being formed by Adoni-Zedek, the king of Jerusalem. The Gibeonites had an uncanny sense that to fight Israel would bring disaster. Perhaps there was a better way to protect themselves and their future.

Rather like Rahab, they had a knowledge of God's doings for they had heard the rumors of how the Israelites had some forty years earlier fled Egypt. Travelers on the caravan routes had told of this strange, nomadic group living in the Sinai Desert. Military intelligence was fairly sophisticated in those days, and Israel was being tracked as it moved on to the east bank of the Jordan. Then came the horror stories of the defeat and total destruction of Jericho. But the rumor was whispered that little Ai had defeated the Israelites. The kings thought that the Israelites might not be so invulnerable after all. Thus, the alliance of the kings formed against Israel, Then the word got out that Ai had been defeated in a second battle, and it appeared that Israel would be moving up into the hills toward Jerusalem.

I tried to put myself and my congregation into the thoughts and feelings of the Gibeonites. If we had lived in those hills, we, too, would have heard the rumors. We, too, would have had to make a choice. Would we fight? Would we run? Or would we sue for peace?

The Gibeonites were sort of like Rahab, but not completely. They had heard as she had about these strange people and their God. But this is where the parallel ends. Rahab not only had a cognitive knowledge about the God of Israel, but she also had a heart open to learn more of Him and worship Him. As far as the Gibeonites were concerned, they apparently had only enough cognitive knowledge to lead them to fear and were willing to do anything to save their necks. What they didn't have was a faith open to honesty, transparently seeking out the God of Israel, coming to personal faith in Him. So they tried to save themselves by deception.

A lying tongue can buy a bit of reprieve, but deception never works permanently. The Gibeonites pulled off their cover-up for all of three days, demonstrating one of the most short-lived deceptions in the annals of military history.

The Gibeonites were not all bad; but wrong, even in the pursuit of good, is not justified. We could build a case that in war anything goes. Deception is the name of the game. We can extend this theme into life and see our relationships as adversarial: do whatever you need to do to save your neck. Many people live according to this Gibeonite ethic of expediency rules. They are basically good people trying to make it through life a day at a time. They do what comes naturally, what is expedient.

At this point, the communicator is free to ask the tough question, "Am I, are you, one of these street-smart people?" Whether one is a Gibeonite of over three thousand years ago, or a Christian living today, the fact of life is that an unexposed cover-up only makes the penalties greater. Suppose the Gibeonites had been honest. They might have been treated like Rahab. We don't know this for certain. But my knowledge of the God of the Old and New Testaments is that those who genuinely seek Him find Him. He is open to all whose hearts are transparently open to receiving His love and grace. Whether the Israelites would have been as kind, we don't know. But the Gibeonites certainly had no reason to believe that the Israelites would be as gracious as they were when they found out the deception. Suppose that we commit ourselves to a transparency of life so that when we get in a jam we do not try to squirm out. We simply say what is true. Are we prepared to make this commitment?

Deception only pays temporarily, never ultimately.

You can win at cards by cheating temporarily. My father-in-law often describes his fraternity days at the University of California at Berkeley. Someone had sold his fraternity a cheating scheme at bridge. It worked for a while until that clever salesman pushed his luck a bit too far and figured that if he could sell it to one fraternity, he could sell it to another. Soon it became apparent that several of the fraternities had purchased the same cheating scheme. Unacquainted, by chance they began playing bridge together and the use of the scheme was soon exposed. And, as you can imagine, they turned their mutual contempt against that clever salesman.

Dishonesty in the intellectual world tears at the very fabric of interpersonal human relationships. Cheating just once to pass that crucial exam can only lead to an intellectual and professional life built on quicksand. Good grades mean nothing at the point at which they really count. They might lead to a better graduate school. Someday, however, the piper will have to be paid. It may be when the knowledge is lacked to win a legal case, or when an engineering mistake costs lives, or when someone has cheated a little bit more than the original cheater, and this person has no ethical grounds on which to state his or her case.

At this point, I shared with my congregation the temptations pastors often face. They looked quite surprised when I said that God is the only One who knows how many copied sermons are pawned off on unsuspecting congregations as original work. We probably know of people who have done this for years and gotten by with it, only to have been ultimately discovered in their habitual deception. There's nothing wrong with good, hard research that learns from the work of others; and in a creative, modest way, a pastor can bring together that research into something helpful, crediting where appropriate those whose work is most extensively used. But to plagiarize, to take the whole work of someone else as our own, pretending to be someone we're not, catches up with us in the ministry just as in any other field.

I shared how every so often I receive a solicitation in the mail from some publishing venture that promises, for a fee, to provide fifty-two sermons a year, plus sermons for special occasions such as weddings and funerals, and to throw in pastoral prayers as a bonus. All of this is done under the rationalization of freeing us to have more time for our pastoral ministry.

I told my congregation about a person I knew who was noted to be an excellent preacher. He returned to his alma mater to speak in the chapel and without giving credit, preached word for word another man's sermon, unaware that the man was sitting in the chapel that same day.

Another of my colleagues, years ago, under pressure to complete his doctorate, plagiarized an obscure dissertation. Now, in the computer era, that deception of all these years has been uncovered by another doctoral candidate, who, researching the same topic, stumbled upon these two dissertations. He compared them and reported the deception. It has cost that man his pulpit and his reputation. Even if he had never been caught, he would have continued to pay the bitter price of shaky self-esteem and the fear of detection.

I tried to interface with the business persons in the congregation and shared some conversations I have had with other business persons who have shared with me their temptations. How easy it is to cut a few corners and make a bit more profit. One contractor told me that people need to watch out for that subtle rationalizing process. Once they start it, they get more and more addicted to it. The kickback from subcontractors and suppliers, the undercutting of bids, all so subtle, can be rationalized as essential to provide for one's family. That's the way it's done, but sooner or later, it catches up with one. Is there anything better than a good reputation, a respected name, a reputation for honesty, even when that honesty is a self-initiated admission of wrongdoing?

How many a person has thought he could get by with moral deception in a marriage? He or she thinks the other spouse will never find out. Some do carry it on for years—at the price of a loss of openness, intimacy, and mutual acceptance. How different it could be if one would simply be transparent, admit one's unfaithfulness, and ask for forgiveness. Better still, how different it would be to remain faithful, acknowledging temptation for what it is and mutually acknowledging that each person is only human.

Track this principle all the way through Scripture. Dishonesty for a good or bad reason may work temporarily—but not permanently.

Jacob found this out in that clandestine negotiation with his mother, Rebekah. He tricked his father, Isaac, into giving him the birthright due to Esau. Years later, Jacob himself ends up the victim of Laban's dishonest treachery.

David thought kings (presidents?) could get by with cover-ups until the bony finger of the prophet Nathan pointed itself in his direction, saying, "You are the man."

Ananias and Sapphira thought that they could look like not only tithers but also great Christian philanthropists by saying that they were giving more than they were actually giving. The Holy Spirit knew differently, and God's judgment fell upon them. Both refused to tell the truth, each at separate times, and died for their deception.

GULLIBILITY

14 Then the men of Israel took some of their provisions; but they did not ask counsel of the LORD. 15 So Joshua made peace with them, and made a covenant with them to let them live; and the rulers of the congregation swore to them.

—*Joshua 9:14–15*

This passage aptly illustrates that, at its very root, gullibility is a deep spiritual problem.

There is a gullibility that is *genuine confusion*. Things simply seem different from what they are. This could be called self-deception. You are sincere but sincerely wrong.

My tendency to do too many things at one time put me into such a state. I had a speaking engagement in another Southern California city, which, under normal circumstances, would have been less than forty-five minutes away, but on this particular evening, it took me that amount of time to simply drive four miles on the crowded freeway. When I finally arrived in the town where I was supposed to speak, I was already a half-hour late. Still thinking that I had the correct directions, I followed them only to arrive at a church that had, a few days earlier, burned down. Obviously, it must have been the wrong place. Heading on a few blocks, stopping people along the way to ask directions, I got no help, so I drove back to the area where I had been and found a building at which some people were meeting.

Assuming I'd come to the right place, I parked my car, took my Bible, and went inside. A man at the door said, "Welcome, Dr. Huffman." As I began to make myself comfortable, obviously late to this 7:30 meeting, another man asked, "By the way, where is Moderator Nelson? Didn't you bring her with you?" Was I ever confused! This man knew me, and I knew who Moderator Nelson was—the moderator of the General Assembly of the Presbyterian Church. I asked him what church this was. "The First Presbyterian Church of Pomona," he said. "I just assumed that you were the one who was bringing the moderator." I said, "No, I'm looking for the First Baptist Church of Pomona." I was at the wrong meeting in the wrong church.

The people to whom we communicate need to be alerted to the fact that it is possible to be sincere but sincerely wrong. Joshua was sincere. He thought things were different from the way they really were and made the assumption that the Gibeonites were telling the truth. He concluded that he had all the facts.

There's also a gullibility that comes from a *misplaced confidence.* Investors discover this, usually the hard way. They must watch out for wrong counsel. I have a very dear friend who trusted a financial counselor and, in the process, lost a fortune. He had put his confidence in a good man, but it was simply misplaced. It just so happened that this good man wasn't a good financial counselor. We have to learn that we can't trust everybody.

Then there's a gullibility that comes from *overconfidence.* Lee Iacocca tells how in 1956 the Ford Motor Company decided to promote auto safety rather than automotive power. The company introduced a safety package that included padding for the dashboard. The company had produced a film to show how much safer the new padding was in the event a passenger hit his head on the dashboard. To illustrate the point, the narrator of the film claimed that the padding was so thick that if you dropped an egg on it from a two-story building, the egg would bounce right off without breaking.

Iacocca tells how he decided to use this piece of information in one of his regional sales meetings. Instead of having the salesmen learn about safety padding from the film, he would make the point far more dramatically by actually dropping an egg onto the padding.

Eleven hundred men sat in the audience as he began to make his pitch about the terrific new safety padding offered in the 1956 models. He climbed a high ladder with a carton of fresh eggs. The very first egg missed the padding and splattered on the wooden floor. He said he took more careful aim with the second. His assistant, who was holding the ladder, chose this moment to move in the wrong direction. As a result, the egg bounced off his shoulder. By now, the audience was roaring with delight and wild applause. The third and fourth eggs landed exactly where they were supposed to. Iacocca states, "Unfortunately, they broke on impact. Finally, with the fifth egg, I achieved the desired result—and got a standing ovation. I learned two lessons that day. First, never use eggs at a sales rally. Second, never go before your customers without rehearsing what you want to say—as well as what you're going to do—to help sell your product."[3]

When we are overconfident we tend to take shortcuts.

Joshua's gullibility involved self-deception, misplaced confidence, and overconfidence. But underneath all three of these is a much deeper problem. At its very root, gullibility is a deep spiritual problem—the failure to consult God and His Word. Joshua listened to the Gibeonites, making his initial queries, deceiving himself. He misplaced his confidence in them and in his colleagues. He acted with overconfidence. The Bible says that he and his colleagues *"took some of their provisions; but they did not ask counsel of the LORD"* (v. 14).

Joshua had done this once before in the battle with Ai. He had made incorrect assumptions then, and now he does it again. He has taken things into his own hands and has neglected God. Ironically, he does this right after having inscribed part of the law on the rocks at Mount Ebal and having read the entire law to the people of Israel. Satan has a way of hitting us at the moment of victory. And Joshua had victory at Jericho and at Ai. Perhaps he thought this matter wasn't big enough to ask God's counsel.

There's an ironic footnote. Though the oath he swore to the Gibeonites was sworn in the name of God, the action had been carried out without consulting God. As men and women of God, we are privileged to stay in constant contact with Him, to seek His help, to find it, to be faithful to Him, and to challenge those with whom we are endeavoring to communicate to do the same.

INTEGRITY

16 And it happened at the end of three days, after they had made a covenant with them, that they heard that they were their neighbors who dwelt near them. 17 Then the children of Israel journeyed and came to their cities on the third day. Now their cities were Gibeon, Chephirah, Beeroth, and Kirjath Jearim. 18 But the children of Israel did not attack them, because the rulers of the congregation had sworn to them by the LORD God of Israel. And all the congregation complained against the rulers.

19 Then all the rulers said to all the congregation, "We have sworn to them by the LORD God of Israel; now therefore, we may not touch them. 20 This we will do to them: We will let them live, lest wrath be upon us because of the oath which we swore to them." 21 And the rulers said to them, "Let them live, but let them be woodcutters and water carriers for all the congregation, as the rulers had promised them."

22 Then Joshua called for them, and he spoke to them, saying, "Why have you deceived us, saying, 'We are very far from you,' when you dwell near us? 23 Now therefore, you are cursed, and none of you shall be freed from being slaves— woodcutters and water carriers for the house of my God."

24 So they answered Joshua and said, "Because your servants were clearly told that the LORD your God commanded His servant Moses to give you all the land, and to destroy all the inhabitants of the land from before you; therefore we were very much afraid for our lives because of you, and have done this thing. 25 And now, here we are, in your hands; do with us as it seems good and right to do to us." 26 So he did to them, and delivered them out of the hand of the children of Israel, so that they did not kill them. 27 And that day Joshua made them woodcutters and water carriers for the congregation and for the altar of the LORD, in the place which He would choose, even to this day.

—Joshua 9:16–27

This is a story of integrity. It's an illustration that two wrongs don't make a right. We are to keep our word even if we've made a mistake and that mistake proves to be costly. We shouldn't ever give up because, when we're right with God, He can turn even a curse into a blessing.

Joshua was put on the spot by the people when they discovered the Gibeonites' deception and Joshua's gullibility. They discovered it in just three days. The Scripture says, *"And all the congregation complained against the rulers"* (v. 18). Joshua and his colleagues had been gullible. Instead of giving a lot of excuses and repudiating the covenant Joshua had made with the Gibeonites, he acknowledged it. He had made this covenant in the name of God and took his word seriously. Perhaps he could have repudiated it on the basis that the Gibeonites had not been honest. Yet Joshua knew that God had always warned about oath taking and then breaking the oath. It's better not to take a vow than to take a vow and break it. To break it only compounds the problem.

Instead of looking for loopholes, Joshua held steady. Instead of bending to the wishes of the crowd who, in its narrow nationalism, wanted to wipe out the Gibeonites, canceling the vows taken, Joshua was prepared to acknowledge that God was the Protector of these foreigners. A covenant was a covenant. He declared emphatically to the people, *"We have sworn to them by the LORD God of Israel; now therefore, we may not touch them. This we will do to them: We will let them live, lest wrath be upon us because of the oath which we swore to them"* (vv. 19–20). The vow held, and the Gibeonites turn out to be a blessing. They paid the price of their deception—cursed to be slaves, hewers of wood and drawers of water to the house of God. But they also were protected, and we continue to read about them throughout the rest of the Old Testament.

Integrity is a word we need to hear more often today. Two wrongs don't make a right. After having made a commitment, is it right to break that commitment because of a mistake? This is a powerful question to direct to the people with whom we are endeavoring to share God's Word.

This situation also applies to marriage. Many in our congregations are married to Gibeonites, nonbelievers. The Bible clearly instructs us, saying, "Do not be unequally yoked together with unbelievers. For what fellowship has righteousness with lawlessness? And what communion has light with darkness?" (2 Cor. 6:14). At the same time, this provides no excuse for the believing partner to leave the unbelieving spouse. Paul just as clearly urges the believing partner to keep the commitment:

> But to the rest I, not the Lord, say: If any brother has a wife who does not believe, and she is willing to live with him, let him not divorce her. And a woman who has a husband who does not believe, if he is willing to live with her, let her not divorce him. For the unbelieving husband is sanctified by the wife, and the unbelieving wife is sanctified by the husband; otherwise your children would be unclean, but now they are holy (1 Cor. 7:12–14).

There are those to whom we are communicating who are living with some of the painful consequences of not having consulted God about a marriage. They'd like to break the vow they've made, but they need to be reminded that God is in the business of helping them honor that vow. He wants them to have a sanctifying influence on their unbelieving partner. Integrity is so important.

The same thing happens in business. Someone makes a commitment, but it doesn't turn out the way he thought it would. Does he cancel it? We're reminded to let our yeas be yea and our nays be nay. Integrity is a commodity that is all too scarce these days.

This story of the Gibeonites shows how important it is to keep our commitments, even when it's tough. The well-being of others depends on it. A Christian shouldn't technically ever have to put anything in writing. His or her word should be his or her bond. Are you known for this kind of integrity? Are we challenging our people to be known for this kind of integrity? It's a fascinating study to trace the use of the words "vow" and "oath" through the Scriptures. How important it is not to enter into covenants lightly. And, how crucial it is once they are established to keep them with integrity.

A dear farmer friend of mine told me about another farmer with whom he and his family had done business for many years. This other farmer had made a gentleman's agreement to buy some produce at a certain price. Then the market value went down. That man could have claimed altered circumstances; but because he had already agreed to the higher price, he kept his word and paid it. On another occasion, this same farmer had made a promise to sell some produce at a particular price. Between the time of the verbal agreement and the delivery of the produce, the price went up. Out of Christian character and integrity, he insisted on accepting the lower price, knowing the person with whom he was doing business would have been making a sacrifice to buy it from him for more than he would have paid on the open market at the time of the agreement. This farmer's Christian integrity went even beyond what was required. The result is that to this day he is respected for his Christian grace and character by those with whom he has done business.

NOTES

1. Hamlin, *Inheriting the Land*, pp. xiii—xvi.

2. Ibid., pp. 74, 84.

3. Lee lacocca, *Iacocca* (New York: Bantam Books, 1984), p. 39.

CHAPTER ELEVEN—WHEN ON GOD'S SIDE
JOSHUA 10:1–15

Scripture Outline

You Will Face Opposition (10:1–5)

You Will Discover That God Keeps His Covenant (10:6–11)

You Have Supernatural Resources (10:12–15)

Chapters 10, 11, and 12 deal with Joshua's conquest of the land. It is a struggle to know precisely how one should best deal with these chapters. The preacher could endeavor to treat these in historical detail, sketching and analyzing them battle by battle. In a magnificently executed plan, Joshua moved westward through the midsection of the Promised Land, cutting off the north from the south. Then he moved southward in rapid deployment of his resources. After defeating the kings of the south, he then moved northward. It was a superb military strategy. We will allude to it on occasion.

As communicators, however, we will be conveying God's Word to men and women who are not necessarily fascinated by military strategy. These historical facts can be dealt with on several levels of understanding. My endeavor is to extract from these three chapters teachings that are relevant to how people live today. At this point, the communicator is privileged to take these Old Testament battle accounts and discover spiritual principles that are applicable to today.

Initially, I thought I could cover all three chapters in one sermon, but it was impossible. There simply are too many practical teachings highly relevant to today's Christian life. Instead, I limited my first message to verses 1–15 in chapter 10, dealing with one particular battle which I did not even carry through to its finish.

Read the speeches of historic kings, presidents, and generals, speeches written in times of war, and you'll discover an interesting similarity. Most of these leaders have endeavored to mobilize their constituencies to battle with the promise "God is on our side."

One of the most classic evidences of this is the slogan used by the Germans in their twentieth-century wars against the Allies. This phrase appeared in their speeches, and I've even seen it prominently attached to a soldier's helmet: "GOTT MIT UNS"—"God with us."

Germany is not the only modern nation that has justified its actions with this phrase. Study the inaugural addresses of most American presidents, and you will quickly see that frequent reference is made to the Divine Being functioning on our side. It is quite presumptuous to make God a German, an American, or a Britisher. It's as if we give Him honorary citizenship.

In many ways, this kind of "sloganeering" can end up being the Achilles heel of the Christian. I can rationalize my doing what I want to do by deceiving myself into thinking that God is on my side. This is the ultimate idolatry. What a narrow perspective it brings to life. How self-centered and destructive this can be. When I say that God is on my side, I'm declaring that I am the center of the universe, a very important universe. The very Creator and Sustainer of that universe is mobilized by me to function at my whim. All too much of contemporary Christianity smacks of this provincial egocentricity.

I am told that Abraham Lincoln had another way of looking at this issue during the Civil War when both sides were claiming God's help. Lincoln anguished, observing how divided his nation had become: "The key issue is not whether God is on my side but whether I am on God's side." Do you find yourself as fascinated as I by that very subtle distinction in the use of words which produces a massive difference in one's self-understanding?

Joshua is now a veteran of life. He and his colleague Caleb are the only two Israelites who remember Egypt. They know the struggles of having been slaves in an affluent, power-hungry environment. They know what it was like to have been a minority whose standard of living went down, while the standard of living for the majority went up. As slaves, they were a significant part of enabling that rise in the standard of living. "Might makes right" was the attitude of the pharaohs. As a young Hebrew slave, Joshua watched as the Egyptians claimed to have the gods on their side—various gods who served at their beck and call.

The God of the Hebrews didn't seem that strong. The God of Abraham, Isaac, and Jacob, the God of Sarah, Rebekah, and Rachel must have appeared to be impotent. If He was as strong as the gods of Egypt, He would have been of greater help. But then Joshua's imagination was captured by the rumor that an adopted son of Pharaoh had some years before declared himself to be a Hebrew. That man, Moses, had disappeared into the wilderness after failing to bring deliverance to the Israelites by his own human power. Then, much to everybody's amazement, Moses returned, eighty years old, to organize and lead the slaves out of bondage. Joshua, as a young man, had observed the ten plagues and that battle between Jehovah and the Egyptian gods. Finally, he and the rest of his people were led out of Egypt in a miraculous deliverance to spend forty years in the wilderness.

There had been times when God had seemed so close, and then times when God had seemed so distant. There was something strange about this God. He was elusive, and Joshua couldn't quite hold onto Him. Sometimes when he needed Him, He was there; other times when he needed Him, He wasn't.

Forty years now have gone by. God gave Joshua some promises. Joshua knew these promises were conditional. But he had to learn it the hard way, existentially. At first, Joshua functioned as if God was on his side. It worked at Jericho, but it didn't work at Ai. Perhaps it was because God was no longer on his side. Or perhaps, much more significantly, it was because Joshua was no longer on God's side. He had presumed on the Deity and hadn't sought God's counsel. How strange it was, and is, how much better things go when we don't take God for granted but live in daily conversation with Him. When we do, we discover those Achans in our lives, those hidden sins that God cannot tolerate. We are drawn to repentance, to renewal, to spiritual energy.

Joshua learned his lesson and defeated Ai in the second battle. Joshua learned to be on God's side when it came to battles. But he forgot this lesson when it came to making treaties. He was tricked and duped by the Gibeonites because he hadn't consulted the Lord. He entered into the covenant with Gibeon only to discover that he had been deceived. Joshua kept his vow, though, because he had learned his lesson—the lesson of obedience. Joshua was going to do things God's way, rather than expect God to do things his way.

When he had this straight, Joshua was ready for battle—not just the isolated battle, but the conquest. He was ready to move in and occupy the land originally given to Abraham, once again promised to Moses, and now to be taken by Joshua.

There are three specific messages here for those of us who have learned what it is to be on God's side.

YOU WILL FACE OPPOSITION

10:1 Now it came to pass when Adoni-Zedek king of Jerusalem heard how Joshua had taken Ai and had utterly destroyed it—as he had done to Jericho and its king, so he had done to Ai and its king—and how the inhabitants of Gibeon had made peace with Israel and were among them, ² that they feared greatly, because Gibeon was a great city, like one of the royal cities, and because it was greater than Ai, and all its men were mighty. ³ Therefore Adoni-Zedek king of Jerusalem sent to Hoham king of Hebron, Piram king of Jarmuth, Japhia king of Lachish, and Debir king of Eglon, saying, ⁴ "Come up to me and help me, that we may attack Gibeon, for it has made peace with Joshua and with the children of Israel." ⁵ Therefore the five kings of the Amorites, the king of Jerusalem, the king of Hebron, the king of Jarmuth, the king of Lachish, and the king of Eglon, gathered together and went up, they and all their armies, and camped before Gibeon and made war against it.

—*Joshua 10:1–5*

When on God's side, you will face opposition. God's people are always threatened by those who are not on God's side. When you have a sincere relationship with the Lord, the word has a way of getting out. The sincerity of your commitment is challenged. Even God's power is measured.

Adoni-Zedek, the king of Jerusalem, heard how Joshua had taken Ai as well as Jericho and how a peace treaty had been established with the Gibeonites. So he and his people *"feared greatly, because Gibeon was a great city, like one of the royal cities, and because it was greater than Ai, and all its men were mighty"* (v. 2).

Gibeon should have been one of Adoni-Zedek's allies, but it wasn't because it had established a treaty with Israel. Alarmed, Adoni-Zedek intensified his efforts at building an alliance with the kings of Hebron, Jarmuth, Lachish, and Eglon. He was determined to crush any help the Israelites might eventually get from the

Gibeonites. Instead of marching on Joshua, Adoni-Zedek and his allies marched on Gibeon. He was not about to let the Gibeonite-Israelite covenant go unchallenged. He would crush the Gibeonites while the Israelites were still camped thirty-two kilometers down the Judean hillside, along the Jordan River at Gilgal.

I've noticed in my life that a commitment to the status quo provides a more placid, easy-going lifestyle. Set your sights high, commit yourself to changing people's lives, and you'll immediately stimulate opposition. People are threatened by change, so they end up making strange alliances. The kings that Adoni-Zedek brought together were actually natural enemies. But they quickly became allies when they heard the Israelites were coming. The reputation of Joshua and Israel was traveling in advance of them and was spreading fear and terror in the hearts of the enemy. If Joshua had been content simply to camp at Gilgal, setting up his own city-state, there probably wouldn't have been as much initial opposition. It was this energetic commitment to obey God and occupy the land that God had given to Israel that stirred up the opposition.

I observed something similar to this happen in the church. Several years ago, my good friend John Guest received a call to become the rector of St. Stephen's Episcopal Church in Sewickley, Pennsylvania. Up to that point, John had been a wandering Christian troubadour, singing and preaching the gospel of Jesus Christ. With his long hair and winsome British accent, he attracted many confused American young people. Somehow they saw in John a kind of Paul McCartney turned spiritual. John, who had his own rock band, instituted beach ministries at popular summer resorts. In the off-season, he worked in the diocese of Pittsburgh as an Episcopal youth minister. His primary responsibilities were at St. Stephen's Church, a staid, affluent, play-it-safe, status-quo congregation where a modest number of people attended church on Sunday. On those few occasions that the rector allowed this young minstrel his chance to preach, the church filled up. The men, especially, related to John and the challenge he gave. And the women loved seeing their men come to church.

One day the long-term rector retired. The "search committee" went on a nationwide hunt for a new rector, and in the face of considerable criticism, they called John Guest.

That's not quite the end of the story. John meant business with God. He had been converted to Jesus Christ as a tough kid off the streets of London, England, through the evangelistic ministry of Billy Graham. Fire burned in his bosom. Certainly it was an honor as a young man to be placed as rector of that sophisticated, wealthy, prestigious Sewickley church, made up of so many of the heirs of America's great industrial barons. But a good salary and a prestigious post were not what John wanted. He wanted people to come to a personal relationship with Jesus Christ. He wanted them to grow in their faith and to be deployed in servant ministries to others. He wanted to see renewal in that local congregation and within the national Episcopalian church. His was a no-nonsense ministry with a radical New Testament message: that all have sinned and come short of the glory of God; that Jesus Christ is God become man to die for the sins of the world; that Jesus Christ bodily rose from the dead; that He is coming again; and that each of us will stand before Him in the judgment day, accountable as to whether or not we repented of sin and put our trust in Him.

Everything exploded. The church was divided, polarized by this young pastor who was serious about God and was faithfully preaching His Word. John refused to "play church" the conventional way. He was on God's side. He would stand with courage and faithfully preach His Word, when a watered-down word would have been more palatable. John was both vilified and hero-ized. Some stalwart church members of decades worked to get him removed, and some eventually left.

At this same time, God was very much at work through John's ministry. Many were coming alive in Christ for the first time. God's word spread and was contagious. Many hungering for religious reality were attracted to that church. Many of the old-time members were converted. The church grew numerically, and a building program was announced. Again, controversy broke out. People argued that it would take too much money and that it couldn't be done. By this time, there were hard-core, dedicated Christian men and women who had caught the vision, who meant business, and who were prepared to face the opposition with John in the knowledge that they were on God's side.

As I wrote this chapter, I was at Oglebay Lodge near Wheeling, West Virginia, ministering to several hundred energetic men and women from John's church on a weekend retreat. It is exciting to see how God is at work in the lives of many men and women as a result of John's willingness to stand alone against tremendous opposition.

Not only John Guest, but every faithful servant of Jesus Christ such as he, is going to face strong opposition. Don't ever forget this!

YOU WILL DISCOVER THAT GOD KEEPS HIS COVENANT

⁶ And the men of Gibeon sent to Joshua at the camp at Gilgal, saying, "Do not forsake your servants; come up to us quickly, save us and help us, for all the kings of the Amorites who dwell in the mountains have gathered together against us."

⁷ So Joshua ascended from Gilgal, he and all the people of war with him, and all the mighty men of valor. ⁸ And the LORD said to Joshua, "Do not fear them, for I have delivered them into your hand; not a man of them shall stand before you." ⁹ Joshua therefore came upon them suddenly, having marched all night from Gilgal. ¹⁰ So the LORD routed them before Israel, killed them with a great slaughter at Gibeon, chased them along the road that goes to Beth Horon, and struck them down as far as Azekah and Makkedah. ¹¹ And it happened, as they fled before Israel and were on the descent of Beth Horon, that the LORD cast down large hailstones from heaven on them as far as Azekah, and they died. There were more who died from the hailstones than the children of Israel killed with the sword.
—*Joshua 10:6–11*

When on God's side, you'll discover that God keeps His covenant. If God will stand behind a covenant worked out by duplicity between the Gibeonites and the Israelites, how much more He will stand behind His covenant with Israel and with us, His new Israel?

Verses 6–11 tell a fantastic story. The men of Gibeon look out and see the alliance of those five kings led by Adoni-Zedek, the king of Jerusalem, moving toward them across the Judean hills. They observe the enemy soldiers begin to set up for war outside the city gates, knowing that they could not prevail on their own against as strong a city as Gibeon. So they slipped messengers out the city gates down to Gilgal where Joshua was encamped. Their urgent message said, *"Do not forsake your servants; come up to us quickly, save us and help us, for all the kings of the Amorites who dwell in the mountains have gathered together against us"* (v. 6).

Joshua didn't establish a long-range planning task force to evaluate whether or not it would be wise to follow through on the covenant established with Gibeon. He was a man of integrity and a servant of the Lord who had integrity. Joshua had given his word to the Gibeonites in the name of the Lord. So he called together his troops and alerted them that they were going to march immediately.

As they were organizing for that march, Joshua opened his heart once again to God in prayer; this time, before the battle. And God said, *"Do not fear them, for I have delivered them into your hand; not a man of them shall stand before you"* (v. 8).

Joshua led his troops up those thirty-two plus kilometers of winding trails, climbing from thirteen hundred feet below sea level to close to three thousand feet above sea level, under the cover of darkness. It took them eight to ten hours as they rapidly covered the same terrain that had previously taken them three days at a more leisurely pace.

The five kings and their soldiers were thrown into a panic before Israel, and many were killed. Those who weren't were chased farther up the hillside and then down the descent toward Beth Horon. Then *"the LORD cast down large hailstones from heaven on them as far as Azekah, and they died. There were more who died from the hailstones than the children of Israel killed with the sword"* (v. 11).

Never forget that God is a God of integrity who keeps His word. Some of His promises have conditions. We have seen the price that Joshua paid when he did not live up to the conditions. Our God, in His Word, describes the alternatives so clearly. We can live according to our own value schemes, independent of His love and His covenant, but we'll pay the price. Or, we can elect to be faithful to Him and discover His faithfulness. Most of the troubles we have are the results of our own stubborn unfaithfulness to the covenant. Or, they result from the stubborn unfaithfulness of someone else whose resistance to God's will impacts our lives. This is a spiritual principle we are privileged to share with those with whom we are in communication.

There are many ways we can illustrate this. We can give illustrations of marriage partners who are in rebellion against God and can cause a lot of pain for their partner. We can describe situations of rebellious children who create havoc in the family. There are church leaderships that do not live under the authority of God's Word and can spiritually paralyze a congregation. There are no limits to the types of illustrations we can give to make this point that the Christian life is not an easy life. At the same time, there are no limits to the illustrations that we can give of those who have found God's faithfulness in times of great difficulty. God keeps His covenant.

Even in the darkest hour, one solitary believer who has kept the faith can experience the peace of God which passes all understanding. We are now discovering case after case of this kind among believers in Red China who, for decades now, have experienced God's faithfulness to His covenant in the most trying of circumstances.

This is how the prophet Jeremiah could write words of hope at a time when Jerusalem had been devastated by Nebuchadnezzar in 586 B.C. He was boxed in with gloom, his proud city destroyed, his friends taken captive, once beautiful people left rotting in the streets, infants with parched tongues cleaving to the rooves of their mouths, some so hungry that they turned to cannibalism. In this desperate moment, in what has been called his "Easter Eve" of the human soul, when all was lost, Jeremiah sensed hope within hopelessness. His soul, weighed down by God's judgment, sprang forward with a confidence in the Lord's unconquerable mercy as he wrote:

> This I recall to my mind,
> Therefore I have hope.
> Through the Lord's mercies we are not consumed,
> Because His compassions fail not.
> They are new every morning;
> Great is Your faithfulness.
>
> —*Lamentations 3:21–23*

It is from this passage we receive the inspiring words of the hymn:

> Great is Thy faithfulness!
> Great is Thy faithfulness!
> Morning by morning new mercies I see;
> All I have needed Thy hand hath provided—
> Great is Thy faithfulness, Lord, unto me!

Jeremiah and Joshua both had learned that God keeps His covenant with those who are faithful to Him. We cannot emphasize this enough to our people.

YOU HAVE SUPERNATURAL RESOURCES

12 Then Joshua spoke to the LORD in the day when the LORD delivered up the Amorites before the children of Israel, and he said in the sight of Israel:
"Sun, stand still over Gibeon;
And Moon, in the Valley of Aijalon."

13 So the sun stood still,
And the moon stopped,
Till the people had revenge
Upon their enemies.

Is this not written in the Book of Jasher? So the sun stood still in the midst of heaven, and did not hasten to go down for about a whole day. 14 And there has been no day like that, before it or after it, that the LORD heeded the voice of a man; for the LORD fought for Israel.

15 Then Joshua returned, and all Israel with him, to the camp at Gilgal.

—*Joshua 10:12–15*

When on God's side, we have supernatural resources. We are not limited strictly to that which makes sense in the terms of this world. We are in relationship with a God of supernatural power who uses His power to achieve His ends.

This supernatural dimension appears in this particular military venture. God has communicated His promise to Joshua in a supernatural communication, a conversation in prayer between God and man. So large were the hailstones that bombarded the fleeing enemy that more were killed by these "great stones from heaven" than by conventional, military weapons. Then Joshua asked the Lord for the sun to stand still and for the moon to stay until the battle could be completed: *"So the sun stood still,/And the moon stopped,/Till the people had revenge/Upon their enemies"* (v. 13). God heard the cry for help and answered it with supernatural intervention.

Many theories have been advanced as to what actually happened that day. Some have declared that this is a fanciful notion, for any intelligent person knows that it is not the sun that moves but the earth that rotates on its axis around the sun. It's interesting to note that the same cynical people will refer to the sun "rising in the morning and setting in the evening." Descriptive language continues to be used by the most scientific people.

There is also a difference in opinion among scholars as to precisely what happened. The Hebrew word *dâmam* is translated in a number of the versions "stand still." It also can be translated "be silent." The Hebrew word ʿāmad—which usually means "to stand still" and in The New King James Version is translated "stopped"—can also mean "to cease doing something." A few scholars believe that Joshua was actually claiming a continuation of the darkness that had aided him in his surprise attack upon the alliance. The majority opinion is that Joshua was calling for continued light so as to finish the battle. Many a sermon or Bible lesson has concentrated on this being the "longest day."

In my opinion, this is not at all the major point. Either theory is acceptable to me. Whether or not God was prolonging the darkness or the light, we do know that God had supernaturally intervened in the way in which He was keeping His promise, giving His military help, and providing the ideal atmospheric conditions under which to complete the battle.

We cannot stress too much that our God gives supernatural resources to us when we are on His side. This assertion does raise many a question in the minds of the people to whom we are communicating. Their natural reaction is, "That was nice way back when, but God doesn't work that way today." We are privileged to counter that response and to challenge those who have a difficult time believing in God's supernatural interaction. Encourage the individuals in your congregation or class to take a look at their own lives, particularly at those times—and they may not have been easy—in which they have been most faithful to the Lord. Challenge them to see if they can observe a pattern to God's divine intervention in ways that validate His faithfulness to His covenant.

From my own personal experience, I can relate events and circumstances that are nothing short of the miraculous.

I lose my breath just thinking back to what it took for my wife, Anne, and me ever to have met, let alone what it took for the providential encounter that lasted no more than ten minutes between a young man from Boston and a young woman from Los Angeles in a military chapel in Taipei, Formosa, in 1963, to mature eventually into marriage.

I look back amazed at how God led me through Wheaton College to Princeton Seminary and brought about my pastorates in Key Biscayne, Florida; Pittsburgh, Pennsylvania; and Newport Beach, California, but not some that I coveted more. There is no way that I could have arranged events and circumstances to work out the way they did. At the time, I thought that God had let me down. I was afraid He was not there, not interested, or perhaps asleep. Now I can see what He was doing. What appeared to be coincidence and chance now has the mark of supernatural intervention. Illustrations from your own life will stimulate thinking in your people.

One man in my congregation has just experienced a terrible disappointment. For months now, he has been interviewing for a job for which he is highly qualified, and it appeared that he would be the person offered that position. Then at the last moment, through certain political machinations, he was edged out, and someone else was brought in to fill that important post. He was crushed. My reference to my past disappointments ministered to him at his existential point of need, helping him to trust the Lord. Perhaps what appeared to be failure was actually God's supernatural intervention. It gave him hope that some day he, too, would sing "Great is Thy faithfulness" with eyes able to see that faithfulness was at work in this specific situation.

There is a little-known story of our building program. Several years ago, we had a congregational meeting to discuss whether or not there should be a building program. It seemed impossible that we could raise the amount of money needed. The afternoon of the congregational meeting, my secretary called and alerted me that someone was driving down from Los Angeles just to see me for ten minutes and wondered if I could make time yet that afternoon. To my recollection, I'd only met that person once before. I had no idea of what would cause such urgency. I made room in my schedule, and an hour and a half later, that person walked into my study and said, "I can't be at the congregational meeting tonight, however, God has told me to do something and to do it today. I've been blessed in receiving a large amount of money that I never dreamed would be mine. God has told me to pledge one million dollars to the building program. My name must be kept anonymous, but you are free to tell about this pledge at the congregational meeting this evening."

I would never have guessed that this person had that kind of money. And, if I had known it, I never would have thought that this person's heart would be touched to give a gift of that size to St. Andrew's Presbyterian Church. The final $150,000 has been transferred to the church. The pledge is paid in full. Without this miracle gift, there would have been no building program. It was that announcement that stimulated the congregation's affirmative vote.

What of the supernatural can you see in your life and challenge those to whom you are communicating to see in theirs? What significant ways has God intervened in answered prayer and special direction?

I've seen healings of a supernatural nature. My friend Werner Burklin, dying of cancer in the late 1960s, after having had major internal organs partially removed surgically, is alive and vital today in the service of Jesus Christ. My dear friend Norm Cook, stricken with encephalitis on the mission field several years ago, is vital and healthy today. One of our own members, Bob Curtis, had heart problems, with an apparent 70 percent blockage of three heart valves. He came through his angiogram with the very words of his doctor: "Bob, you had the miracle you prayed for. Your tests show no blockage whatsoever." It doesn't hurt to remind our people of the specificity of God's supernatural interaction in the lives of people they know.

At the same time, we have to acknowledge honestly to the people with whom we are communicating that God doesn't always do what we want when we want it in a supernatural way. It's at this point that we come right back to our basic thesis. The question is not whether God is on my side but whether I am on God's side. Am I determined to have Him do what I want when I want it, or am I willing to submit myself to His sovereignty to see Him do what He wants in my life? I have had serious physical illnesses that did not receive what people would call supernatural healing. I have friends who are just as sincere Christians as those I have mentioned whose ultimate healings were not physical but spiritual or emotional or even death.

But what we can say with all the authority of God's Word is that ours is a God of supernatural power. He uses this power to achieve His ends. When you are on God's side, you are part of those ends and are part of the victory that is His.

CHAPTER TWELVE—COMPLETING THE CONQUEST

JOSHUA 10:16—12:24

Scripture Outline

A Life of Ongoing Warfare (10:16–21)

A Spiritual Battle to Death with Christ as Victor (10:22–42)

A Spiritual Home Base (10:43)

The Responsibility of Completing the Conquest (11:1—12:24)

God is right now in the process of waging war with evil, and the struggle is cosmic. The question here again is not whether or not God is on our side but whether we are on God's side. Both in relationship to ancient Israel and to contemporary men and women, this question has perpetual relevance.

E. John Hamlin refers to a "stereoscopic view" of God's warfare. God fights for Israel as part of His battle against the powers of death and sin; He works for salvation in the whole world. The reverse can also be said—God fights against Israel at the point that God's people have joined the forces of chaos and destruction and are no longer on the side of His new creation.[1]

This continues to be the case and is the reason it is so important that we bring ourselves into conformity with God's will instead of trying to bring God into conformity with our wills. When Joshua enlisted God on his side without consulting God's will, he both lost the battle with Ai and was deceived by Gibeon. So far in chapter 10, as Joshua consulted God, desperately desiring to be on God's side, he had resources going beyond his own natural resources.

In Joshua 10:1–14, we learned three important lessons about what happens when we are on God's side. First, we will face opposition. God has enemies, and just being on His side means that we will share the same enemies. Second, we will discover that God keeps His covenant. He has integrity and stood by the promises made in His name to Gibeon. If He will do that for deceitful people, how much more He will keep His promise to those of us who have accepted His gift of mercy and grace? Third, we will have supernatural resources. The sun and the moon were made to stand still so as to enable God to prevail as He worked out His will through His people, Israel.

God normally uses human agents to do His work on earth. I am constantly amazed at the fact that the very God of the universe has chosen primarily to work through weak, sinful human beings. He has entrusted His world to us. He has set natural laws in place, within which we live during the normal sequence of events. However, He still reserves the right to be God. His resources are of a supernatural nature, and, when He sees fit in His sovereignty, God deploys those supernatural resources to accomplish the ends He wants, both through us and for us.

Through the rest of chapter 10 and on into chapters 11 and 12, Joshua completes the major part of the conquest. The defeat of Adoni-Zedek, the king of Jerusalem, and his four colleague-kings is not the end of the story. A major battle was still going on, only part of which was finished. We now pick up the sequence and carry it on through the rest of the conquest.

These three chapters contain a true story of battle after battle. The question is, how do we deal with these stories in a way that we will find helpful to those with whom we are endeavoring to communicate? I resist the tendency to allegorize them, reading into them certain symbolic meanings of a conjectural nature. Some commentators attach great significance to the numerical fact that there were five kings. They try to draw a parallel between Adoni-Zedek, the king of Jerusalem, and the high priest Melchizedek of Abraham's era. Melchizedek is seen as being an Old Testament type of Christ, and Adoni-Zedek as an Old Testament type of the Antichrist spoken of in the Book of Revelation. I simply am not able with certainty to make such an identification. I find these speculations fascinating, but I also am convinced that it is dangerous to make too specific an association.

I am prepared, however, to take the historical events that happened over three thousand years ago and see fascinating spiritual parallels with the Christian life today. God did not give us His written word to make us knowledgeable historians of specific details in the life of obscure, ancient people. Those historical details are important, both for the people called Israel and for God's people living in the twenty-first century, the new Israel. It is important that we study how God worked in ancient times so as to discover how He works in contemporary times.

The experience of ancient Israel parallels the experience of the new Israel. Knowledge of this "holy history" is imperative for Holy Spirit–guided insights into contemporary Christian living. Too many Christians have lost sight of valuable spiritual truths because they have restricted themselves to the specific New Testament spiritual and ethical teachings of Jesus and Paul. They are missing the richness of the Old Testament revelation of how God has worked and continues to work in the lives of His covenant people. We as preachers have the privilege of introducing our people to the richness of these Old Testament historical narratives.

In this chapter we will look at four additional contemporary teachings that come out of chapters 10, 11, and 12, as we observe Israel completing the conquest.

A LIFE OF ONGOING WARFARE

16 But these five kings had fled and hidden themselves in a cave at Makkedah. 17 And it was told Joshua, saying, "The five kings have been found hidden in the cave at Makkedah."

18 So Joshua said, "Roll large stones against the mouth of the cave, and set men by it to guard them. 19 And do not stay there yourselves, but pursue your enemies, and attack their rear guard. Do not allow them to enter their cities, for the LORD your God has delivered them into your hand." 20 Then it happened, while Joshua and the children of Israel made an end of slaying them with a very great slaughter, till they had finished, that those who escaped entered fortified cities. 21 And all the people returned to the camp, to Joshua at Makkedah, in peace.

No one moved his tongue against any of the children of Israel.

—Joshua 10:16–21

The Christian life is one of ongoing warfare. Joshua led a sneak attack, aided by the cover of darkness, upon the five kings who were encamped against Gibeon. They panicked and fled, pursued both by the swords of the Israelites and the enormous hailstones from heaven. The five kings observed the horrendous military defeat as their soldiers retreated. They wanted to save their own necks so they hid themselves in a cave at Makkedah. Word of this came to Joshua, and he gave the order that great stones be rolled against the mouth of the cave with soldiers assigned to guard it while the rest of his soldiers pursued the enemy, completing the victory. Joshua wasn't content to win the battle; he knew that he was engaged in an ongoing warfare and was determined to press the advantage.

Frequent reference is made throughout the entire Bible to the warfare that marks the life of God's people. We are not engaged in an occasional skirmish, but an ongoing struggle. Paul urges us to "fight the good fight of faith, lay hold on eternal life, to which [we] were also called and have confessed the good confession in the presence of many witnesses" (1 Tim. 6:12). There is an ongoing dimension of struggle to our confession of faith in Jesus Christ. Toward the end of his earthly life, Paul had this to say about himself: "I have fought the good fight, I have finished the race, I have kept the faith. Finally, there is laid up for me the crown of righteousness, which the Lord, the righteous Judge, will give to me on that Day, and not to me only but also to all who have loved His appearing" (2 Tim. 4:7–8).

Too often, I run into young Christians who define their relationship with Jesus Christ in simplistic terms. They assume that since they are now "born again" and have received Christ's forgiveness, their problems will evaporate. They may have even discovered that the question isn't whether God is on our side but whether we are on God's side and would quickly confess to being on God's side. But they've missed one very important biblical teaching: when we are on God's side, we are engaged with Him in this ongoing warfare with sin and Satan. We are instructed:

> Finally, my brethren, be strong in the LORD and in the power of His might. Put on the whole armor of God, that you may be able to stand against the wiles of the devil. For we do not wrestle against flesh and blood, but against principalities, against powers, against the rulers of the darkness of this age, against spiritual hosts of wickedness in the heavenly places (Eph. 6:10–12).

That is heavy teaching, isn't it? We need to alert the people for whom we have responsibility in communication of the embattled nature of the Christian life. How sad it would be if someday they could justly accuse us of never having warned them. So much teaching today is entertaining. The results of this somewhat flippant approach to the Christian life and the joy that is ours in Christ can be the false promise of a trouble-free existence. We need to stress the fact that being on God's side makes one all the more subject to Satan's attack. The more on God's side one is, the more Satan hates that person and the more he will try to seduce that one with temptation.

Satan hit Jesus hard in the wilderness. He was vicious in his attack upon godly Job. He went after his money and the rest of his earthly possessions; he attacked Job's children and wife; and finally, he attacked Job's physical body and his emotional being. We must communicate forcefully to our people that there is struggle in the Christian life. They must be warned to avoid teaching that urges them simply to bring all their problems to Jesus and expect they will go away. Satan isn't going to waste his energy on lukewarm, nominal Christians who are playing church. He has them right where he wants them as they "claim a form of godliness but deny the power thereof." His onslaught will be against those who are serious in their faith.

This is why it is so important to know that we are engaged in an ongoing warfare and to be armed for it. Paul wrote in Ephesians 6:13–18:

> Therefore take up the whole armor of God, that you may be able to withstand in the evil day, and having done all, to stand. Stand therefore, having girded your waist with truth, having put on the breastplate of righteousness, and having shod your feet with the preparation of the gospel of peace; above all, taking the shield of faith with which you will be able to quench all the fiery darts of the wicked one. And take the helmet of salvation, and the sword of the Spirit, which is the word of God; praying always with all prayer and supplication in the Spirit, being watchful to this end with all perseverance and supplication for all the saints.

A SPIRITUAL BATTLE TO DEATH WITH CHRIST AS VICTOR

[22] Then Joshua said, "Open the mouth of the cave, and bring out those five kings to me from the cave." [23] And they did so, and brought out those five kings to him from the cave:

the king of Jerusalem, the king of Hebron, the king of Jarmuth, the king of Lachish, and the king of Eglon.

24 So it was, when they brought out those kings to Joshua, that Joshua called for all the men of Israel, and said to the captains of the men of war who went with him, "Come near, put your feet on the necks of these kings." And they drew near and put their feet on their necks. 25 Then Joshua said to them, "Do not be afraid, nor be dismayed; be strong and of good courage, for thus the LORD will do to all your enemies against whom you fight." 26 And afterward Joshua struck them and killed them, and hanged them on five trees; and they were hanging on the trees until evening. 27 So it was at the time of the going down of the sun that Joshua commanded, and they took them down from the trees, cast them into the cave where they had been hidden, and laid large stones against the cave's mouth, which remain until this very day.

28 On that day Joshua took Makkedah, and struck it and its king with the edge of the sword. He utterly destroyed them—all the people who were in it. He let none remain. He also did to the king of Makkedah as he had done to the king of Jericho.

29 Then Joshua passed from Makkedah, and all Israel with him, to Libnah; and they fought against Libnah. 30 And the LORD also delivered it and its king into the hand of Israel; he struck it and all the people who were in it with the edge of the sword. He let none remain in it, but did to its king as he had done to the king of Jericho.

31 Then Joshua passed from Libnah, and all Israel with him, to Lachish; and they encamped against it and fought against it. 32 And the LORD delivered Lachish into the hand of Israel, who took it on the second day, and struck it and all the people who were in it with the edge of the sword, according to all that he had done to Libnah. 33 Then Horam king of Gezer came up to help Lachish; and Joshua struck him and his people, until he left him none remaining.

34 From Lachish Joshua passed to Eglon, and all Israel with him; and they encamped against it and fought against it. 35 They took it on that day and struck it with the edge of the sword; all the people who were in it he utterly destroyed that day, according to all that he had done to Lachish.

36 So Joshua went up from Eglon, and all Israel with him, to Hebron; and they fought against it. 37 And they took it and

struck it with the edge of the sword—its king, all its cities, and all the people who were in it; he left none remaining, according to all that he had done to Eglon, but utterly destroyed it and all the people who were in it.

38 Then Joshua returned, and all Israel with him, to Debir; and they fought against it. 39 And he took it and its king and all its cities; they struck them with the edge of the sword and utterly destroyed all the people who were in it. He left none remaining; as he had done to Hebron, so he did to Debir and its king, as he had done also to Libnah and its king.

40 So Joshua conquered all the land: the mountain country and the South and the lowland and the wilderness slopes, and all their kings; he left none remaining, but utterly destroyed all that breathed, as the Lord God of Israel had commanded. 41 And Joshua conquered them from Kadesh Barnea as far as Gaza, and all the country of Goshen, even as far as Gibeon. 42 All these kings and their land Joshua took at one time, because the Lord God of Israel fought for Israel.

—Joshua 20:22–42

Ours is a spiritual battle to death with Christ being the ultimate Victor.

Joshua's order in verse 24 is fascinating. In the Middle East, there are great Egyptian and Assyrian murals and sculptures. They are historic records of ancient wars; and frequently, the specific action is recorded. The conquering king's or general's act of placing his foot on the neck of the defeated general or king was the ancient symbol of victory. The court artists would record such scenes so that all passersby might see just who was the victor. Not only has God told Joshua that he will win this battle (v. 8), but now Joshua, who is on God's side, is prophetically declaring to his military aides that God will continue to give them victory as they are faithful to Him. In verse 25 he rearticulates to the people the promise earlier given to him.

References of this nature appear all through the Scriptures. In 1 Kings 5:3 we read, *"until the Lord put his foes under the soles of his feet."* The psalmist saw present victories as a promise of a day when God would make *"Your enemies Your footstool"* (110:1; referring to the Messiah). The apostle Paul picks up the same phrase in 1 Corinthians 15:24–25, referring to Jesus Christ's ultimate victory over sin and death, writing: "Then comes the end, when He delivers the kingdom to God the Father, when He puts an end to all rule and all authority and power. For He must reign till He has put all enemies under His feet."

What hope we as believers in Jesus Christ can attach to the answers to that deep, deep question of each of our hearts: "Who shall separate us from the love of Christ? Shall tribulation, or distress, or persecution, or famine, or nakedness, or peril, or sword?" (Rom. 8:35). We must never forget the clear-cut answer, and we must communicate this over and over again to those for whom we bear pastoral responsibility. There will be tribulation, distress, persecution, famine, nakedness, peril, and sword. We are never told that we will not have difficulty. We are engaged in a spiritual battle to death with Christ as the Victor:

> Yet in all these things we are more than conquerors through Him who loved us. For I am persuaded that neither death nor life, nor angels nor principalities nor powers, nor things present nor things to come, nor height nor depth, nor any other created thing, shall be able to separate us from the love of God which is in Christ Jesus our Lord (Rom. 8:37–39).

We must never forget that He who is in us is more powerful than he who is in the world.

And we must remember that victory entails putting to death the enemy. We shouldn't pity those five kings. But something within us says, "Wouldn't humiliating them have been enough? Why did Joshua have to kill them, hang them on five trees, and then throw their dead bodies back into the cave, rolling the stones back up against the cave? That's awfully severe, isn't it?" The Hebrew word *ḥêrem* appears sprinkled all through this passage. It refers to what is separated or banned from ordinary use or contact. These kings were *ḥêrem* and were to be destroyed. They would have come back to conquer at some future date. Even in modern times, Middle-Eastern kings or dictators are assassinated and their bodies are placed on public display. In 1958, King Faisal of Iraq was impaled in the city square of Baghdad along with his uncle who was prime minister. It tells the world who is in charge.

It was not enough to leave those five kings lurking in a cave; they had to be slain. In a similar way, we are to put to death that sin that so easily besets us. I have to ask myself what sinister thoughts and actions are hidden within the cave of my life. What are they, empowered by Satan, planning to do to me? Empowered by the Holy Spirit, I am privileged to rip those stones away from the front of that cave, grab those demons by their throats, and crucify them in the name of Jesus Christ, confessing my need of His forgiveness and my power to live with Christ as Victor in my life. What a privilege we have of communicating this spiritual truth to our people.

A SPIRITUAL HOME BASE

43 Then Joshua returned, and all Israel with him, to the camp at Gilgal.

—*Joshua 10:43*

Ours is the privilege of having a spiritual home base. Gilgal, the place where Joshua had set up the twelve stones of memory after the crossing of the Jordan, was also the place of circumcision before the battle of Jericho. It was the home base after the defeat and victory at Ai. The Gibeonites came to woo Joshua at Gilgal. The Israelites moved forth from Gilgal to fight the battle. After Joshua slew the five kings, he moved on to Makkedah, Libnah, Lachish, Eglon, Hebron, Debir, defeating the whole land, the hill country, and the Negev to the south, from the lowlands over to the Mediterranean Sea.

Returning to the camp at Gilgal, these soldiers must have been exhausted. Every kind of warfare takes its toll. God pity the mercenary who has no great cause and is in it only for the money, or pity the soldier without a home, or the Christian without his Gilgal, a place to which he or she can return.

Do you have a Gilgal to which you periodically return? I have had one in just about every community in which I have served. It has been my own private place of quietness, a place in which I can be alone with God. If you have such a place, tell your people about it, and encourage them to have places of their own.

But Gilgal is more than a private place; it also has community significance. It is a sanctuary where God's people are gathered to hear His Word. Ours is not an individualistic campaign. We have colleagues in the fight. We reconnoiter as the church to share our war stories. As Joshua's conquest was carried on, each of the individual tribes could have spun off from the main force when their own land was captured according to the allocation of land in the pentateuchal record. But they stayed together and returned to Gilgal.

There they not only found rest and energy for future battles that they would unselfishly wage together, but they also strategized. The Israelites had moved into the midsection of the land, conquered the south, and then moved northward. Gilgal was a place of rest, of energy, and of strategy.

The British expositor Alan Redpath makes a fascinating parallel between Gilgal and Calvary. He writes:

> May I remind you of the great words of New Testament truth and salvation which have their roots deeply imbedded in Gilgal. Here they are; refresh your memory. It was a place of remembrance, where all of God's people together went down unto death; it was a place of resurrection, where together they came up with their leader into life. It was a place of renunciation, where they cast off the carnal existence of the wilderness; it was a place of restoration, where they came again into fellowship with the Lord. It was the place of realization, where they began to taste of the strong food of the land; it was the place of revelation, where they met their Captain with a drawn sword.
>
> The Christian life has its own roots firmly imbedded in Calvary, the place where we died with Jesus and rose with Him, where we have deliberately renounced carnality and have entered into a living fellowship with our Lord, where we have begun to take the strong food of His Word and to realize every moment of our lives that the Captain of the Lord's hosts is with us.[2]

THE RESPONSIBILITY OF COMPLETING THE CONQUEST

11:1 And it came to pass, when Jabin king of Hazor heard these things, that he sent to Jobab king of Madon, to the king of Shimron, to the king of Achshaph, 2 and to the kings who were from the north, in the mountains, in the plain south of Chinneroth, in the lowland, and in the heights of Dor on the west, 3 to the Canaanites in the east and in the west, the Amorite, the Hittite, the Perizzite, the Jebusite in the mountains, and the Hivite below Hermon in the land of Mizpah. 4 So they went out, they and all their armies with them, as many people as the sand that is on the seashore in multitude, with very many horses and chariots. 5 And when all these kings had met together, they came and camped together at the waters of Merom to fight against Israel.

6 But the LORD said to Joshua, "Do not be afraid because of them, for tomorrow about this time I will deliver all of them slain before Israel. You shall hamstring their horses and burn their chariots with fire." 7 So Joshua and all the people of war with him came against them suddenly by the waters of Merom, and they attacked them. 8 And the LORD delivered them into the hand of Israel, who defeated them and chased them to Greater Sidon, to the Brook Misrephoth, and to the Valley of Mizpah eastward; they attacked them until they left none of them remaining. 9 So Joshua did to them as the LORD had told him: he hamstrung their horses and burned their chariots with fire.

10 Joshua turned back at that time and took Hazor, and struck its king with the sword; for Hazor was formerly the head of all those kingdoms. 11 And they struck all the people who were in it with the edge of the sword, utterly destroying them. There was none left breathing. Then he burned Hazor with fire.

12 So all the cities of those kings, and all their kings, Joshua took and struck with the edge of the sword. He utterly destroyed them, as Moses the servant of the LORD had commanded. 13 But as for the cities that stood on their mounds, Israel burned none of them, except Hazor only, which Joshua burned. 14 And all the spoil of these cities and the livestock, the children of Israel took as booty for themselves; but they struck every man with the edge of the sword until they had destroyed them, and they left none breathing. 15 As the LORD had commanded Moses his servant, so Moses commanded Joshua, and so Joshua did. He left nothing undone of all that the LORD had commanded Moses.

16 Thus Joshua took all this land: the mountain country, all the South, all the land of Goshen, the lowland, and the Jordan plain—the mountains of Israel and its lowlands, 17 from Mount Halak and the ascent to Seir, even as far as Baal Gad in the Valley of Lebanon below Mount Hermon. He captured all their kings, and struck them down and killed them. 18 Joshua made war a long time with all those kings. 19 There was not a city that made peace with the children of Israel, except the Hivites, the inhabitants of Gibeon. All the others they took in battle. 20 For it was of the LORD to harden their

hearts, that they should come against Israel in battle, that He might utterly destroy them, and that they might receive no mercy, but that He might destroy them, as the LORD had commanded Moses.

21 And at that time Joshua came and cut off the Anakim from the mountains: from Hebron, from Debir, from Anab, from all the mountains of Judah, and from all the mountains of Israel; Joshua utterly destroyed them with their cities.
22 None of the Anakim were left in the land of the children of Israel; they remained only in Gaza, in Gath, and in Ashdod.

23 So Joshua took the whole land, according to all that the LORD had said to Moses; and Joshua gave it as an inheritance to Israel according to their divisions by their tribes. Then the land rested from war.

12:1 These are the kings of the land whom the children of Israel defeated, and whose land they possessed on the other side of the Jordan toward the rising of the sun, from the River Arnon to Mount Hermon, and all the eastern Jordan plain:
2 One king was Sihon king of the Amorites, who dwelt in Heshbon and ruled half of Gilead, from Aroer, which is on the bank of the River Arnon, from the middle of that river, even as far as the River Jabbok, which is the border of the Ammonites,
3 and the eastern Jordan plain from the Sea of Chinneroth as far as the Sea of the Arabah (the Salt Sea), the road to Beth Jeshimoth, and southward below the slopes of Pisgah. 4 The other king was Og king of Bashan and his territory, who was of the remnant of the giants, who dwelt at Ashtaroth and at Edrei, 5 and reigned over Mount Hermon, over Salcah, over all Bashan, as far as the border of the Geshurites and the Maachathites, and over half of Gilead to the border of Sihon king of Heshbon.

6 These Moses the servant of the LORD and the children of Israel had conquered; and Moses the servant of the LORD had given it as a possession to the Reubenites, the Gadites, and half the tribe of Manasseh.

7 And these are the kings of the country which Joshua and the children of Israel conquered on this side of the Jordan, on the west, from Baal Gad in the Valley of Lebanon as far as Mount Halak and the ascent to Seir, which Joshua gave to the tribes of Israel as a possession according to their divisions, 8 in the mountain country, in the lowlands, in the Jordan plain, in the slopes, in the wilderness, and in the South—the Hittites,

the Amorites, the Canaanites, the Perizzites, the Hivites, and the Jebusites: [9] the king of Jericho, one; the king of Ai, which is beside Bethel, one; [10] the king of Jerusalem, one; the king of Hebron, one; [11] the king of Jarmuth, one; the king of Lachish, one; [12] the king of Eglon, one; the king of Gezer, one; [13] the king of Debir, one; the king of Geder, one; [14] the king of Hormah, one; the king of Arad, one; [15] the king of Libnah, one; the king of Adullam, one; [16] the king of Makkedah, one; the king of Bethel, one; [17] the king of Tappuah, one; the king of Hepher, one; [18] the king of Aphek, one; the king of Lasharon, one; [19] the king of Madon, one; the king of Hazor, one; [20] the king of Shimron Meron, one; the king of Achshaph, one; [21] the king of Taanach, one; the king of Megiddo, one; [22] the king of Kedesh, one; the king of Jokneam in Carmel, one; [23] the king of Dor in the heights of Dor, one; the king of the people of Gilgal, one; [24] the king of Tirzah, one—all the kings, thirty-one.

—Joshua 11:1—12:24

Ours is a responsibility of completing the conquest. As the Israelites moved northward, they ran into tough resistance. The people of the northern cities also were organized. Jabin, the king of Hazor, gathered together a great alliance, kings who were determined to crush Joshua. These kings had horses and chariots and came out by numbers like sand upon the seashore (11:4). They had hardened hearts (v. 20) and giants called Anakim among them (v. 21). Decades earlier, ten of the twelve spies had reported with great fear to Moses that there were giants in the land. The Israelites were like grasshoppers before them. Only Joshua and Caleb had believed that God could give them victory.

As we preach and teach, we must be aware that many to whom we speak are ready to throw in the towel. In fact, we are also often at that point. We must remind ourselves and those with whom we are communicating to hang in there. We will prevail—not because we are tough but because we are on God's side. I love this fascinating statement attributed to Napoleon: "Alexander, Caesar, Charlemagne, and myself founded empires, but upon what did we rest the creations of our genius? Upon force. Jesus Christ alone founded his kingdom upon love, and at this day millions of men would die for him."[3]

Dr. V. Raymond Edman, for many years president of Wheaton College, would frequently remind the student body, "It's always too soon to quit." We must urge our people not to give up too soon.

A friend of mine in the ministry was deserted by his wife for another man. For seven years, she alienated herself from him. Two of those years, he slept in the same bed with her. During that time, she never let him touch her sexually. In human terms, he had every reason to find another woman for he had been deserted. In the midst of his terrible pain, he endeavored to learn lessons of adaptability and faithfulness. One summer, he was on retreat at a conference center where Corrie ten Boom happened to be speaking. Someone had told her about his circumstances, and he returned to his room one evening to see a letter tucked under his door. It was from Corrie ten Boom, who had been deeply touched by the torture he was experiencing. Although she had never met him, she was inspired to write him a note of comfort, telling him that even though he might not at times feel it, he was covered by God's wings. "When you are covered by God's wings, it can get pretty dark." Those words brought hope to my friend. Today this man and his wife have a restored love, because God was faithful. Not only that, but also because he never gave up. He was more than a conqueror through Christ who strengthened him.

I have been doing a lot of thinking about my own life and ministry in the church I serve. I happened across Harold Lindsell's biography of Dr. Harold John Ockenga, for many decades the minister of the Park Street Congregational Church in Boston, founder of Fuller Theological Seminary, and president of Gordon-Conwell Divinity School. Although Dr. Ockenga died in 1985, this biography was written in 1951, when he was in his mid-forties. Dr. Lindsell observed that if Harold Ockenga continued to live, he had another twenty years or so of ministry ahead of him. He noted that his path had been marked by incalculable difficulty and opposition along many fronts and that Ockenga was endeavoring to wear the armor described by the apostle Paul. Then Lindsell noted that this armor makes no provision nor protection for one's back. It protects only the one who faces the enemy.[4]

As communicators, you and I are called to a deepening commitment to Jesus Christ, a greater understanding. We are engaged in a warfare—a spiritual battle to death. We have the privilege of the church as our home base, our Gilgal. We have the responsibility to complete the spiritual warfare in which we are engaged on God's side. Someday we will stand before Christ the Victor who will look us in the eyes and say, "Well done, thou good and faithful servant.

Enter into thy eternal rest." For now, we have the special privilege and opportunity to communicate this biblical understanding of Christian life in very frank, personal terms to those for whom the Lord has given us a sense of responsibility.

NOTES

1. Hamlin, *Inheriting the Land*, p. 96.

2. Redpath, *Victorious Christian Living*, p. 153.

3. Harmon, *The Interpreter's Bible*, p. 603.

4. Harold Lindsell, *Park Street Prophet: The Story of Harold Ockenga* (Wheaton, Ill.: Van Kampen Press, 1951), p. 174.

CHAPTER THIRTEEN—THE ARCHIVES SPEAK

JOSHUA 13:1—19:51

Scripture Outline

> We Never Fully Arrive in This Life (13:1–7)
>
> God Gives and Holds Accountable (13:8—14:5)
>
> Faithfulness to the Covenant (14:6—15:19)
>
> Women's Rights (15:20—17:13)
>
> The Alternative to Complaining About One's Lot in Life (17:14–18)
>
> The Disposition of the Remaining Land (18:1—19:51)

In one way, nothing is more boring than to be stuck in a room filled with dusty old volumes filled with land transactions, wills, epitaphs, out-of-date maps, and records of boundary markings.

That's precisely what we have in chapters 13 through 19. Very few pastors ever preach out of these seven chapters, with the exception of an occasional message on God's promise, delayed but fulfilled, to Caleb. I doubt that I would have ever preached out of these somewhat ponderous, archival chapters if I had not committed myself to preaching through the entire Book of Joshua and to writing this commentary. In the world of practical, contemporary significance, what can we as preachers discover from a study of page after page of musty, old Jewish archives describing which of the twelve tribes got which part of the land at the end of the conquest? Frankly, I dreaded coming to this part of my Joshua study. Scholars, writing critical commentaries, might find these materials to be of technical interest. But what about those of us who are endeavoring to communicate to contemporary people? Is there anything here of value to them? Are we foolish even to attempt to make any pulpit or popular classroom comments on these materials? I have to admit that such archives can be boring.

Archives, however, also have hidden in them exciting messages. When appropriately approached, archives speak. So instead of trying to preach a verse-by-verse exposition of these seven chapters, which would have been counterproductive to the creative use of the pulpit I fill, I decided to let the theme "The Archives Speak" be my message. This way, I would not be tied down to the mechanical aspects of the land distribution, but I could share in one message the importance of archives. And I could illustrate that even the most technical and detailed biblical materials have hidden within them practical, up-to-date messages.

I was working through these seven chapters during the height of the world's curiosity as to the whereabouts of the Nazi war criminal Joseph Mengele. This gave me a perfect opportunity to emphasize the way archives can speak messages that rivet the world's attention. The most sophisticated researchers in the world were analyzing scraps of decayed clothing, letters, photographs, and bone fragments. Handwriting experts were comparing penmanship from the late 1930s and early 1940s with penmanship from more than thirty years later. Not many would have found fifty-year-old dental records of any interest. But the records took on enormous significance as the world gathered around that cemetery plot in the town of Embu, some twenty-five miles south of Sao Paulo, Brazil, to observe the exhumation of what was reported to be the remains of "the angel of death." The notorious Nazi death-camp doctor had sent some four hundred thousand victims to their death at Auschwitz-Birkenau in Poland and used thousands of others as guinea pigs for his gruesome genetic research. Archives do speak; and, on occasion, the world listens.

Then I shared with my congregation my own teenage fascination with graveyards. I had discovered that I could learn a lot about death and life from reading the grave markers of those who had gone on before. When I was a student at Princeton Theological Seminary, I occasionally dated a coed from Wellesley College who shared my strange fascination. On more than several occasions, we hiked through cemeteries, ranging from old burial grounds in Boston to rural cemeteries on a hillside in New Hampshire, reading tombstones. Then we would philosophize, in our own little re-creation of history, from those bottom-line glimpses into the lives etched in stone in a few words describing their ultimate commitment, their names, their dates, and their proximity to others in the family, and their environment. All gave intriguing insights into life, its dreams, its expectancies, its joys, its sorrows, and then death and the importance of never forgetting its inevitability. Even when driving alone (I have never been able to interest my wife in this somewhat morbid activity), I find myself occasionally pulling off the main road at a cemetery, parking the car, and drifting off into history as I go to read those markers.

You could write the history of fortunes made and fortunes lost just by browsing through county courthouse archival records. These dusty old materials tell stories and teach truths in very special ways. So I urged the members of my congregation not to discount the value of biblical archival material, which may at first glance appear tedious, dry, dusty, and unimportant. Such materials can be boring, but at the same time, there are a few things that are quite exciting capsuled within Joshua's verse-after-verse sections that name tribes, people, cities, bodies of water, and boundary markings. The archives do speak; they contain true insights for contemporary Christian living.

So instead of getting caught up in the stuff of biblical scholars who specialize in Jewish tribal history or biblical mapmakers who technically study tribal boundaries, I used these seven chapters as an opportunity to illustrate how Joshua's archival material, as well as many of the other biblical archival passages, do speak. I arbitrarily chose five insights into contemporary living. In no way did I exhaust the many possibilities that are in these seven chapters of Joshua.

For example, the passing mention of the Israelite execution of Balaam in Joshua 13:22 could open up the entire vista of the Scriptures dealing with the fascinating story in Numbers 22—25. This story teaches us to watch out for "preachers for hire," who as mercenaries blend truth and evil, ultimately corrupting the faith and practice of God's people. The communicator could trace these teachings about Balaam through the New Testament, which develops this story further. In 2 Peter 2:15 Balaam is described as a prophet for hire. Jude describes the ways of false prophets who are only interested in profit. Revelation 2:14 quotes Jesus as alerting His church to guard itself against those who teach the false doctrine of Balaam, putting a stumbling block before God's people, teaching them to eat things sacrificed to idols and to commit sexual immorality. I, personally, did not feel entitled to the luxury of lingering, preaching through these seven chapters at length.

Instead, I picked the following five themes and dealt with them briefly within the context of one sermon.

WE NEVER FULLY ARRIVE IN THIS LIFE

13:1 Now Joshua was old, advanced in years. And the LORD said to him: "You are old, advanced in years, and there remains very much land yet to be possessed. **2** This is the land that yet remains: all the territory of the Philistines and all that of the Geshurites, **3** from Sihor, which is east of Egypt, as far as the border of Ekron northward (which is counted as Canaanite); the five lords of the Philistines—the Gazites, the Ashdodites, the Ashkelonites, the Gittites, and the Ekronites; also the Avites; **4** from the south, all the land of the Canaanites, and Mearah that belongs to the Sidonians as far as Aphek, to the border of the Amorites; **5** the land of the Gebalites, and all Lebanon, toward the sunrise, from Baal Gad below Mount Hermon as far as the entrance to Hamath; **6** all the inhabitants of the mountains from Lebanon as far as the Brook Misrephoth, and all the Sidonians—them I will drive out from before the children of Israel; only divide it by lot to Israel as an inheritance, as I have commanded you. **7** Now therefore, divide this land as an inheritance to the nine tribes and half the tribe of Manasseh."

—Joshua 13:1–7

These archives tell us that we never completely arrive in this life.

Verse 1 tells us that Joshua is now an old man. It hadn't been too long since he had seemed young as he succeeded his mentor, Moses. Now he bears the scars of battle. Leadership has taken its toll. As much as he had endeavored to do a thorough job, his work was not yet completed. It comes as a startling moment of truth when we realize our own human limitations, discovering that we may never accomplish all we had planned to accomplish in this life.

The Philistine area had not been conquered with its five great cities of Gaza, Ashdod, Ashkelon, Gath, and Ekron. What a thorn in the flesh the Philistines would be over the next three hundred years until a young King David emerged to complete what Joshua couldn't in his time. Neither had Jerusalem nor some of the hill country to the north, toward Mount Hermon, been conquered. The coast of Phoenicia, which is now southern Lebanon, had not been taken. And even within those territories that had been conquered, there were Canaanites living with whom there would be an ongoing struggle for coexistence.

Joshua might have been discouraged because of his age, knowing his work wasn't completed. But this was not the case. Joshua was a man of spiritual understanding. He had observed Moses—that great law-giver, that great leader of the people—as he went up to the top of Mount Nebo and looked westward into the Promised Land, knowing that his duties were done, although there were still many things to be accomplished. Another would have to carry on.

This is the stuff of the Christian life. We never completely arrive in this life. This fact is alien to our contemporary mindset as goal-oriented, management-by-objective people. This is a perfect opportunity to point out that life continues even though we don't accomplish all that we wish. Urge those with whom you'll be sharing this message to take a good walk through a cemetery, if only to remind themselves that life goes on and that we are not the center of the universe.

The apostle Paul realized this; and he was a most energetic, task-oriented person. Fortunately, early in his ministry, he came to see himself as an ambassador for Christ, a person under orders. Paul realized that God's work is bigger than one person. He would do his best to be faithful, fighting the good fight and running the race. He would finish the course, only to hand the baton to someone else. It is the result of this understanding that Paul could write from his prison cell in Rome these perceptive words to his fellow believers in the metropolitan center of Philippi in Northern Greece: "Not that I have already attained, or am already perfected; but I press on, that I may lay hold of that for which Christ Jesus has also laid hold of me" (Phil. 3:12).

Christian maturity becomes ours as we are willing to have our names added to the honor roll of faith in Hebrews 11. What kind of epitaph could be carved into our gravestones? Raise this question to those with whom you communicate. Would it reflect the summary statement covering that great honor roll of faith in Hebrews 11? Some of God's greatest saints never lived to see their work completed: "These all died in faith, not having received the promises, but having seen them afar off were assured of them, embraced them and confessed that they were strangers and pilgrims on the earth" (Heb. 11:13).

When we discover that we never completely arrive in this life, we are set free to be. We understand that this life is a struggle—

never easy. Psychiatrist M. Scott Peck opens his book *The Road Less Traveled* with a straightforward statement. It is well worth quoting:

> Life is difficult.
>
> This is a great truth, one of the greatest truths. It is a great truth because once we truly see this truth, we transcend it. Once we truly know that life is difficult—once we truly understand and accept it—then life is no longer difficult. Because once it is accepted, the fact that life is difficult no longer matters.
>
> Most do not fully see this truth that life is difficult. Instead they moan more or less incessantly, noisily or subtly, about the enormity of their problems, their burdens, and their difficulties as if life were generally easy, as if life should be easy. They voice their belief, noisily or subtly, that their difficulties represent a unique kind of affliction that should not be and that has somehow been especially visited upon them, or else upon their families, their tribe, their class, their nation, their race, or even their species, and not upon others. I know about this moaning because I have done my share.
>
> Life is a series of problems. Do we want to moan about them or solve them? Do we want to teach our children to solve them?[1]

During the time that I worked on this book, I spent four weeks in Egypt, Israel, Greece, and Scotland. I left for my trip totally exhausted. That final week of study, reflection, golf, jogging, and sleep at St. Andrews, Scotland, brought me total refreshment. I came back from my study leave ready to tackle life anew only to confront a pile of difficulties on my desk. I am discovering that I can't settle back and take it easy. Ministry is tough, and life is difficult. God will never give us more resources than we need to live one day at a time. If perchance we think we have more, we tend to get spoiled.

Hopefully, next Sunday, I will look back on seven days of growth, which will be an ongoing and continuing process. And there will be others who will pick up the standard and carry it when we have been put to our eternal rest. Far from being a discouraging fact, I am finding it to be an exciting reality. Not allowing myself to wallow in the realization that life is difficult, I find myself thrilled with the challenge that, for these few moments in time, we are privileged together to carry the baton that we have received from a previous generation and that we will hand on to another generation, as did Joshua.

GOD GIVES AND HOLDS ACCOUNTABLE

8 With the other half-tribe the Reubenites and the Gadites received their inheritance, which Moses had given them, beyond the Jordan eastward, as Moses the servant of the LORD had given them: 9 from Aroer which is on the bank of the River Arnon, and the town that is in the midst of the ravine, and all the plain of Medeba as far as Dibon; 10 all the cities of Sihon king of the Amorites, who reigned in Heshbon, as far as the border of the children of Ammon; 11 Gilead, and the border of the Geshurites and Maachathites, all Mount Hermon, and all Bashan as far as Salcah; 12 all the kingdom of Og in Bashan, who reigned in Ashtaroth and Edrei, who remained of the remnant of the giants; for Moses had defeated and cast out these.

13 Nevertheless the children of Israel did not drive out the Geshurites or the Maachathites, but the Geshurites and the Maachathites dwell among the Israelites until this day.

14 Only to the tribe of Levi he had given no inheritance; the sacrifices of the LORD God of Israel made by fire are their inheritance, as He said to them.

15 And Moses had given to the tribe of the children of Reuben an inheritance according to their families. 16 Their territory was from Aroer, which is on the bank of the River Arnon, and the city that is in the midst of the ravine, and all the plain by Medeba; 17 Heshbon and all its cities that are in the plain: Dibon, Bamoth Baal, Beth Baal Meon, 18 Jahaza, Kedemoth, Mephaath, 19 Kirjathaim, Sibmah, Zereth Shahar on the mountain of the valley, 20 Beth Peor, the slopes of Pisgah, and Beth Jeshimoth— 21 all the cities of the plain and all the kingdom of Sihon king of the Amorites, who reigned in Heshbon, whom Moses had struck with the princes of Midian: Evi, Rekem, Zur, Hur, and Reba, who were princes of Sihon dwelling in the country. 22 The children of Israel also killed with the sword Balaam the son of Beor, the soothsayer, among those who were killed by them. 23 And the border of the children of Reuben was the bank of the Jordan. This was the inheritance of the children of Reuben according to their families, the cities and their villages.

24 Moses also had given an inheritance to the tribe of Gad, to the children of Gad according to their families. 25 Their territory was Jazer, and all the cities of Gilead, and half the land of the Ammonites as far as Aroer, which is before Rabbah, 26 and from Heshbon to Ramath Mizpah and Betonim, and from Mahanaim to the border of Debir, 27 and in the valley Beth Haram, Beth Nimrah, Succoth, and Zaphon, the rest of the kingdom of Sihon king of Heshbon, with the Jordan as its border, as far as the edge of the Sea of Chinnereth, on the other side of the Jordan eastward. 28 This is the inheritance of the children of Gad according to their families, the cities and their villages.

29 Moses also had given an inheritance to half the tribe of Manasseh; it was for half the tribe of the children of Manasseh according to their families: 30 Their territory was from Mahanaim, all Bashan, all the kingdom of Og king of Bashan, and all the towns of Jair which are in Bashan, sixty cities; 31 half of Gilead, and Ashtaroth and Edrei, cities of the kingdom of Og in Bashan, were for the children of Machir the son of Manasseh, for half of the children of Machir according to their families.

32 These are the areas which Moses had distributed as an inheritance in the plains of Moab on the other side of the Jordan, by Jericho eastward. 33 But to the tribe of Levi Moses had given no inheritance; the LORD God of Israel was their inheritance, as He had said to them.

14:1 These are the areas which the children of Israel inherited in the land of Canaan, which Eleazar the priest, Joshua the son of Nun, and the heads of the fathers of the tribes of the children of Israel distributed as an inheritance to them. 2 Their inheritance was by lot, as the LORD had commanded by the hand of Moses, for the nine tribes and the half-tribe. 3 For Moses had given the inheritance of the two tribes and the half-tribe on the other side of the Jordan; but to the Levites he had given no inheritance among them. 4 For the children of Joseph were two tribes: Manasseh and Ephraim. And they gave no part to the Levites in the land, except cities to dwell in, with their common-lands for their livestock and their property. 5 As the LORD had commanded Moses, so the children of Israel did; and they divided the land.

—Joshua 13:8—14:5

The archives also tell us that God is the One who gives us the land, and He has some ideas about how we should use it.

Two Hebrew words are important in their usage here. One is the word *lākad*. It is a verb used for the act of capturing cities, describing how Jericho, Ai, Lachish, Eglon, Hebron, Debir, Hazor, Kiriath-Arba, and Leshem and "all their kings" were taken. It literally means to "take" by force "in battle." The Hebrew word *lāqah* is best translated "receive," as we see it in verse 8. This would be the most accurate translation of the same word in chapter 11, verses 16 and 23.

The idea is that God gives victory in battle so that His people are able to take *(lākad)* cities and kings. When it comes to land, it is God who gives it. The people receive *(lāqah)* the gift. Enemies may be conquered and their cities captured, but the land is not seized but rather received as a gift from God. The land belongs to God, and His people have it in trust as their inheritance. This has an enormous significance for the way in which one uses what God has given. It reminds us of the biblical theme of stewardship. What God has shared with us, we have a responsibility to use for His glory. Since God is the One who has given us the land, we are responsible to use it as good stewards. We do not have the right to exploit the land in a way that minimizes its usefulness for others.

A new society was being created by God, which had some distinctive characteristics when contrasted with the previous Canaanite society. Land reform marked this new society. In Canaan, the city kings were the owners of the land around the city, which was under their power. An aristocracy made up of business, religious, and government officials, representing only 2 percent of the population, had control over at least 50 percent of the land. These holdings were worked by slaves or sharecropping peasants. The land was tilled by villagers, who paid heavy taxes to support the urban elite. But in this new society, God was seen as the ultimate landowner, giving the whole land not to a king but to all the people. Tribe by tribe, family by family, God treated the people impartially. There was no privileged class. Even Joshua received a small grant. This is one reason God was so resistant to having the Hebrews appoint a king, as kings tend to assume arbitrary power.

The new society was marked by kinship associations. In the old Canaanite society, the poor were heavily burdened by debt slavery, sharecropping, and economic hardship. They were pushed to the edge of society and their existence made marginal. In the new society, there was an emphasis on family relationships. The land was to be used by all of the people for the benefit of all of the people, not just for a few. The land was parceled out to the tribes, and the tribes bore responsibility to see that each family within the tribe had its own land. There would be a periodic redistribution. Every seven years, there was a minor adjustment. Then on the fiftieth year, the land reverted to its previous family ownership. The loans to a poor family were to be interest free. There was a principle of mutual assistance. Military action was to be handled by mutual defense action. This was to avoid the establishment of standing armies that could be arbitrary in their power and become displaced from a responsibility for the land itself. Peace was a desired objective; the nation was not to see itself destined to be permanently at war.

The new society also put a premium on village life. Canaanite society had concentrated the power in cities, so village life had been disrupted. The Israelites used cities primarily as market places and administrative centers and sites of refuge in dangerous times. Judicial and religious functions were shared with the villages. The extended family was encouraged. The sharing of physical resources was institutionalized.

And the new society described in the seven chapters we are discussing emphasized a strong respect for the boundaries that limited living space. The boundaries defined areas of responsibility, the limits of control, and the protection against aggression. The respect for boundaries is one way of defining the last five of the Ten Commandments. Private property was to be respected. No king was, by fact of his power, privileged to take another person's land, wife, or other possessions. This was a radical understanding of society. This careful allotment of the land to the tribes was God's way of instituting a new society, a society in which righteousness and justice would prevail.

This new society was to be expanding. There were those territories such as the Philistine area, the Phoenician Coast, the Plain of Esdraelon, northern Trans-Jordan, and even the city of Jerusalem, that would need to come under this new perspective. The responsibility of the people was to receive the land that God intended for them to have and treat it with faithful stewardship. A helpful expansion of some of these concepts can be found in *Inheriting the Land*, by E. John Hamlin.[2]

FAITHFULNESS TO THE COVENANT

6 Then the children of Judah came to Joshua in Gilgal. And Caleb the son of Jephunneh the Kenizzite said to him:

"You know the word which the LORD said to Moses the man of God concerning you and me in Kadesh Barnea. [7] I was forty years old when Moses the servant of the LORD sent me from Kadesh Barnea to spy out the land, and I brought back word to him as it was in my heart. [8] Nevertheless my brethren who went up with me made the heart of the people melt, but I wholly followed the LORD my God. [9] So Moses swore on that day, saying, 'Surely the land where your foot has trodden shall be your inheritance and your children's forever, because you have wholly followed the LORD my God.' [10] And now, behold, the LORD has kept me alive, as He said, these forty-five years, ever since the LORD spoke this word to Moses while Israel wandered in the wilderness; and now, here I am this day, eighty-five years old. [11] As yet I am as strong this day as on the day that Moses sent me; just as my strength was then, so now is my strength for war, both for going out and for coming in. [12] Now therefore, give me this mountain of which the LORD spoke in that day; for you heard in that day how the Anakim were there, and that the cities were great and fortified. It may be that the LORD will be with me, and I shall be able to drive them out as the LORD said."

[13] And Joshua blessed him, and gave Hebron to Caleb the son of Jephunneh as an inheritance. [14] Hebron therefore became the inheritance of Caleb the son of Jephunneh the Kenizzite to this day, because he wholly followed the LORD God of Israel. [15] And the name of Hebron formerly was Kirjath Arba (Arba was the greatest man among the Anakim). Then the land had rest from war.

15:1 So this was the lot of the tribe of the children of Judah according to their families:

The border of Edom at the Wilderness of Zin southward was the extreme southern boundary. [2] And their southern border began at the shore of the Salt Sea, from the bay that faces southward. [3] Then it went out to the southern side of the Ascent of Akrabbim, passed along to Zin, ascended on the south side of Kadesh Barnea, passed along to Hezron, went up to Adar, and went around to Karkaa. [4] *From there* it passed toward Azmon and went out to the Brook of Egypt; and the border ended at the sea. This shall be your southern border.

[5] The east border was the Salt Sea as far as the mouth of the Jordan. And the border on the northern quarter began at the bay of the sea at the mouth of the Jordan. [6] The border

went up to Beth Hoglah and passed north of Beth Arabah; and the border went up to the stone of Bohan the son of Reuben. [7] Then the border went up toward Debir from the Valley of Achor, and it turned northward toward Gilgal, which is before the Ascent of Adummim, which is on the south side of the valley. The border continued toward the waters of En Shemesh and ended at En Rogel. [8] And the border went up by the Valley of the Son of Hinnom to the southern slope of the Jebusite city (which is Jerusalem). The border went up to the top of the mountain that lies before the Valley of Hinnom westward, which is at the end of the Valley of Rephaim northward. [9] Then the border went around from the top of the hill to the fountain of the water of Nephtoah, and extended to the cities of Mount Ephron. And the border went around to Baalah (which is Kirjath Jearim). [10] Then the border turned westward from Baalah to Mount Seir, passed along to the side of Mount Jearim on the north (which is Chesalon), went down to Beth Shemesh, and passed on to Timnah. [11] And the border went out to the side of Ekron northward. Then the border went around to Shicron, passed along to Mount Baalah, and extended to Jabneel; and the border ended at the sea.

[12] The west border was the coastline of the Great Sea. This is the boundary of the children of Judah all around according to their families.

[13] Now to Caleb the son of Jephunneh he gave a share among the children of Judah, according to the commandment of the LORD to Joshua, namely, Kirjath Arba, which is Hebron (Arba was the father of Anak). [14] Caleb drove out the three sons of Anak from there: Sheshai, Ahiman, and Talmai, the children of Anak. [15] Then he went up from there to the inhabitants of Debir (formerly the name of Debir was Kirjath Sepher).

[16] And Caleb said, "He who attacks Kirjath Sepher and takes it, to him I will give Achsah my daughter as wife." [17] So Othniel the son of Kenaz, the brother of Caleb, took it; and he gave him Achsah his daughter as wife. [18] Now it was so, when she came to him, that she persuaded him to ask her father for a field. So she dismounted from her donkey, and Caleb said to her, "What do you wish?" [19] She answered, "Give me a blessing; since you have given me land in the South, give me also springs of water." So he gave her the upper springs and the lower springs.

—Joshua 14:6—15:19

The archives tell us that faithfulness to the covenant pays rich, ultimate dividends.

This section of Joshua tells the story of Caleb. Apparently, his roots were originally outside the covenant, for he is referred to as *"Caleb the son of Jephunneh the Kenizzite"* (v. 6).

The story of Caleb goes back to Numbers 13:30. He was one of the twelve spies along with Joshua sent out by Moses. Only Caleb and Joshua came back with a favorable report. Ten of the spies acknowledged that the land was a magnificent land flowing with milk and honey. But they were afraid of the military might, the fortified cities, and the giants who lived in the land. It was Caleb, supported by Joshua, who had the courage to say, "Let us go up at once and take possession, for we are well able to overcome it" (Num. 13:30). He had a strong confidence in the Lord. But his position did not prevail. The judgment of God came upon the Israelites for their faintheartedness. God declared that those adults who had seen His glory and signs in Egypt and yet had bickered with Him in the wilderness, ten times, would not have the privilege of going into the Promised Land—except for Joshua and Caleb. God said, "'But My servant Caleb, because he has a different spirit in him and has followed Me fully, I will bring into the land where he went, and his descendants shall inherit it'" (Num. 14:24).

Now some forty-five years later, Caleb lives to see the covenant fulfilled. The very land most peopled with the giants is the land that Caleb wants. He now is going to claim the Lord's help to defeat the Anakim and to possess the land that he knew God would give to His people. What a strong lesson describing God's faithfulness to His covenant and His yearning for us to stay faithful to our commitments to Him. So, at age eighty-five, Caleb received that for which he had trusted God all those years.

I don't know what vows you've made, what commitments of life are yours. And you and I do not know what vows the people with whom we are communicating have made to God. But we do know that the Lord has committed himself to us and to all those who have repented of sin and put their trust in Jesus Christ. We need to remind ourselves and those for whom we bear communicative responsibility that God will keep His end of the covenant and will reward our faithfulness. At the same time, we need to remind ourselves and others that He doesn't promise immediate results. Caleb was forty years old when God made His promise. Over half a lifetime later, at age eighty-five, Caleb received tangibly that which he had trusted God for all those years.

In a fascinating encounter with his daughter and son-in-law (15:13–19), Caleb shows a flexibility. He had given his daughter in marriage to Othniel, who had helped him defeat the inhabitants of the land. Achsah, his daughter, and Othniel received their inheritance of the dry land of the Negeb. Knowing the importance of water, Achsah approached her father and asked him for some source of fresh water. In the same loving way in which God had worked with him, Caleb reciprocated that generosity and gave to his daughter and son-in-law the upper springs and the lower springs so that their land could be productive. What a contrast with those of us who keep the best for ourselves, giving away to others only what is no longer of prime usefulness.

WOMEN'S RIGHTS

20 This was the inheritance of the tribe of the children of Judah according to their families:

21 The cities at the limits of the tribe of the children of Judah, toward the border of Edom in the South, were Kabzeel, Eder, Jagur, 22 Kinah, Dimonah, Adadah, 23 Kedesh, Hazor, Ithnan, 24 Ziph, Telem, Bealoth, 25 Hazor, Hadattah, Kerioth, Hezron (which is Hazor), 26 Amam, Shema, Moladah, 27 Hazar Gaddah, Heshmon, Beth Pelet, 28 Hazar Shual, Beersheba, Bizjothjah, 29 Baalah, Ijim, Ezem, 30 Eltolad, Chesil, Hormah, 31 Ziklag, Madmannah, Sansannah, 32 Lebaoth, Shilhim, Ain, and Rimmon: all the cities are twenty-nine, with their villages.

33 In the lowland: Eshtaol, Zorah, Ashnah, 34 Zanoah, En Gannim, Tappuah, Enam, 35 Jarmuth, Adullam, Socoh, Azekah, 36 Sharaim, Adithaim, Gederah, and Gederothaim: fourteen cities with their villages; 37 Zenan, Hadashah, Migdal Gad, 38 Dilean, Mizpah, Joktheel, 39 Lachish, Bozkath, Eglon, 40 Cabbon, Lahmas, Kithlish, 41 Gederoth, Beth Dagon, Naamah, and Makkedah: sixteen cities with their villages; 42 Libnah, Ether, Ashan, 43 Jiphtah, Ashnah, Nezib, 44 Keilah, Achzib, and Mareshah: nine cities with their villages; 45 Ekron, with its towns and villages; 46 from Ekron to the sea, all that lay near Ashdod, with their villages; 47 Ashdod with its towns and villages, Gaza with its towns and villages—as far as the Brook of Egypt and the Great Sea with its coastline.

48 And in the mountain country: Shamir, Jattir, Sochoh, 49 Dannah, Kirjath Sannah (which is Debir), 50 Anab, Eshtemoh, Anim, 51 Goshen, Holon, and Giloh: eleven cities with their villages; 52 Arab, Dumah, Eshean, 53 Janum, Beth

Tappuah, Aphekah, [54] Humtah, Kirjath Arba (which is Hebron), and Zior: nine cities with their villages; [55] Maon, Carmel, Ziph, Juttah, [56] Jezreel, Jokdeam, Zanoah, [57] Kain, Gibeah, and Timnah: ten cities with their villages; [58] Halhul, Beth Zur, Gedor, [59] Maarath, Beth Anoth, and Eltekon: six cities with their villages; [60] Kirjath Baal (which is Kirjath Jearim) and Rabbah: two cities with their villages.

[61] In the wilderness: Beth Arabah, Middin, Secacah, [62] Nibshan, the City of Salt, and En Gedi: six cities with their villages.

[63] As for the Jebusites, the inhabitants of Jerusalem, the children of Judah could not drive them out; but the Jebusites dwell with the children of Judah at Jerusalem to this day.

16:1 The lot fell to the children of Joseph from the Jordan, by Jericho, to the waters of Jericho on the east, to the wilderness that goes up from Jericho through the mountains to Bethel, [2] then went out from Bethel to Luz, passed along to the border of the Archites at Ataroth, [3] and went down westward to the boundary of the Japhletites, as far as the boundary of Lower Beth Horon to Gezer; and it ended at the sea.

[4] So the children of Joseph, Manasseh and Ephraim, took their inheritance.

[5] The border of the children of Ephraim, according to their families, was thus: The border of their inheritance on the east side was Ataroth Addar as far as Upper Beth Horon.

[6] And the border went out toward the sea on the north side of Michmethath; then the border went around eastward to Taanath Shiloh, and passed by it on the east of Janohah. [7] Then it went down from Janohah to Ataroth and Naarah, reached to Jericho, and came out at the Jordan.

[8] The border went out from Tappuah westward to the Brook Kanah, and it ended at the sea. This was the inheritance of the tribe of the children of Ephraim according to their families. [9] The separate cities for the children of Ephraim were among the inheritance of the children of Manasseh, all the cities with their villages.

[10] And they did not drive out the Canaanites who dwelt in Gezer; but the Canaanites dwell among the Ephraimites to this day and have become forced laborers.

17:1 There was also a lot for the tribe of Manasseh, for he was the firstborn of Joseph: namely for Machir the firstborn of Manasseh, the father of Gilead, because he was a man of war;

therefore he was given Gilead and Bashan. 2 And there was a lot for the rest of the children of Manasseh according to their families: for the children of Abiezer, the children of Helek, the children of Asriel, the children of Shechem, the children of Hepher, and the children of Shemida; these were the male children of Manasseh the son of Joseph according to their families.

3 But Zelophehad the son of Hepher, the son of Gilead, the son of Machir, the son of Manasseh, had no sons, but only daughters. And these are the names of his daughters: Mahlah, Noah, Hoglah, Milcah, and Tirzah. 4 And they came near before Eleazar the priest, before Joshua the son of Nun, and before the rulers, saying, "The LORD commanded Moses to give us an inheritance among our brothers." Therefore, according to the commandment of the LORD, he gave them an inheritance among their father's brothers. 5 Ten shares fell to Manasseh, besides the land of Gilead and Bashan, which were on the other side of the Jordan, 6 because the daughters of Manasseh received an inheritance among his sons; and the rest of Manasseh's sons had the land of Gilead.

7 And the territory of Manasseh was from Asher to Michmethath, that lies east of Shechem; and the border went along south to the inhabitants of En Tappuah. 8 Manasseh had the land of Tappuah, but Tappuah on the border of Manasseh belonged to the children of Ephraim. 9 And the border descended to the Brook Kanah, southward to the brook. These cities of Ephraim are among the cities of Manasseh. The border of Manasseh was on the north side of the brook; and it ended at the sea.

10 Southward it was Ephraim's, northward it was Manasseh's, and the sea was its border. Manasseh's territory was adjoining Asher on the north and Issachar on the east. 11 And in Issachar and in Asher, Manasseh had Beth Shean and its towns, Ibleam and its towns, the inhabitants of Dor and its towns, the inhabitants of En Dor and its towns, the inhabitants of Taanach and its towns, and the inhabitants of Megiddo and its towns—three hilly regions. 12 Yet the children of Manasseh could not drive out the inhabitants of those cities, but the Canaanites were determined to dwell in that land. 13 And it happened, when the children of Israel grew strong, that they put the Canaanites to forced labor, but did not utterly drive them out.

—Joshua 15:20—17:13

Four verses in the midst of these archives—Joshua 17:3–6—tell us that women have their inheritance rights too. This may not seem like much today, but it was revolutionary in that society because male chauvinism was supreme.

One man, by the name of Zelophehad of the tribe of Manasseh, had five daughters and no sons. Verses 3–6 describe how these five daughters came to Eleazar, the priest, and Joshua, asserting their rights. They reminded Joshua, *"The LORD commanded Moses to give us an inheritance among our brothers"* (v. 4). So, in good faith, Joshua made certain that there were inheritance rights for women so that the land would stay in the family.

As modest as it seems in contemporary terms, this had expansive, radical implications for that day. And it gives us an insight into how God views women. Obviously, there are many other passages of the Scriptures that deal more specifically with this theme. The church may continue to debate on into future generations whether or not there are specific roles for men and for women. One fact stands certain. In God's eyes, male and female are equal, and both have their rights. Neither is by arbitrary power to lord it over the other or by clever manipulation to selfishly get his or her way.

THE ALTERNATIVE TO COMPLAINING
ABOUT ONE'S LOT IN LIFE

14 Then the children of Joseph spoke to Joshua, saying, "Why have you given us only one lot and one share to inherit, since we are a great people, inasmuch as the LORD has blessed us until now?"

15 So Joshua answered them, "If you are a great people, then go up to the forest country and clear a place for yourself there in the land of the Perizzites and the giants, since the mountains of Ephraim are too confined for you."

16 But the children of Joseph said, "The mountain country is not enough for us; and all the Canaanites who dwell in the land of the valley have chariots of iron, both those who are of Beth Shean and its towns and those who are of the Valley of Jezreel."

17 And Joshua spoke to the house of Joseph—to Ephraim and Manasseh—saying, "You are a great people and have great power; you shall not have only one lot, 18 but the mountain country shall be yours. Although it is wooded, you shall cut it down, and its farthest extent shall be yours; for you shall drive

out the Canaanites, though they have iron chariots and are
strong."

—*Joshua 17:14–18*

The archives also tell us not to complain about our lot in life
but to maximize it. When the tribe of Joseph saw what land they
were given, they came to Joshua complaining. They felt that they
had not been given enough land to take care of their people.
Joshua refused to humor them and told them, "Get to work and
clear the hills of that brush. You'll have plenty of land when you
are done taking care of the land you've been given."

They responded, saying that the hill country was not enough;
and the Canaanites lived in the plains and had chariots of iron. So
Joshua once again confronted them directly, telling them not to
worry about the Canaanites. Once they were done clearing the
land, they should organize themselves and go to battle against the
Canaanites. Their need for expanded territory would then be met
if they would simply discipline themselves for the struggle ahead.
It wouldn't be easy, but the battle would be theirs if they were
faithful to the Lord.

Many a contemporary analogy could be made here. How often
we have complained to God that we have not really been given
fair treatment. We want something more or different than God
has seen fit to give us. How many times I, in my own whimpering
way, have made my complaints to God, and He has given me the
same word Joshua gave to the tribe of Joseph. He has told me to
use faithfully the resources He has given me and to quit complaining about my lot in life. God has made it clear that if half the
energy I spent in complaining would be spent in doing something
constructive about my circumstances, they would radically
improve.

I am forced to contrast my own complaining ways, as one graciously gifted by God, with that very special woman, Joni Eareckson
Tada. Imagine diving into the Chesapeake Bay as a lively teenager
but surfacing to spend the rest of your life as a quadriplegic.
Whenever I am tempted to complain about my circumstances, I
think of her. She must have her low days and her periodic struggles,
but she has done something about her life. She has taken charge,
refusing to let her bed confine her. Taking an initiative, Joni has
picked up a paint brush with her teeth and created works of great
art under the most impossible of circumstances. She has refused to
become preoccupied with her limitations and has developed her

personality over these decades of paralysis. She has made herself so attractive that a very special man considered it a privilege for her to say yes to his marriage proposal. And they've built a healthy life together. Far from uttering drab sounds of complaint, Joni sings beautiful music of faith, hope, and God's faithfulness in all circumstances.

THE DISPOSITION OF THE REMAINING LAND

18:1 Now the whole congregation of the children of Israel assembled together at Shiloh, and set up the tabernacle of meeting there. And the land was subdued before them. ² But there remained among the children of Israel seven tribes which had not yet received their inheritance.

³ Then Joshua said to the children of Israel: "How long will you neglect to go and possess the land which the LORD God of your fathers has given you? ⁴ Pick out from among you three men for each tribe, and I will send them; they shall rise and go through the land, survey it according to their inheritance, and come back to me. ⁵ And they shall divide it into seven parts. Judah shall remain in their territory on the south, and the house of Joseph shall remain in their territory on the north. ⁶ You shall therefore survey the land in seven parts and bring the survey here to me, that I may cast lots for you here before the LORD our God. ⁷ But the Levites have no part among you, for the priesthood of the LORD is their inheritance. And Gad, Reuben, and half the tribe of Manasseh have received their inheritance beyond the Jordan on the east, which Moses the servant of the LORD gave them."

⁸ Then the men arose to go away; and Joshua charged those who went to survey the land, saying, "Go, walk through the land, survey it, and come back to me, that I may cast lots for you here before the LORD in Shiloh." ⁹ So the men went, passed through the land, and wrote the survey in a book in seven parts by cities; and they came to Joshua at the camp in Shiloh. ¹⁰ Then Joshua cast lots for them in Shiloh before the LORD, and there Joshua divided the land to the children of Israel according to their divisions.

¹¹ Now the lot of the tribe of the children of Benjamin came up according to their families, and the territory of their lot came out between the children of Judah and the children of Joseph. ¹² Their border on the north side began at the Jordan, and the border went up to the side of Jericho on the

north, and went up through the mountains westward; it ended at the Wilderness of Beth Aven. [13] The border went over from there toward Luz, to the side of Luz (which is Bethel) southward; and the border descended to Ataroth Addar, near the hill that lies on the south side of Lower Beth Horon.

[14] Then the border extended around the west side to the south, from the hill that lies before Beth Horon southward; and it ended at Kirjath Baal (which is Kirjath Jearim), a city of the children of Judah. This was the west side.

[15] The south side began at the end of Kirjath Jearim, and the border extended on the west and went out to the spring of the waters of Nephtoah. [16] Then the border came down to the end of the mountain that lies before the Valley of the Son of Hinnom, which is in the Valley of the Rephaim on the north, descended to the Valley of Hinnom, to the side of the Jebusite city on the south, and descended to En Rogel. [17] And it went around from the north, went out to En Shemesh, and extended toward Geliloth, which is before the Ascent of Adummim, and descended to the stone of Bohan the son of Reuben. [18] Then it passed along toward the north side of Arabah, and went down to Arabah. [19] And the border passed along to the north side of Beth Hoglah; then the border ended at the north bay at the Salt Sea, at the south end of the Jordan. This was the southern boundary.

[20] The Jordan was its border on the east side. This was the inheritance of the children of Benjamin, according to its boundaries all around, according to their families.

[21] Now the cities of the tribe of the children of Benjamin, according to their families, were Jericho, Beth Hoglah, Emek Keziz, [22] Beth Arabah, Zemaraim, Bethel, [23] Avim, Parah, Ophrah, [24] Chephar Haammoni, Ophni, and Gaba: twelve cities with their villages; [25] Gibeon, Ramah, Beeroth, [26] Mizpah, Chephirah, Mozah, [27] Rekem, Irpeel, Taralah, [28] Zelah, Eleph, Jebus (which is Jerusalem), Gibeath, and Kirjath: fourteen cities with their villages. This was the inheritance of the children of Benjamin according to their families.

19:1 The second lot came out for Simeon, for the tribe of the children of Simeon according to their families. And their inheritance was within the inheritance of the children of Judah. [2] They had in their inheritance Beersheba (Sheba), Moladah, [3] Hazar Shual, Balah, Ezem, [4] Eltolad, Bethul, Hormah, [5] Ziklag, Beth Marcaboth, Hazar Susah, [6] Beth

Lebaoth, and Sharuhen: thirteen cities and their villages; [7] Ain, Rimmon, Ether, and Ashan: four cities and their villages; [8] and all the villages that were all around these cities as far as Baalath Beer, Ramah of the South. This was the inheritance of the tribe of the children of Simeon according to their families.

[9] The inheritance of the children of Simeon was included in the share of the children of Judah, for the share of the children of Judah was too much for them. Therefore the children of Simeon had their inheritance within the inheritance of that people.

[10] The third lot came out for the children of Zebulun according to their families, and the border of their inheritance was as far as Sarid. [11] Their border went toward the west and to Maralah, went to Dabbasheth, and extended along the brook that is east of Jokneam. [12] Then from Sarid it went eastward toward the sunrise along the border of Chisloth Tabor, and went out toward Daberath, bypassing Japhia. [13] And from there it passed along on the east of Gath Hepher, toward Eth Kazin, and extended to Rimmon, which borders on Neah. [14] Then the border went around it on the north side of Hannathon, and it ended in the Valley of Jiphthah El. [15] Included were Kattath, Nahallal, Shimron, Idalah, and Bethlehem: twelve cities with their villages. [16] This was the inheritance of the children of Zebulun according to their families, these cities with their villages.

[17] The fourth lot came out to Issachar, for the children of Issachar according to their families. [18] And their territory went to Jezreel, and included Chesulloth, Shunem, [19] Haphraim, Shion, Anaharath, [20] Rabbith, Kishion, Abez, [21] Remeth, En Gannim, En Haddah, and Beth Pazzez. [22] And the border reached to Tabor, Shahazimah, and Beth Shemesh; their border ended at the Jordan: sixteen cities with their villages. [23] This was the inheritance of the tribe of the children of Issachar according to their families, the cities and their villages.

[24] The fifth lot came out for the tribe of the children of Asher according to their families. [25] And their territory included Helkath, Hali, Beten, Achshaph, [26] Alammelech, Amad, and Mishal; it reached to Mount Carmel westward, along the Brook Shihor Libnath. [27] It turned toward the sunrise to Beth Dagon; and it reached to Zebulun and to the Valley of Jiphthah El, then northward beyond Beth Emek and Neiel, bypassing Cabul which was on the left, [28] including

Ebron, Rehob, Hammon, and Kanah, as far as Greater Sidon. ²⁹ And the border turned to Ramah and to the fortified city of Tyre; then the border turned to Hosah, and ended at the sea by the region of Achzib. ³⁰ Also Ummah, Aphek, and Rehob were included: twenty-two cities with their villages. ³¹ This was the inheritance of the tribe of the children of Asher according to their families, these cities with their villages.

³² The sixth lot came out to the children of Naphtali, for the children of Naphtali according to their families. ³³ And their border began at Heleph, enclosing the territory from the terebinth tree in Zaanannim, Adami Nekeb, and Jabneel, as far as Lakkum; it ended at the Jordan. ³⁴ From Heleph the border extended westward to Aznoth Tabor, and went out from there toward Hukkok; it adjoined Zebulun on the south side and Asher on the west side, and ended at Judah by the Jordan toward the sunrise. ³⁵ And the fortified cities are Ziddim, Zer, Hammath, Rakkath, Chinnereth, ³⁶ Adamah, Ramah, Hazor, ³⁷ Kedesh, Edrei, En Hazor, ³⁸ Iron, Migdal El, Horem, Beth Anath, and Beth Shemesh: nineteen cities with their villages. ³⁹ This was the inheritance of the tribe of the children of Naphtali according to their families, the cities and their villages.

⁴⁰ The seventh lot came out for the tribe of the children of Dan according to their families. ⁴¹ And the territory of their inheritance was Zorah, Eshtaol, Ir Shemesh, ⁴² Shaalabbin, Aijalon, Jethlah, ⁴³ Elon, Timnah, Ekron, ⁴⁴ Eltekeh, Gibbethon, Baalath, ⁴⁵ Jehud, Bene Berak, Gath Rimmon, ⁴⁶ Me Jarkon, and Rakkon, with the region near Joppa. ⁴⁷ And the border of the children of Dan went beyond these, because the children of Dan went up to fight against Leshem and took it; and they struck it with the edge of the sword, took possession of it, and dwelt in it. They called Leshem, Dan, after the name of Dan their father. ⁴⁸ This is the inheritance of the tribe of the children of Dan according to their families, these cities with their villages.

⁴⁹ When they had made an end of dividing the land as an inheritance according to their borders, the children of Israel gave an inheritance among them to Joshua the son of Nun. ⁵⁰ According to the word of the LORD they gave him the city which he asked for, Timnath Serah in the mountains of Ephraim; and he built the city and dwelt in it.

[51] These were the inheritances which Eleazar the priest, Joshua the son of Nun, and the heads of the fathers of the tribes of the children of Israel divided as an inheritance by lot in Shiloh before the LORD, at the door of the tabernacle of meeting. So they made an end of dividing the country.

—Joshua 18:1—19:51

The text printed just above completes the seven chapters that are the subject of this commentary chapter.

Research scholars would treat these seven chapters of Joshua quite differently. The majority of the twenty-five commentaries I have on Joshua detail the parceling out of the land to the Israelites. Those details don't have too much to say to contemporary congregations. But the archives do speak. Tucked within these most obscure parts of the Scripture are truths of a contemporary significance. I urge you as a fellow preacher to consider musing on some of these thoughts and others contained in these chapters, using them as a primer in the methodology of biblical study. Urge your people to read through passages such as this for key names, phrases, and places. Alert them to the fact that the archives will speak to us if we take the time to leaf through these dusty pages, opening ourselves to the truths of God held therein.

NOTES

1. M. Scott Peck, *The Road Less Traveled* (New York: Simon & Schuster, 1978), p. 15.

2. Hamlin, *Inheriting the Land*, pp. 99–129.

CHAPTER FOURTEEN—CREATING TWO KINDS OF CITIES

JOSHUA 20:1—21:45

Scripture Outline

A Place of Legal Safety (20:1–9)

A Place of Spiritual Community (21:1–45)

We now come to two of the most fascinating chapters in the Bible. Why do I say this? Because we see God as He creates two kinds of cities—two cities that show us much about the nature of God and how He prioritizes human values on planet earth.

A PLACE OF LEGAL SAFETY

20:1 The LORD also spoke to Joshua, saying, 2 "Speak to the children of Israel, saying: 'Appoint for yourselves cities of refuge, of which I spoke to you through Moses, 3 that the slayer who kills a person accidentally or unintentionally may flee there; and they shall be your refuge from the avenger of blood. 4 And when he flees to one of those cities, and stands at the entrance of the gate of the city, and declares his case in the hearing of the elders of that city, they shall take him into the city as one of them, and give him a place, that he may dwell among them. 5 Then if the avenger of blood pursues him, they shall not deliver the slayer into his hand, because he struck his neighbor unintentionally, but did not hate him beforehand. 6 And he shall dwell in that city until he stands before the congregation for judgment, and until the death of the one who is high priest in those days. Then the slayer may return and come to his own city and his own house, to the city from which he fled.' "

7 So they appointed Kedesh in Galilee, in the mountains of Naphtali, Shechem in the mountains of Ephraim, and Kirjath Arba (which is Hebron) in the mountains of Judah. 8 And on the other side of the Jordan, by Jericho eastward, they assigned Bezer in the wilderness on the plain, from the tribe of Reuben, Ramoth in Gilead, from the tribe of Gad, and Golan in Bashan, from the tribe of Manasseh. 9 These were the cities appointed for all the children of Israel and for the stranger who dwelt among them, that whoever killed a person accidentally might flee there, and not die by the hand of the avenger of blood until he stood before the congregation.

—*Joshua 20:1–9*

One kind of city is a place of legal safety. Nothing is more frightening to me than the thought of living in a society where terrorism reigns.

I have made over twenty trips to the Middle East. Many of these have been as a leader responsible for the people traveling with me. During these years, there has probably been no part of the world more frequently mentioned on the front page of newspapers for its various crises. People ask, "Is it safe to go?" My usual response is that, actuarially speaking, you have a much greater chance of physical injury while driving through a major metropolitan area in the United States than you do traveling through the Middle East. People give me a somewhat puzzled look; they can't quite believe it. But it's a fact. I've been there in times just before or following revolutions or when wars were being waged in neighboring countries, only to find out more about those situations when reading the international edition of *Time* magazine a few days later than I knew on the days in which those events were happening. In the meantime, people at home were worried for our safety.

One major exception was in 1970 when I canceled a tour. Forty-five of us were to leave the following Sunday from Miami when the headlines carried the news that a Swiss Air plane, carrying Holy Land passengers, had been blown up by Arab terrorists. At just about the same time, an Israeli tour bus, filled with American passengers, had been attacked by terrorists while it was driving along the Tel Aviv-Haifa Road. A minister's wife was killed, and several other passengers were injured. Although everyone had paid for the trip in full and we were to leave in four days, on Wednesday of that week I canceled the tour. When the law of the jungle takes over, and people resort to terrorism to adjust perceived injustices, nobody is safe.

At the time that I was writing this chapter, the eyes of the world were focused on Beirut as, daily, we chronicled the tragic events in the lives of TWA hostages captured on that fateful flight out of Athens. They did nothing to deserve their scenario of horrors. They didn't bomb Beirut or create refugee camps. They didn't illegally appropriate Arab lands. They weren't necessarily pro-Israel and anti-Arab. But their nightmare went on day upon day upon day. Even the tough-talking president of the United States—who had been so critical of his predecessor's impotency under similar circumstances in the Iranian hostage crisis—found himself incapable of dealing with such irrational-rational behavior. One misstep, one logical action intended to bring fairness, could cost the lives of innocents. Yet to release several hundred prisoners in exchange for helpless victims didn't seem fair. So once again, one part of the world reverted to the law of the jungle. The law was taken into the hands of the few. Those who felt wrongs had been perpetrated against them had grabbed the reigns of justice, arguing their cause in the most unjust of ways. In the meantime, what was going to be a record summer in the number of Americans traveling through Greece became a shambles of cancelations. Greek cruise lines, hotels, and tour operators panicked as they saw their anticipated profits slip through their fingers.

At the same time, a bomb went off in the luggage area at Tokyo International Airport, killing two baggage handlers and injuring a few more. Experts believe that it had been timed to go off in midair. Fortunately, the flight had arrived ahead of schedule. The same day, an Air India flight exploded in midair over Ireland. Random terrorism is frightening.

This twentieth chapter of Joshua underlines the fact that God understands this law of the jungle, having observed it from the earliest of times. It wasn't long after Adam and Eve disobeyed Him that one of their sons killed his brother in a momentary jealous rage. The life of Abel, which was sacred, was snuffed out by an angered brother. This kind of lawless act has been going on ever since.

The oldest law of crime and punishment in the Old Testament is found in Genesis 4:23–24. It is a song of Lamech—a vendetta. It tells of indiscriminate killing as each person takes the law into his own hands.

Then comes a more responsible ethic articulated in Exodus 21:23–25: "But if any harm follows, then you shall give life for life, eye for eye, tooth for tooth, hand for hand, foot for foot, burn for burn, wound for wound, stripe for stripe." The harshness of indiscriminate vendettas is brought into ethical control. Punishment shall be in proportion to the crime. Whatever wrong has been done, it shall, in turn, be done to the criminal. At least there are some controls in force, some limits to retribution.

Then we come to a third stage of ethical development. If by accident a person kills someone, the slayer may seek a refuge in the sanctuary by the altar (Ex. 21:12–14). It becomes apparent that the person guilty of premeditated murder is subject to capital punishment. If the murder was not premeditated, his or her life shall be protected. This worked well during the wilderness journey when the tabernacle was close at hand for all the people.

Now as the Israelites moved into the Promised Land, God specified that there would be six cities of refuge, safe places of compassion to which a person could flee. Anyone who killed another person unintentionally could immediately flee to the gate of one of these cities where he would be given a preliminary hearing by the elders. If it could be established that he had committed the crime in a fit of passion or by accident, he would be given the right of asylum. He would then live in the city until he received a public hearing. If it was found that the crime was without premeditation, then that community would become responsible for him as long as he lived in the city. No one could harm him while he continued in residence there until the high priest died. Then he could return in safety to his own community to be restored as a free man.

God's intention is for His people to live in peace. A land becomes poisoned when terror reigns. Anyone who takes the life of another person, whether in a premeditated way, in an act of passion, or in an accident, must be dealt with in a way that is fair to that person and to the society. The establishment of such cities of refuge does not repudiate capital punishment. It is God's way of endeavoring to guarantee that both justice and mercy prevail. Only the innocent are to be protected, not the guilty.

These six cities—which included Kadesh in the hill country of Galilee, Shechem in the hill country of Ephraim, and Hebron in the hill country of Judah—were strategically located so that there would be easy access to all persons seeking refuge. And there were to be three more cities beyond the Jordan River that would provide good access for those living in Trans-Jordan. Those cities were Bezer in Reuben; Ramoth in Gilead, from the tribe of Gad; and

Golan in Bashan, from the tribe of Manasseh. Verse 9 states, *"These were the cities appointed for all the children of Israel and for the stranger who dwelt among them, that whoever killed a person accidentally might flee there, and not die by the hand of the avenger of blood until he stood before the congregation."*

These safe places were not only for Jews. They also provided equal access for the foreigner who was guilty of accidental manslaughter. That person was entitled to the same justice, welcome, living place, protection, and atoning grace as the native-born Israelite.

God is determined to build in a protection against the abuses of the *lex talionis*, that "eye for an eye" approach that makes the next of kin an avenger. There are some values to that approach, but emotions can get carried away. History is marked with numerous abuses in which whole tribes and clans have been decimated as emotionally stimulated retribution was carried out in an unending, downward spiral.

In the establishment of these cities of refuge, God was setting the wheels in motion for what ultimately would become the due process of law. Our Western legal system finds its roots in this ethical teaching which declares that a person is innocent until proven guilty.

But beyond the legal and ethical implications for a society, there are also spiritual implications. As one who shies away from too quickly seeing Jesus Christ in each Old Testament passage, I am struck with the similarities of the safety provided in these cities of refuge and the safety we have when we take our refuge in Jesus Christ.

Many hymns pick up this theme of the Old Testament city of refuge and articulate it in relationship to our Savior. Cleland B. McAfee's words in his hymn "There Is a Place of Quiet Rest" capture this concept, as do the words poetically expressed in this familiar hymn:

> How firm a foundation, ye saints of the Lord,
> Is laid for your faith in His excellent Word!
> What more can He say than to you He hath said,
> To you who for refuge to Jesus have fled?

The Bible expositor Arthur W. Pink carries on this analogy into very specific terms. He sees the cities of refuge as a manifest type of Christ as He is presented and offered to sinners in the gospel.

First, these cities were *appointed by God Himself,* not by man's devising. God also appointed Christ to be the Savior of sinners, the "slain from the foundation of the world" (Rev. 13:8).

Second, the cities were *given to provide shelter from the avenger.* Pity the sinner who thinks he can successfully defy God's eternal scheme of justice. There is no way we can save ourselves unless we flee to Jesus.

Third, these cities were *placed on a height.* They were built on hills or mountains so that they could be readily seen. Even as Jesus was lifted up on the cross and is now exalted at the right hand of God the Father, we as pastors are responsible to lift Him up.

Fourth, the *road* to the city of refuge was *plainly marked.* Jewish writers say that there was a law in Israel that, one day in every year, people were sent to repair the roads leading to these cities so as to remove all stumbling stones and to make certain that the signposts were clear. We, too, are to make certain that the gospel is fully and plainly declared.

Fifth, there was *easy access* to these cities. They were not in remote corners, but could be reached within a day. The application is obvious: "The LORD is near to those who have a broken heart,/And saves such as have a contrite spirit" (Ps. 34:18).

Sixth, the city of refuge provided *protection* from the revenger of blood for *only the accidental homicide.* The deliberate murderer was excluded. The Scriptures teach us that there is no salvation in Christ for presumptuous sinners, those who still go on deliberately in their sins. There is no shelter in the Savior for those who are in love with sin. But for those who flee to Him from their sin, there is His generous redemption.

Seventh, the one who took refuge in that city *had to remain there.* This reminds us not to make use of Christ only at the time of our conversion but throughout our entire lives. We are to abide in Him always.

Eighth, the city of refuge was *available for Gentiles as well as Jews.* Christ's invitation is universal; He extends His "whosoever will may come" to all.

Ninth, it was the *death of the high priest that secured full and final deliverance.* It is in the death of Jesus Christ that our full redemption has been accomplished.

Even the names of these cities speak of what the believer has in Christ. Kadesh signifies "holy"; Shechem means "shoulder"; Hebron means "fellowship"; Bezer means a "fortified place"; Ramoth means "height" or "exultation"; and Golan means "exultation" or "joy."[1]

What powerful relevance these cities of refuge have for us today.

A PLACE OF SPIRITUAL COMMUNITY

21:1 Then the heads of the fathers' houses of the Levites came near to Eleazar the priest, to Joshua the son of Nun, and to the heads of the fathers' houses of the tribes of the children of Israel. ² And they spoke to them at Shiloh in the land of Canaan, saying, "The LORD commanded through Moses to give us cities to dwell in, with their common-lands for our livestock." ³ So the children of Israel gave to the Levites from their inheritance, at the commandment of the LORD, these cities and their common-lands:

⁴ Now the lot came out for the families of the Kohathites. And the children of Aaron the priest, who were of the Levites, had thirteen cities by lot from the tribe of Judah, from the tribe of Simeon, and from the tribe of Benjamin. ⁵ The rest of the children of Kohath had ten cities by lot from the families of the tribe of Ephraim, from the tribe of Dan, and from the half-tribe of Manasseh.

⁶ And the children of Gershon had thirteen cities by lot from the families of the tribe of Issachar, from the tribe of Asher, from the tribe of Naphtali, and from the half-tribe of Manasseh in Bashan.

⁷ The children of Merari according to their families had twelve cities from the tribe of Reuben, from the tribe of Gad, and from the tribe of Zebulun.

⁸ And the children of Israel gave these cities with their common-lands by lot to the Levites, as the LORD had commanded by the hand of Moses.

⁹ So they gave from the tribe of the children of Judah and from the tribe of the children of Simeon these cities which are designated by name, ¹⁰ which were for the children of Aaron, one of the families of the Kohathites, who were of the children of Levi; for the lot was theirs first. ¹¹ And they gave them Kirjath Arba (Arba was the father of Anak), which is Hebron, in the mountains of Judah, with the common-land surrounding it. ¹² But the fields of the city and its villages they gave to Caleb the son of Jephunneh as his possession.

¹³ Thus to the children of Aaron the priest they gave Hebron with its common-land (a city of refuge for the slayer), Libnah with its common-land, ¹⁴ Jattir with its common-land,

Eshtemoa with its common-land, ¹⁵ Holon with its common-land, Debir with its common-land, ¹⁶ Ain with its common-land, Juttah with its common-land, and Beth Shemesh with its common-land: nine cities from those two tribes; ¹⁷ and from the tribe of Benjamin, Gibeon with its common-land, Geba with its common-land, ¹⁸ Anathoth with its common-land, and Almon with its common-land: four cities. ¹⁹ All the cities of the children of Aaron, the priests, were thirteen cities with their common-lands.

²⁰ And the families of the children of Kohath, the Levites, the rest of the children of Kohath, even they had the cities of their lot from the tribe of Ephraim. ²¹ For they gave them Shechem with its common-land in the mountains of Ephraim (a city of refuge for the slayer), Gezer with its common-land, ²² Kibzaim with its common-land, and Beth Horon with its common-land: four cities; ²³ and from the tribe of Dan, Eltekeh with its common-land, Gibbethon with its common-land, ²⁴ Aijalon with its common-land, and Gath Rimmon with its common-land: four cities; ²⁵ and from the half-tribe of Manasseh, Tanach with its common-land and Gath Rimmon with its common-land: two cities. ²⁶ All the ten cities with their common-lands were for the rest of the families of the children of Kohath.

²⁷ Also to the children of Gershon, of the families of the Levites, from the other half-tribe of Manasseh, they gave Golan in Bashan with its common-land (a city of refuge for the slayer), and Be Eshterah with its common-land: two cities; ²⁸ and from the tribe of Issachar, Kishion with its common-land, Daberath with its common-land, ²⁹ Jarmuth with its common-land, and En Gannim with its common-land: four cities; ³⁰ and from the tribe of Asher, Mishal with its common-land, Abdon with its common-land, ³¹ Helkath with its common-land, and Rehob with its common-land: four cities; ³² and from the tribe of Naphtali, Kedesh in Galilee with its common-land (a city of refuge for the slayer), Hammoth Dor with its common-land, and Kartan with its common-land: three cities. ³³ All the cities of the Gershonites according to their families were thirteen cities with their common-lands.

³⁴ And to the families of the children of Merari, the rest of the Levites, from the tribe of Zebulun, Jokneam with its common-land, Kartah with its common-land, ³⁵ Dimnah with its common-land, and Nahalal with its common-land: four

cities; ³⁶ and from the tribe of Reuben, Bezer with its common-land, Jahaz with its common-land, ³⁷ Kedemoth with its common-land, and Mephaath with its common-land: four cities; ³⁸ and from the tribe of Gad, Ramoth in Gilead with its common-land (a city of refuge for the slayer), Mahanaim with its common-land, ³⁹ Heshbon with its common-land, and Jazer with its common-land: four cities in all. ⁴⁰ So all the cities for the children of Merari according to their families, the rest of the families of the Levites, were by their lot twelve cities.

⁴¹ All the cities of the Levites within the possession of the children of Israel were forty-eight cities with their common-lands. ⁴² Every one of these cities had its common-land surrounding it; thus were all these cities.

⁴³ So the LORD gave to Israel all the land of which He had sworn to give to their fathers, and they took possession of it and dwelt in it. ⁴⁴ The LORD gave them rest all around, according to all that He had sworn to their fathers. And not a man of all their enemies stood against them; the LORD delivered all their enemies into their hand. ⁴⁵ Not a word failed of any good thing which the LORD had spoken to the house of Israel. All came to pass.

—Joshua 21:1–45

The second kind of city that God has created is a place of spiritual community. Whereas there needed to be cities of refuge to offer legal safety and compassion, there also needed to be cities that would be centers of spiritual activity.

God called for the establishment of forty-eight Levitical cities. In a way, these cities can be seen as a substitute for the idolatrous high places, shrines, altars, and all of the pagan paraphernalia that were present in the land at the time of the conquest. The Levites were to replace the pagan worship with a saturation presence in the land, a constant reminder of the God who had brought His people out of the bondage of Egypt and the wanderings in the wilderness. These cities also were to be centers of teaching for those such as Rahab who had become part of the covenant people and did not have a historic background in the faith.

The Levites began with Levi, one of the sons of Jacob. He was not a particularly honorable character, so it was not because of his godliness that the tribe bearing his name became the priestly clan. Apparently, sometime during the Egyptian captivity, the Levites made a transition from that of tribal status to that of religious guild.

The tribe of Levi consisted of three main branches corresponding to Levi's three sons—Kohath, Gershon, and Merari. The Kohathites (Num. 3:17) were the most distinguished. Moses and Aaron were of that branch. As Levites, the Kohathites had responsibility for the ark and its sacred furniture, guarding it at all times and carrying it from place to place during the wilderness journey. The Gershonites were in charge of the tabernacle, with its cords, curtains, and coverings. The sons of Merari had charge of the more solid parts of the tabernacle, its boards and bars, its pillars and pins, and all the vessels that were part of the tabernacle worship.

The many duties of the Levites, as they are detailed in the Pentateuch, were outlined primarily for the wilderness journey. Now that Joshua had brought the people into the Promised Land, the tabernacle would be established at Shiloh, and the duties of the Levites would undergo change. The Gibeonites were retained to be "hewers of wood and drawers of water for the congregation and for the altar of the Lord," doing the more laborious part of the work at Shiloh. It was important that the spiritual leaders, with their transtribal character, be dispersed through the entire land, not just concentrated at one place. They were not tied to any particular location, boundary lines, or tribal group. Instead of being given land by Joshua, we are told, "But the Levites have no part among you, for the priesthood of the LORD is their inheritance" (18:7). They became the teachers, theologians, storytellers, counselors, and inspired preachers in this new society. They were responsible for integrating into a coherent body the tradition and history of God's people.

It is interesting to note that, although they were not given tribal lands, they were given living space in each of these forty-eight cities that are listed in chapter 21. It was clear that they needed land and provisions to sustain them if they were adequately to infiltrate the land. God made this provision, having specified during the time of Moses that land was to be set aside for them. Chapter 21 tells how the heads of the fathers' houses of the Levites came to Eleazar the priest, and to Joshua the son of Nun, and to the heads of the various houses of the tribes of the people of Israel, and at Shiloh declared, *"The LORD commanded through Moses to give us cities to dwell in, with their common-lands for our livestock.' So the children of Israel gave to the Levites from their inheritance, at the commandment of the LORD, these cities and their commonlands"* (vv. 2–3). So we see a willingness on the part of the other tribes to give specific city land and pasture land outside of the cities to the Levites so that the presence of God's teaching would be dispersed throughout the land.

This alerts us to the importance of provision being made for spiritual leadership. Through the centuries, God has set certain persons aside for full-time ministry. And God has instructed His people to make provision for those who are called to full-time work for Him.

There is an additional fascinating insight into the utilization of land. When these Levitical cities were planned, provision was made not only for the population but also for the agricultural land surrounding them so that the Levites could become self-sufficient and self-sustaining. Each of these forty-eight cities had around it a green belt for cattle and gardening. Some scholars have made interesting note that, over three thousand years later, we are waking up to the necessity to plan in our cities significant areas for trees and grass. Urban intensification must be relieved in places where people can rediscover a contact with the land. It is interesting to note that each of these six cities of refuge also happens to be one of the forty-eight Levitical cities. The priests had a significant part in guaranteeing safety and due process of hearing to those who fled to the refuge spots.

Is there anything that parallels these Levitical cities today? I am convinced that it quickly becomes quite apparent that God today has established His church in its local congregational expression as such a place of spiritual community.

The Swiss psychiatrist Paul Tournier has written a remarkable book, *A Place for You*, underlining the importance of each of us having a place of safety. In it, he gives case examples of people who psychologically and spiritually have needed to discover a place where they can be at home, accepted, and understood. He states:

> The ideal support, then, is a presence, a vigilant, unshakeable, indefectible, presence, but one that is discreet, gentle, silent, and respectful. We want help in our struggle, but do not want our personal responsibility to be taken from us. A look, a smile, an intense emotion—these are the things that can help us to win our victories over ourselves.[2]

Although the church is not always that, what better place is there to find this kind of safety? We should be able to discover it in the home; but the home is not always a safe place. It's important that we acknowledge this fact as we endeavor to communicate God's Word, as there are many with whom we are communicating that are doing their best to make their homes a safe place but, due to circumstances beyond their control, who are not experiencing this safety. What we may not always be able to accomplish in the home, we can hopefully work toward accomplishing in the church.

The church can be a safe place in that it provides the opportunity for corporate worship. We are told in Scripture not to neglect the assembling of ourselves together. There is something that happens when the people of God are gathered together, expressing our hymns of praise, giving our offerings, being led in pastoral prayers, and being challenged through Word and sacrament in a way that helps us realize our identity in Christ. We are privileged to be part of this extended family—the family of God in worship.

The church can be a safe place in that it is where we can come for teaching. These Levitical cities were designed to provide a place where people could come for instruction. How important education is that helps us learn, that helps us grow in our knowledge as well as in our love of Jesus Christ.

The church can be a safe place in that it is where we can come for counsel. Hannah went to the priest Eli, describing her anguish as a woman who could not conceive. Throughout the past several thousand years, what would men and women have done if they could not have gone to a representative of the Lord with their problems? Each of us needs an eloquent ear that will listen to us and guide us at pivotal points in our lives. This gives us as pastors the opportunity to declare our commitment to our people and our desire to help them work through their struggles. God pity the pastor who is too busy to see people in need. Both he and the people he is called to serve will shrivel up spiritually if the church becomes big business, insensitive to individual human need and the privilege of giving pastoral counsel and care.

The church can be a safe place in that it provides the intimacy of small covenant groups. I was privileged to work on the staff of two New York City churches during my Princeton Theological Seminary years. One was the Marble Collegiate Church. For two years, each Sunday, I heard Dr. Norman Vincent Peale declare, either verbally to the congregation or in printed form in the bulletin: "This is the one place in Manhattan where old-fashioned friendliness still survives." In my final year in seminary, I served with Dr. Bryant Kirkland at the Fifth Avenue Presbyterian Church. Sunday after Sunday, Dr. Kirkland stated, "You can't go it alone in Manhattan. You need a church, and the church needs you!" That's a simple fact of life. We need each other, and we are privileged to know and care for each other.

God pity the person who does not have a covenant-sharing community for worship, for instruction, for counsel, and for mutual support.

During a visit to Israel, our group was addressed by Becky and Wes Pippert. Becky was the noted speaker and author of the Inter Varsity Press book on evangelism *Out of the Saltshaker and into the World.* Wes had been the head of the United Press International Israel news bureau for several years. They were immersed in that culture so fraught with tension between Arabs and Jews. We asked Wes whether he was pro-Jew or pro-Arab. His response was profound. I paraphrase him:

> I am neither pro-Jew nor pro-Arab. Although the Jews are obviously God's special people, God does not excuse unjust behavior—theirs or anyone else's. As I read the Old Testament, the words *justice, mercy,* and *righteousness* seem to go together. God encourages all of us to this high standard and holds us accountable. Even His people in Old Testament times were judged when they were unjust, unmerciful, and unrighteous. And they were blessed when justice, mercy, and righteousness prevailed. The same holds for today. God is pro all people who are faithful to Him, and He judges our unfaithfulness.

How significant it is for us to discover that the God of all creation, as He led His people into the Promised Land, made two kinds of provision that He continues to make today. One: He created cities of refuge to become places of legal safety. Two: He created Levitical cities that became places of spiritual community. And to the very present moment, the heart of God continues to beat with a deep desire for His people to practice and experience justice and to practice and experience community.

NOTES

1. Arthur W. Pink, *Gleanings in Joshua* (Chicago Moody Press, 1964), pp. 382–84.

2. Paul Tournier, *A Place for You* (New York: Harper & Row, 1968), p. 192.

CHAPTER FIFTEEN—AN ALTAR OF RUMOR

JOSHUA 22:1–34

Scripture Outline

Transitions (22:1–9)

Rumors (22:10–29)

Peacemaking (22:30–34)

Tucked away here in the midst of Joshua is one of the least known but most fascinating stories in the Bible. I found very little in the way of homiletical help in the many commentaries I consulted. After reading the chapter in story form as the Scripture lesson of the morning, I conducted a brief survey. I asked how many of the close to two thousand people in my congregation had any familiarity with this story. The question was not whether they had read the entire Book of Joshua, but whether they remembered any part of this story. Fewer than ten acknowledged any memory of it. Obviously, it has had little attention.

This brings both a challenge and a significant opportunity to the communicator. This story is just as relevant today as when it happened. It is a story of transitions, of rumors, and of peacemaking.

TRANSITIONS

22:1 Then Joshua called the Reubenites, the Gadites, and half the tribe of Manasseh, **2** and said to them: "You have kept all that Moses the servant of the LORD commanded you, and have obeyed my voice in all that I commanded you. **3** You have not left your brethren these many days, up to this day, but have kept the charge of the commandment of the LORD your God. **4** And now the LORD your God has given rest to your brethren, as He promised them; now therefore, return and go to your tents and to the land of your possession, which Moses the servant of the LORD gave you on the other side of the Jordan. ⁵ But take careful heed to do the commandment and the law which Moses the servant of the LORD commanded you, to love the LORD your God, to walk in all His ways, to keep His commandments, to hold fast to Him, and to serve Him with all your heart and with all your soul." ⁶ So Joshua blessed them and sent them away, and they went to their tents.

⁷ Now to half the tribe of Manasseh Moses had given a possession in Bashan, but to the other half of it Joshua gave a possession among their brethren on this side of the Jordan, westward. And indeed, when Joshua sent them away to their tents, he blessed them, ⁸ and spoke to them, saying, "Return with much riches to your tents, with very much livestock, with silver, with gold, with bronze, with iron, and with very much clothing. Divide the spoil of your enemies with your brethren."

⁹ So the children of Reuben, the children of Gad, and half the tribe of Manasseh returned, and departed from the children of Israel at Shiloh, which is in the land of Canaan, to go to the country of Gilead, to the land of their possession, which they had obtained according to the word of the LORD by the hand of Moses.

—*Joshua 22:1–9*

This is a story of transitions.

Transitions are difficult in the best of circumstances. Transitions signal the end of one era and the beginning of another.

I recently was musing with several friends about the psychological dynamics of change. For some of us, change comes as a violent shock to our systems. One woman bluntly stated her own experience in making the fifty-mile move from Los Angeles down to Newport Beach. "As excited as I was about my move, it took me five years after coming to Newport Beach until I got over leaving my old home and began really to love my new house. The move wasn't easy."

I have also observed this phenomenon as I have moved from one part of the United States to another. I spent the first fourteen years of my life in Boston, Massachusetts. When my family moved to Wheaton, Illinois, I looked forward to the change only to find that the adjustment took longer than I expected. As a teenager abruptly removed from my environment, I dreamed nightly for months of my friends back home in New England. My moves from Illinois to Princeton, New Jersey, after eight years, then to Tulsa, Oklahoma, after three years, and then to Key Biscayne, Florida, after three more years, came with less difficulty. But yanking up the roots after six years of established family living and moving to Pittsburgh, Pennsylvania, had its difficulties. And the move after five years to Newport Beach, California, as marvelous a beach community as this is, had its way of tearing at the fabric of our family's existence. I don't ever want to move again. I hope it is not just because I am getting more and more conservative the older I get, but just that change and transition are painful.

I've watched as our congregation moved from our old sanctuary into our new sanctuary. We worked hard to make this move possible. It was a twenty-year goal of St. Andrew's, but the change wasn't easy for some of us. The longer one has been here the more difficult the adjustment has been. As one who worked hard to make this change possible, I, too, had my struggles during the transition. I met with a young couple for their first premarital counseling session prior to their forthcoming wedding. At the end of the meeting, they mentioned that they had been attending St. Andrew's Presbyterian Church regularly for the last three months. They asked, "Whatever happened to your old sanctuary?" I said, "It's still here. It's that A-frame brick building." They responded, "Oh, that. We thought that was the chapel. You mean that was the sanctuary?" Their response administered a momentary shock to my system. I couldn't quite believe that these two very sincere people had arrived so recently on the scene of our church's life that they had no connectedness with the substantial part of our historic past that was fleshed out in the old sanctuary. Something within me felt a sense of loss. Actually, this was why we built the new sanctuary—to reach out to new people in growing ministry.

Transitions obviously involve more than a change in physical surroundings. They also involve changes in relationships. Some are quite apparent, such as those brought about by death, illness, financial loss, or divorce. Some are much more subtle, such as transitions brought about when a person begins to look introspectively into himself or herself. When one member of a family goes through therapy, what initially appears to be a very smooth transition can end up producing major changes in that family's dynamics.

Transitions are both a *high point* and a *low point* in the life of a person and of a community.

Transitions are a high point in that they are celebrative moments. We see this in what happened as Israel began its demobilization at the end of the formal military conquest. Moses had allowed the Reubenites, the Gadites, and the half-tribe of Manasseh to occupy the east bank of the Jordan. He had done it on the condition that the warriors of those two and one-half tribes would cross over the Jordan and help the other nine and one-half tribes conquer the land. We saw specific reference to this situation in Joshua 1:12–18. Their faithfulness to this promise was confirmed as under Joshua they fulfilled the commitment made to Moses. They crossed over the Jordan with Joshua and won their badges of courage. They refused to take the easy way and sit out the conquest with their wives and children in Trans-Jordan.

Now came the transition. Joshua summoned the Reubenites, the Gadites, and the half-tribe of Manasseh, releasing them from any more military service. He affirmed them for their faithfulness and sent them home to their wives and children with honor medals for the way in which they stood by their brothers and sisters in the toughest times of battle. He noted their obedience in a sort of commencement address.

Commencement speakers usually wax eloquent in telling of commonly shared past joys and sorrows. The ceremony becomes a celebrative moment mingled with a touch of nostalgia as the graduates go home and then on to other places. The school will never be the same. Commencements, installations, and commissionings mark both an end and a beginning. This is why we have farewell banquets and why we have charges and challenges articulated by guest speakers. Our comings and our goings do have great significance.

Not only did Joshua thank these tribes for a job well done, but he also called on them to continue to obey the commands of the Lord. He said:

> And now the LORD your God has given rest to your brethren, as He promised them; now therefore, return and go to your tents and to the land of your possession, which Moses the servant of the LORD gave you on the other side of the Jordan. But take careful heed to do the commandment and the law which Moses the servant of the LORD commanded you, to love the LORD your God, to walk in all His ways, to keep His commandments, to hold fast to Him, and to serve Him with all your heart and with all your soul (vv. 4–5).

Then Joshua blessed them and sent them away. They went to their homes in Trans-Jordan.

It was in this final blessing and charge that Joshua inadvertently sowed the seed of a future problem. He had warned them not to forget the Lord God as they returned to their families on the other side of the Jordan. To us, the miles are not too many between the hills of Judea and the hills of Trans-Jordan. The Rift Valley, which goes right down the heart of the Middle East and on into the continent of Africa, makes a major divide. The hills on either side of the Jordan River go up to about thirty-five hundred feet above sea level. The Jordan itself empties into the Dead Sea at thirteen hundred feet below sea level. In that day, those miles, which can now be covered by car in a couple of hours, seemed like an eternity.

Joshua wanted to be sure that the tribes living in Trans-Jordan remained faithful to the Lord. In this celebrative moment, he urged them to share the wealth—the cattle, the silver, the gold, the bronze, the iron, and the clothing that represented the spoils of their battle—with those who had stayed behind. He was articulating both the importance of community and the willingness of those in prominent leadership positions or who have received great material blessings to share their gains with others whose tasks are less noticed. It was a high point of celebration as those Reubenites, Gadites, and the half-tribe of Manasseh marched from Shiloh, where they had been demobilized by Joshua, down through the Judean hills into the Jordan Valley and back up into the hills of Gilead. They couldn't wait to get home. You can imagine their sounds of celebration.

But transitions also are a *low point,* because things can often begin to come unraveled. Unity is a great oneness that is often present when men and women are drawn together by a common task. When that task is completed—the athletic season is over, the battle is finished, or the academic year has ended—the team or the army or the student body disperses. The family breaks up. This is why those of us who occasionally lead tours to the Holy Land always have a final banquet the last night of the tour. I always share verbally the obvious fact that we never again will be together in quite the way we have been during these intensive days of travel. So now is the time to say what the group members want to say to each other so as to freeze forever in their memories what was special about this event. I warn them that the minute they hit the ground in the United States they will grab for their luggage and head through customs no longer with a group solidarity but as forty to forty-five separate individuals.

It is the common task that keeps the group together, as Israel discovered when they conquered the Holy Land. Israel continues to discover the reality of this truth, boxed in as it is by Egypt, Jordan, Syria, Lebanon, and the rest of the Arab world. When Israel was trying to establish its national identity in the late 1940s and early 1950s, there was seldom a word of dissent. Each individual Jew had his private opinions. Those opinions were subordinated to the ultimate good of recovering from the Holocaust and establishing a national identity, a homeland for their scattered people. Decades later, Israelis are no longer the little minority standing alone but together against the world; now they are seen as powerful, one of the world's greatest fighting forces. Their incursion into Lebanon and their years of running battles with Palestinian militants have caused a disruption of national unity. Opinions on domestic and international policies within Israel vary widely today.

The key is to recognize that it is impossible to stay always on a war footing. A people cannot be mobilized forever. But some dictators, who want to stay in power, refuse to acknowledge this fact. To them, national unity is much more important than peace. So they continue to antagonize other nations and to agitate their own population into a constant frenzy directed at an external foe so as to maintain a national oneness that ensures their leadership incumbency. In short, they always have an external enemy so as to orchestrate peace at home.

Some live forever in the fear of transition and do everything they can to maintain the status quo because it is comfortable. Transitions are the high points and the low points in the life of any family. A wedding is celebrated with laughter and in a way is ·mourned with tears. Things will never be the same again. We tell ourselves, "We've not lost a daughter, but we've gained a son." This is often our way of trying to reassure ourselves that we will survive the transition.

This biblical story in Joshua 22 demonstrates both the celebrative aspect of transition and the ways that transitions rip and tear at the fabric of normal existence. The moment those two and one-half tribes headed east and crossed the Jordan River, something changed in Israel. The nation would never again be quite the same, because, no matter how emphatic had been the charge of Joshua, the farther they got from the altar at Shiloh, the farther they might end up from the presence of God and the unity of His people who lived on the other side of the Jordan. Perhaps they might even forget about the God of Abraham, Isaac, and Jacob.

RUMORS

10 And when they came to the region of the Jordan which is in the land of Canaan, the children of Reuben, the children of Gad, and half the tribe of Manasseh built an altar there by the Jordan—a great, impressive altar. 11 Now the children of Israel heard someone say, "Behold, the children of Reuben, the children of Gad, and half the tribe of Manasseh have built an altar on the frontier of the land of Canaan, in the region of the Jordan—on the children of Israel's side."
12 And when the children of Israel heard of it, the whole congregation of the children of Israel gathered together at Shiloh to go to war against them.

13 Then the children of Israel sent Phinehas the son of Eleazar the priest to the children of Reuben, to the children of Gad, and to half the tribe of Manasseh, into the land of Gilead, 14 and with him ten rulers, one ruler each from the chief house of every tribe of Israel; and each one was the head of the house of his father among the divisions of Israel.
15 Then they came to the children of Reuben, to the children of Gad, and to half the tribe of Manasseh, to the land of Gilead, and they spoke with them, saying, 16 "Thus says the whole congregation of the LORD: 'What treachery is this that you have committed against the God of Israel, to turn away this day from following the LORD, in that you have built for yourselves an altar, that you might rebel this day against the LORD? 17 Is the iniquity of Peor not enough for us, from which we are not cleansed till this day, although there was a plague in the congregation of the LORD, 18 but that you must turn away this day from following the LORD? And it shall be, if you rebel today against the LORD, that tomorrow He will be angry with the whole congregation of Israel. 19 Nevertheless, if the land of your possession is unclean, then cross over to the land of the possession of the LORD, where the LORD's tabernacle stands, and take possession among us; but do not rebel against the LORD, nor rebel against us, by building yourselves an altar besides the altar of the LORD our God. 20 Did not Achan the son of Zerah commit a trespass in the accursed thing, and

wrath fell on all the congregation of Israel? And that man did not perish alone in his iniquity.' "

21 Then the children of Reuben, the children of Gad, and half the tribe of Manasseh answered and said to the heads of the divisions of Israel: 22 "The LORD God of gods, the LORD God of gods, He knows, and let Israel itself know—if it is in rebellion, or if in treachery against the LORD, do not save us this day. 23 If we have built ourselves an altar to turn from following the LORD, or if to offer on it burnt offerings or grain offerings, or if to offer peace offerings on it, let the LORD Himself require an account. 24 But in fact we have done it for fear, for a reason, saying, 'In time to come your descendants may speak to our descendants, saying, "What have you to do with the LORD God of Israel? 25 For the LORD has made the Jordan a border between you and us, you children of Reuben and children of Gad. You have no part in the LORD." So your descendants would make our descendants cease fearing the LORD.'
26 Therefore we said, 'Let us now prepare to build ourselves an altar, not for burnt offering nor for sacrifice, 27 but that it may be a witness between you and us and our generations after us, that we may perform the service of the LORD before Him with our burnt offerings, with our sacrifices, and with our peace offerings; that your descendants may not say to our descendants in time to come, "You have no part in the LORD."'
28 Therefore we said that it will be, when they say this to us or to our generations in time to come, that we may say, 'Here is the replica of the altar of the LORD which our fathers made, though not for burnt offerings nor for sacrifices; but it is a witness between you and us.' 29 Far be it from us that we should rebel against the LORD, and turn from following the LORD this day, to build an altar for burnt offerings, for grain offerings, or for sacrifices, besides the altar of the LORD our God which is before His tabernacle."

—Joshua 22:10–29

This is a story of rumors. Rumors unattended produce misunderstanding and warfare, and they can be disastrous in dividing further what has been naturally fractionalized by transition and change.

Included in the charge to faithfulness that Joshua gave the Reubenites, the Gadites, and the half-tribe of Manasseh was the seed of later trouble. These tribes took very seriously what Joshua had said and were determined that, in their existence far away from the rest of the ten tribes, they would not lose their identity as part of the nation of Israel. So when they came to the frontier of the land of Canaan on the west bank of the Jordan River, they built a large altar designed to remind them of their identity as Jews and also of the real altar at Shiloh. Their hearts were transparent before God. But the rumors began to spread. Those of the other tribes began to whisper, *"Behold, the children of Reuben, the children of Gad, and half the tribe of Manasseh have built an altar on the frontier of the land of Canaan, in the region of the Jordan—on the children of Israel's side"* (v. 11). The Bible goes on to say, *"And when the children of Israel heard of it, the whole congregation of the children of Israel gathered together at Shiloh to go to war against them"* (v. 12).

Time of transition comes, and change has its effect. The people are no longer closely knit together in a common enterprise. The major conquest is over, and what remains are more individualistic struggles. It would have been awfully hard to spread a dishonest rumor between those with whom they were engaged in a common enterprise. When distance, physical or emotional, is established, communication breaks down. It's when each person is starting to do his or her own thing that misunderstandings arise and are fueled by rumors. We human beings like to act on our emotions. It doesn't make a lot of difference that the flames of those emotions may be fueled by the gasoline of incorrect information.

At this moment in our story, no one wanted to be bothered with the truth. A demobilized people were beginning to miss battle and were yearning once again to pick up their weapons. The tribes who lived west of the Jordan were going to take vengeance on their sister tribes who were so quickly engaging in false worship. They planned to act immediately; they didn't have time for an investigation.

One of the greatest crises in my own Christian life occurred in the early 1960s when I observed a terrible injustice to a person I loved very much. This man, who was involved in several ministries, had his weaknesses; I knew them. Primarily, he wasn't a very good businessman; his talent was in promotion, not in the detail of budgeting and cash-flow. His gifts as a visionary had several years earlier been observed by a major Christian industrialist from whom my friend had raised money for some Christian projects. The industrialist had been looking for a successor to a president of a foundation in which he had invested a lot of money. So, in addition to helping fund those projects, he urged this friend of mine to assist the foundation president on a part-time basis. His thought was that later he would succeed into that position but in the meantime could carry on his other ministries.

I watched as my friend confronted some difficulties that made it impossible for him to be on time meeting some bills he owed. The rumor started that my friend was a crook. The wealthy industrialist heard this, believed the rumors, and immediately cut off his financial support of both the Christian enterprises headed by my friend and arranged for him to be fired from the foundation vice-presidency. As a result, the financial difficulties my friend had experienced in his faithful ministries for Christ intensified. For the next seven years, he was without personal income. His wife went back to work to support the family. The wealthy industrialist for some strange reason never thoroughly checked out the rumors, and he refused an appointment to see my friend. He went to his grave a decade later having written off my friend, sincerely believing him to be dishonest. This man never knew that, about the time of his death, my friend, through careful savings and receipt of some belated back pay, had paid back his creditors.

What just about destroyed me emotionally and threatened my Christian faith was to see two men, both men of Christian integrity, become separated by false rumor. The one who happened to have the power and who could have helped, if he had known the facts, had instead jumped to conclusions that were based on rumors. He never knew the truth. The words of a few of us who tried to get matters straightened out were never heard. The cause of Christ was needlessly damaged.

Unattended rumors can be disastrous in producing misunderstanding. Yet rumors, when investigated, can produce positive results.

In most misunderstandings between people of God, there is truth on both sides. In the case study I have just shared, my friend wasn't the most skilled in financial planning, but he was anything but a thief. He was a man of God, naive about certain kinds of financial affairs. The industrialist was also a man of God. If he had heard the facts, he couldn't possibly have come to the conclusions that he reached. He was genuinely trying to be a good steward of his resources and to rid his organization of someone whom he perceived to be dishonest.

When the Israelites on the west bank organized at Shiloh to move in warfare against the two and a half tribes living on the east bank, they were sincere because they had a valid concern. They had learned their lesson well and were living in the fear of apostasy. Entirely misunderstanding their brothers and sisters, they imagined that those on the other side of the Jordan were setting up a rival worship center. Their perception was precisely the opposite of reality. The altar they saw as divisive and leading to the worship of false gods was intended to remind those on the east bank of the one true God and to help them maintain their identity with the tribes in the newly conquered land.

The case for those who had remobilized on the west bank was a valid concern that had been brought about by various events during the wilderness wanderings and the conquest.

One lesson they had learned at Mt. Peor (Numbers 23—25). There, as the people of Israel were camped in the highlands of Gilead prior to entering the Promised Land, they observed the Midianites who had an outbreak of the bubonic plague. Fearful of contracting this dreaded disease, the Hebrews participated in a pagan ritual designed to halt it. This consisted of sacrificing to the angry spirits of the dead who were believed to have caused the disease, eating a ritual meal, establishing close relationship with the spirits to influence them, and participating in ritual sexual intercourse to please them.

Needless to say, this so-called cure was anything but that. Modern study of the bubonic plague shows us that these three actions only brought about a further disastrous spread of the disease with thousands of Hebrew deaths. Physical contact with the infected Midianites communicated the plague bacillus directly into the lungs of the Hebrews, with a one-day incubation period before death. When a well-meaning Hebrew took what he thought was the most effective step to prevent the epidemic from spreading, he brought a Midianite princess into the inner room of his home for ritual intercourse. The end of the plague was brought about not by this ritual act but by the death of the two at the hand of Phinehas, the priest.

This Old Testament story is not remembered for its medical aspects. As we know from our study of the Pentateuch, God revealed to the Israelites a detailed sanitary code designed to prevent the outbreak and the spread of disease. What became institutionalized into Israelite understanding was the danger of corrupting worship. The Israelites had come to understand that the sin at Peor was that of making the wrong sacrifice on the wrong altar to the wrong god in the wrong way. Psalm 106:23–31 and 1 Corinthians 10:8 warn against turning away from God. The west-bank tribes were not about to let their east-bank counterparts make the same mistake again. They would defend the true religion.

The second experience was fresh on their minds. They had observed in Achan the immoral use of wealth (7:1–26) and had seen the corporate responsibility of one who individually had sinned against God but whose whole family paid the price of that sin. What hurts one hurts all. They could not stand by idly in what appeared to be false worship. They were scared, and rightly so, of spiritual malignancy.

The east-bank tribes, it must be remembered, had a genuine desire to remember who God really was. Their intentions were pure, and theirs was not a false worship. The altar that had created such rumors was not meant to supplant the place of worship at Shiloh. No sacrifices were to be offered upon it. It was to remind themselves and their children and their children's children of their true roots.

If these rumors had been unchecked and the nine and a half tribes had moved in military force against the two and a half tribes, there would have been a bloody civil war, perhaps even a tragic massacre.

Fortunately, reason prevailed. Instead of acting in the white heat of emotion and self-righteousness, the accusers stopped long enough to recognize they might be in error. They chose Phinehas, son of Eleazar the priest, and appointed ten chiefs, one from each of the tribal families of Israel, to go as a delegation to visit the Reubenites, the Gadites, and the half-tribe of Manasseh in the land of Gilead. The delegation raised questions about this perceived apostasy. *"What treachery is this that you have committed against the God of Israel, to turn away this day from following the LORD, in that you have built for yourselves an altar, that you might rebel this day against the LORD?"* (v. 16). The delegation reminded them of the sin at Peor (v. 17) and of Achan and how he did not perish alone for his iniquity (v. 20). And the Reubenites and the Gadites and the half-tribe of Manasseh responded, declaring their heartfelt integrity. They had built the altar to remind themselves who God was. Instead of the rumored altar being a sign of apostasy, it was an altar of witness to the one true God.

What, then, do we learn about rumors?

First, we must learn *never to discount rumors.* They may be true, and we had better take them seriously and get to the heart of them. It's important that we do our reality testing, because a rumor also may not be true. If only that wealthy industrialist had taken the time to track down the rumor, if only he had been willing to listen in an unbiased way to the pleas of my friend and hear his side of the story, something of health could have come. Instead, a broken relationship and shattered dreams were the result.

Second, we should learn to *keep cool while we gather the information*. Warfare among the Israelite tribes could have eclipsed the truth. We need to sit on our emotions when they become white hot and not move to any final action in a moment of fury.

Third, we need to *talk frankly with the one about whom the rumors have spread*. It is important to engage in honest conversation and to listen if we are still not certain. We need to take the rumor, and the person about whom the rumor has spread, to someone with greater objectivity and let that person give us a frank reading on the situation. How sad is a broken relationship.

PEACEMAKING

30 Now when Phinehas the priest and the rulers of the congregation, the heads of the divisions of Israel who were with him, heard the words that the children of Reuben, the children of Gad, and the children of Manasseh spoke, it pleased them. 31 Then Phinehas the son of Eleazar the priest said to the children of Reuben, the children of Gad, and the children of Manasseh, "This day we perceive that the LORD is among us, because you have not committed this treachery against the LORD. Now you have delivered the children of Israel out of the hand of the LORD."

32 And Phinehas the son of Eleazar the priest, and the rulers, returned from the children of Reuben and the children of Gad, from the land of Gilead to the land of Canaan, to the children of Israel, and brought back word to them. 33 So the thing pleased the children of Israel, and the children of Israel blessed God; they spoke no more of going against them in battle, to destroy the land where the children of Reuben and Gad dwelt.

34 The children of Reuben and the children of Gad called the altar, Witness, "For it is a witness between us that the LORD is God."

—Joshua 22:30–34

This really is not just the story of transitions and the story of rumors. In its bottom-line form, it is the story of peacemaking.

When rumors are addressed as rumors and hard realities are sincerely confronted between brothers and sisters, peace and understanding can result.

However, this is not our natural human orientation. There is a kind of Kamikaze tendency in people to carry their convictions so strongly that they jump to hasty conclusions on insufficient evidence. I note my own tendency to savor rumors and to enjoy gossip too readily. I don't like that tendency in myself and would like genuinely to be a very peace-loving person. But I have to admit that there is a latent hostility, a kind of killer instinct, that I must ask the help of the Holy Spirit to hold in check. The deeper my convictions are, the more conscious I must be of my lack of tolerance and my disinclination toward peacemaking. I am haunted, and have been now for over fifteen years, by a one-third-page ad taken out by a New York advertising firm in *Time* magazine during the Vietnam War. I tore out the page, put the word "peace" at the top, circled it, and placed it in a file. Periodically, I reread the quote:

> War is an excuse
>   to kill.
> If you need an excuse,
>   that's a good one.
> Feel free
>   to kill
> and say you kill
>   to be free.
> Freedom is a good excuse
>   if you need one.
> Count the dead:
>   killing
>   by the numbers
>   kills no one
>   in particular,
>   nothing personal,
>   you know,
>   which is a good excuse
>   if you need one.
> The killer
>   needs an excuse, and peace
>   is no excuse.[1]

I just happen to believe that the west-bank tribes reacted to the rumors initially with killer instinct. Basic, human, sinful pride arrogantly came to the surface, stimulated by the distancing that the transition period had created, and rationalized by a desire to maintain truth. Thank God someone stepped forth as a peacemaker and had the courage to jeopardize his own standing in that remobilizing community to label rumors as rumors. Thank God someone was willing to seek the truth and that the people were willing to cool off enough to send the delegation to find out the true facts about that altar of rumor.

The end of the story is beautiful:

> And Phinehas the son of Eleazar the priest, and the rulers, returned from the children of Reuben and the children of Gad, from the land of Gilead to the land of Canaan, to the children of Israel, and brought back word to them. So the thing pleased the children of Israel, and the children of Israel blessed God; they spoke no more of going against them in battle, to destroy the land where the children of Reuben and Gad dwelt. The children of Reuben and the children of Gad called the altar, Witness, "For it is a witness between us that the LORD is God" (vv. 32–34).

Peace, combined with truth, is the highest priority; without truth, it is a compromise. Truth without a desire for peace is brittle legalism.

Jesus said, "Blessed is the peacemaker." Nothing pleases God more than when His people honestly seek truth and peace and when He sees the war fever between brothers and sisters turn to joy and understanding. This is worth our every effort.

NOTE

1.   Harry Pesin, "A Polite Plea for Peace," *Time*, May 11, 1970, p. 66.

CHAPTER SIXTEEN—THE COVENANT AT RISK
JOSHUA 23:1–16

Scripture Outline
> The Promise of Faithfulness (23:1–13)
> The Consequences of Unfaithfulness (23:14–16)

Deathbed conversations are something to take very seriously. Several years ago, my uncle lay dying in an Elkhart, Indiana, hospital room. My father drove down from Chicago to see his older brother. They had a time of candor and openness as sometimes brothers have. When my father emerged from the privacy of that hospital room, he was literally besieged by his nieces, who wanted to know "everything Father said." The fact was that their father had said many things throughout his eighty years. Some were not taken too seriously. After all, words are just words on many occasions. But words in the last hours of a person's life take on a whole new significance.

During his one hundred and ten years, Joshua had spoken many words, but not all were treated as being of equal value. For many of those years, Joshua was Moses' second lieutenant. His words had no ultimate authority. Then when Moses passed on the mantle of leadership and gave his own final words to the people before his death on Mount Nebo, Joshua was ready to take over. Now he too had come to the end of life. Many years had gone by, and the major part of the conquest was long behind him and the people of Israel. Unembarrassed by his elder years, Joshua called the entire leadership of Israel together. Instead of apologizing for his old age, he took advantage of it and spoke with the perspective of the long haul, that steady understanding that comes through long years of accumulated wisdom. His were not casual remarks. When he spoke, he meant business. So now when Joshua spoke, the people listened. We, too, have the privilege of listening to his every word.

As preachers, we have to decide how we should handle chapters 23 and 24. Some scholars feel that chapter 24 should be integrated into the end of chapter 8, verses 30 to 35. I have problems with this approach in that it does include the account of Joshua's death as well as other concluding matters of the Joshua era.

Instead, I join with those who see chapters 23 and 24 as two separate accounts of the same farewell gathering. Instead of trying to pile them into one version, the writer of Joshua included them both. Each has a slightly different perspective, as would your version and mine if we were telling of the same event. Each of these two chapters has something special to tell us. In preaching, I dealt with Joshua 23 on one Sunday and Joshua 24 on the following Sunday. I told a story of an accident that I had observed several nights before in which a young man had been thrown from a motorcycle over a median strip into the oncoming lane of traffic. I had observed the officials as they sought out witnesses to the accident. Then I listened as the three witnesses gave their accounts of the same set of events. Each account described the same events from the particular perspective of each witness. I believe that is what we have here. The writer and editor of Joshua could very well have appreciated the richness of the two accounts. Therefore, they were both included in these concluding chapters.

Joshua's final words reduce themselves to these two combined phrases: *"For the LORD your God is He who has fought for you. . . you shall hold fast to the LORD your God, as you have done to this day"* (vv. 3, 8). We are privileged to hold onto these final words of this elder leader. His admonition is serious, for he understands the covenant. He understands what God has offered us and what it is for us to keep our part of the covenant. Joshua understands that the covenant is always at risk, not because of God, but because of you and me.

The covenant is a pledge that God had made with humankind. The first covenant was God's promise to Adam and Eve in their fall that One would come to crush the head of the serpent. It is rearticulated in the rainbow given to Noah after the flood. God also promised Abraham and Sarah that they would have a son, and his progeny would become a great nation. Its ultimate expression is in the New Covenant that Jesus articulated with His disciples when He took the bread and the cup instituting the sacrament of the Lord's

Supper to be commemorated as the reminder of His life, death, and Resurrection. The call is for us not only to receive His gift of grace but also to be participants in the covenant.

Joshua is dealing here with the theme of faithfulness. First emphasizing God's faithfulness, he then notes the importance of our remaining faithful in the face of so many other pressures to be unfaithful. Joshua speaks with the authority of years as he gives both his positive challenge to faithfulness and his warning of the consequences of unfaithfulness.

THE PROMISE OF FAITHFULNESS

23:1 Now it came to pass, a long time after the LORD had given rest to Israel from all their enemies round about, that Joshua was old, advanced in age. **2** And Joshua called for all Israel, for their elders, for their heads, for their judges, and for their officers, and said to them:

"I am old, advanced in age. **3** You have seen all that the LORD your God has done to all these nations because of you, for the LORD your God is He who has fought for you. **4** See, I have divided to you by lot these nations that remain, to be an inheritance for your tribes, from the Jordan, with all the nations that I have cut off, as far as the Great Sea westward. **5** And the LORD your God will expel them from before you and drive them out of your sight. So you shall possess their land, as the LORD your God promised you. **6** Therefore be very courageous to keep and to do all that is written in the Book of the Law of Moses, lest you turn aside from it to the right hand or to the left, **7** and lest you go among these nations, these who remain among you. You shall not make mention of the name of their gods, nor cause anyone to swear by them; you shall not serve them nor bow down to them, **8** but you shall hold fast to the LORD your God, as you have done to this day. **9** For the LORD has driven out from before you great and strong nations; but as for you, no one has been able to stand against you to this day. **10** One man of you shall chase a thousand, for the LORD your God is He who fights for you, as He promised you. **11** Therefore take careful heed to yourselves, that you love the LORD your God. **12** Or else, if indeed you do go back, and cling to the remnant of these nations—these that remain among you—and make marriages with them, and go in to them and they to you, **13** know for certain that the LORD your God will no longer drive out these nations from before you.

But they shall be snares and traps to you, and scourges on your sides and thorns in your eyes, until you perish from this good land which the LORD your God has given you.

—*Joshua 23:1–13*

Joshua begins with the positive promise of faithfulness. The bottom line of faithfulness to the covenant is that we will succeed. Joshua states it bluntly. But we never fully arrive in this life.

Years had gone by since the major part of Joshua's conquest had been completed. Some land had been allocated to the twelve tribes. This didn't guarantee that the struggle was over. Each of the tribes had to consolidate its own position in the land. I know Christians who do not like the idea that life lived in relationship with Jesus Christ has its incomplete dimension. They would like to come to faith in Jesus and receive life as a neatly wrapped package. The business of living one day at a time, in which we grow toward wholeness in Christ, frustrates them. They want quick, easy answers, a life free of problems, and instant success.

Joshua declared that a *life of faithfulness to the Lord does bring success*. God is in the process of making good on His promises. I love the blunt way Joshua puts it in verses 2–5:

> *"I am old, advanced in age. You have seen all that the LORD your God has done to all these nations because of you, for the LORD your God is He who has fought for you. See, I have divided to you by lot these nations that remain, to be an inheritance for your tribes, from the Jordan, with all the nations that I have cut off, as far as the Great Sea westward. And the LORD your God will expel them from before you and drive them out of your sight. So you shall possess their land, as the LORD your God has promised you."*

Hundreds of years later, the apostle Paul, toward the end of his life, shared similar words of positive confidence from his prison cell in Rome with the believers in Philippi. He looked both backward and forward as he said, "I thank my God upon every remembrance of you, always in every prayer of mine making request for you all with joy, for your fellowship in the gospel from the first day until now, being confident of this very thing, that He who has begun a good work in you will complete it until the day of Jesus Christ" (Phil. 1:3–6). All through Scripture, we see this ongoing nature of Christian living. Whether it is Joshua articulating God's faithfulness to the covenant or the apostle Paul, hundreds of years later, we see this constant, biblical theme that the covenant has its ongoing, day-in and day-out dynamics.

Paul, in a similar fashion, at the end of his life, wrote to his colleague Timothy:

> For I am already being poured out as a drink offering, and the time of my departure is at hand. I have fought the good fight, I have finished the race, I have kept the faith. Finally, there is laid up for me the crown of righteousness, which the Lord, the righteous Judge, will give to me on that Day, and not to me only but also to all who have loved His appearing" (2 Tim. 4:6–8).

Here is a radical understanding of success. Success is not necessarily what bears that designation in worldly terms. We know many people who are "very successful" in business, but their personal and spiritual lives are in shambles. There are others who are, in the world's view, failures in one or two areas but very successful in others. It's important to see the overview. If you were locked up in prison, as was the apostle Paul in Rome, would you see yourself as a failure or a success? Would you see God as faithful to His side of the covenant or not? From our vantage point, it is clear that the Romans had not defeated Paul. In God's eyes, success isn't necessarily success nor is failure necessarily failure. It is when we come to grips with this, and understand the spiritual truth, that we are set free to be all that God created us to be. The bottom line of faithfulness to the covenant is that we will succeed. Let us be certain that that success is success as defined by God.

Joshua mentions four action steps that we can take if we want to achieve success on God's terms.

First, *give God the credit* for all you have and all you are.

Joshua reminded the people, *"'For the LORD your God is He who has fought for you"* (v. 3). My hindsight is not very good. When I am in the middle of a struggle I have a way of depending upon the Lord. When I come out of the struggle in pretty good shape, I have that self-centered, conceited tendency to give myself the credit for having done a pretty good job of handling it. I need to remind myself daily that every good and perfect gift comes from the Lord. He has won the battle with sin and death and has given us life, health, and opportunity.

The Jews who had achieved the major part of the conquest began to credit themselves with their success. After all, they had a superior moral and ethical culture to that of the Canaanites. They had also benefitted from their years of observing the highly organized Egyptian culture. When you are beginning to come out on top, it is easy to credit yourself with the magnificent qualities that produce success. I can become puffed up with pride in my "self-made-man" syndrome, polishing my Horatio Alger award prior to even receiving it. I forget that it is the grace of our Lord Jesus Christ that gives me everything I have. In the account we have been reading, God was in charge, not the arrogant Jewish leadership. There would have been no conquest of the land without God. There would be no viable, lasting success in our lives without the grace of the Lord. Moses discovered this fact when he was utterly defeated and humbled at those moments in his life when he struck out in his own power and success. It was when he was faithful to the covenant that he experienced true victory.

I have been an admirer and follower of Billy Graham since I was a youngster in the mid-1940s. It is not because he is a great speaker, a bright person, or an extremely successful person; he is all of these. But there are great speakers and bright persons who are also extremely successful for whom I have very little respect. As I have watched Dr. Graham, I have been impressed with his humility. His is not an artificial, cosmetic humility. What I have admired and why I give such wholehearted support to his evangelistic crusades is that I know the integrity of this man who endeavors to speak Christ's truths and calls men, women, and children to repentance and trust in the Savior. Dr. Graham also recognizes his weaknesses and humbly seeks the help of the Lord and the counsel of others. I have been privileged to observe him in the posture of prayer, pleading for God's cleansing and anointing and spiritual empowerment, knowing that what the world defines as success can be empty nothingness in the eyes of the sovereign God. He has turned down opportunities to run for vice-president on both the Republican and Democratic tickets and has refused to be flattered into accepting major Hollywood acting roles with all the rationalizations that this could increase his visibility and ministry for Christ. He knows that the full credit for what he has been able to accomplish is the Lord's and must be given back to Him.

When we are able to give our successes back to God as His accomplishments, we are also free from having to take full responsibility for what some might call failure. If we are honestly engaged in enterprises genuinely dedicated to the Lord, we are not as easily caught up in superficial evaluation standards.

Second in achieving success on God's terms, *obey the Lord.*

Joshua, in this farewell address, urged the people, *"Therefore be very courageous to keep and to do all that is written in the Book of the Law of Moses, lest you turn aside from it to the right hand or to the left"* (v. 6).

As preachers, we have the privilege of sharing our own odyssey of endeavoring to obey the Lord. I shared with my congregation the fact that the Bible is the authority upon which I live my life. I do not claim to have mastered it or to understand everything in it. But this does not minimize its importance in my life. My desire is to spend some time each day in this Word. On those days I don't do this, I am depriving myself of the spiritual sustenance so critical to experiencing the true success that God promises. When I keep this word in my heart, when I bathe my very essence of being in the teachings of God's Word and am steadfastly committed to obedience, my life functions much more smoothly, much more creatively than it does when I begin to ape the philosophy of short-cut success.

I am reminded of words attributed to the brilliant pianist Artur Rubinstein. He said something to this effect: "When I miss practicing one day, nobody knows it. Two days, I know it. Three days, and the world knows it." In the early 1960s when I was traveling across the Atlantic Ocean on the *Queen Mary*, Artur Rubinstein was on that same voyage. The rumor got out that he had a piano in his stateroom. I happened to get a glimpse of it; and I can remember walking by that stateroom many times and hearing the great performer hidden away at practice.

I'll be the first to admit that a lot of other philosophies are out there in the world competing for my attention. A lot of other ethics quite persuasively argue against biblical ethics. There are also a lot of highly persuasive temptations that can capture my attention, seducing me with their false promises. I shared as bluntly as I could with my congregation the fact that whenever I have been seduced away from obedience to the Word of God, I have been the loser. Promised power, promised pleasure, promised success are all bubbles that burst at the moment of contact.

If we want to experience true success, we need to open our Bible, read it daily, learn its teachings, and obey the Lord.

Third, live a *life of separation from the world.*

Joshua urged the people to be steadfast in obedience, turning neither to the right hand nor to the left, *"'that you may not be mixed with these nations left here among you'"* (v. 7, RSV).

We are citizens of two worlds. We have our responsibilities as members of the human race and as a particular nation that functions within a community of nations. However, we must be careful not to buy in completely to the values of the society in which we find ourselves. We need to ask the Spirit of God to make it very clear to us wherein God's value system is antithetical to the value system of our culture. How many a person has cut himself or herself loose from deep fellowship with other believers in Christ in the initial intention of leading nonbelievers to faith in Jesus Christ?

There is such a thing as reverse evangelism. Even as we encourage those to whom we communicate to know their neighbors and be involved in the life of the community, we need to know wherein the Christian is different from the nonbeliever. And we need to maintain a home base, to be involved with fellow believers in Jesus Christ who will encourage us to go deeper with the Lord. How sad it would be if the only way people could tell if we were Christians was by seeing the sign of the fish attached to the back of our cars. The question is whether or not our lifestyles are different. Have we let the world squeeze us into its own mold?

I believe I shocked my congregation by stating that there is a luxury in living in a country ruled by an atheistic, totalitarian regime. Why luxury? Because then we would know the difference between ourselves and those who, with contempt, despise all that we stand for as Christians. It is so easy in our American environment to buy into those subtle compromises with the powers of this world. We lose our identity as the people of God. We are called to walk that tightrope in which we have authentic, genuine friendships with persons who are not believers in Jesus Christ. At the same time, we are to nurture and cultivate the fellowship of believers that holds us steady so that we are not gradually absorbed into a watered-down cultural religion that begins to identify Christianity with the American way.

Joshua was desperately afraid of the tendency he saw among his Israelite contemporaries whom he had led into the Promised Land to forget that they really were different from the Canaanites. Some had gone native and had accommodated themselves to the Canaanite culture. There's a deep spiritual truth articulated in James 4:4: "Do you not know that friendship with the world is enmity with God? Whoever therefore wants to be a friend of the world makes himself an enemy of God."

On occasion, I have felt led in my preaching to raise questions about certain actions, statements, or attitudes expressed by political leaders. This has disturbed some in the congregations I have served. I have never, until preaching on this passage, stated my political party membership or the names of candidates for whom I have voted. As a result, some have concluded that, on occasion, I might have been taking "cheap shots" from the pulpit at public leaders of a different party and ideology from mine. I used this passage as an opportunity in a nonelection time of year to assert strongly that I could not yield to the pressure of those who state that religion and politics should be kept separate. I asserted that basic to all of life is that interweaving of deep spiritual and ethical conviction that arises from our biblical and theological reflection and causes us to think "Christianly" on the public issues of our day. I tried to emphasize the point that if we do keep our spiritual and political lives compartmentalized, we can end up functioning with a spiritual impotency that refuses to hold public leaders accountable for their attitudes, rhetoric, and actions. As Christians, our primary allegiance is to Jesus Christ, not to the state. We are to render unto Caesar the things that are Caesar's and unto God the things that are God's. If the two end up in conflict, our ultimate allegiance is to the crucified and risen Christ. Therefore, we as communicators have negated our privileged responsibility to be both pastors and prophets if we adapt our message to contemporary cultural, political, social, and ethical mores. In our benign good naturedness, we can end up not just spiritual and ethical eunuchs but also actual enemies of God.

Joshua gets even more specific. He states,

> "Or else, if indeed you do go back, and cling to the remnant of these nations—these that remain among you—and make marriages with them, and go in to them and they to you, know for certain that the LORD your God will no longer drive out these nations from before you. But they shall be snares and traps to you, and scourges on your sides and thorns in your eyes, until you perish from this good land which the LORD your God has given you" (vv. 12–13).

We often shy away from this tough teaching. It's an Old Testament articulation of the New Testament truth that we are not to be unequally yoked together with unbelievers. It has specific implications for marriage. One of the great benefits of expository preaching and teaching is that it forces us to deal with those topics that we might otherwise avoid. The luxury of it is that it enables us to deal with themes that are superimposed on us by the

Bible as we systematically teach and preach through a given book. People in our congregations are not as likely to feel picked on and singled out in their particular circumstances as they would be if they felt a particular topical sermon was tailor-made for them.

I shared some specific words for singles. I suggested that they determine before the Lord that they would claim Christ's strength to remain single rather than to marry a nonbeliever. There is nothing that will destroy one's joy and fullness in Christ more quickly than to marry a person who does not share the same conviction. He or she may be a marvelous person, very attractive, bringing many wonderful traits to the marriage. But the fact is that marriage between a believer and a nonbeliever is the only truly mixed marriage. The Bible does not speak against interracial marriages or transcultural marriages. The Bible enthusiastically includes Rahab, the Canaanite prostitute, in the very lineage of Christ. Obviously, there had been a marriage that qualified her to be the great-great-grandmother of King David. What the Scripture speaks against is one who is numbered among the people of God marrying one who does not share that same family identity. So many Christians I know who make this compromise live with the pain of loving someone, being part of someone, who, at a significant point, is alien to who they are. So a tug-of-war exists. Over a period of years, someone wins that tug-of-war, and often it is the nonbeliever.

I struggle with this as a pastor. In our Protestant tradition, marriage is an ordinance, not a sacrament. Whereas the sacraments are available only to believers in Jesus Christ, an ordinance is that which is designed by God for all humankind. Nonbelievers have a right to get married also. So, on occasion, I marry nonbelievers, two people who have chosen not to receive Jesus Christ as Savior. In premarital counseling, I share with them the claims of Christ and urge them to make this commitment. But I am reluctant to make them jump through hoops to please me so that I will marry them. I would rather marry them as nonbelievers, with it being very clear that it may be a wedding ceremony carried on by a minister, but the ceremony does not make it a Christian marriage. I readily marry all couples who are both believers in Jesus Christ unless there is a complex divorce situation or emotional dynamics that need extensive time and counseling to unravel. Where I receive the greatest pain is when one is a believer in Jesus Christ and the other is a nonbeliever. It's with great anguish that I feel responsible to confront these two partners with the fact that they are headed toward a mixed marriage that will have troubles for both because it is not in accordance with God's Word and with the psychological and spiritual realities that lead to wholeness.

If the preacher chooses to address this matter of mixed marriage from the pulpit, giving strong warning to those who are single Christians to avoid marrying a nonbeliever, he or she must be aware of those who are already married to nonbelievers. We must point out clearly that our endeavor is not to stimulate guilt. Nor are we endeavoring to encourage the breakup of a mixed marriage. At this point in my exposition, I urged a reading of 1 Corinthians 7:10–16, which speaks so clearly to the one involved in a mixed marriage. It urges the believer to be faithful to the unbelieving partner, to do everything one can to live a life of godliness and Christian example in the home so that he or she will have a sanctifying influence on his or her partner and children. Just as pathetic as a believer who intentionally chooses to marry an unbeliever is a believer who is married to an unbeliever and uses it as an excuse to be miserable, difficult, and even leave the unbeliever.

Teaching on separation from the world is one of the most neglected teachings today. It is a difficult teaching because we are called to be the salt of the world. We are called to have relationships that are redemptive in nature. But we are warned against anything that leads to accommodation. The believer in Christ is different, and this differentness should be maintained.

The many-decades-old words of William C. Blaikie were helpful in crystalizing my homiletical thoughts on this topic:

> Joshua was very emphatic in forbidding intermarriage and friendly social intercourse with Canaanites. He saw much need for the prayer, "Lead us not into temptation." He understood the meaning of enchanted ground. He knew that between the realm of holiness and the realm of sin there is a kind of neutral territory, which belongs strictly to neither, but which slopes towards the realm of sin, and in point of fact most commonly furnishes recruits not a few to the army of evil. Alas, how true is this still! Marriages between believers and unbelievers; friendly social fellowship, on equal terms, between the Church and the world; partnership in business between the godly and the ungodly—who does not know the usual result? In a few solitary cases, it may be, the child of the world is brought into the kingdom; but in how many instances do we find the buds of Christian

promise nipped, and lukewarmness and backsliding, if not apostasy, coming in their room! There is no better help for the Christian life, no greater encouragement to fellowship with God, than congenial fellowship with other Christians, especially in the home, as there is no greater hindrance to these things than an alien spirit there.[1]

Fourth in attaining success in God, *avoid pagan worship.*

Perhaps very little needs to be said about this. Few of us are oriented toward pagan worship. Who of us practices sacrificing to idols? Who of us would think of killing our children in religious worship as did the Canaanites? How many of us name the names of false gods? How many of us involve ourselves in immoral sexual worship practices with temple prostitutes? Joshua tells the people that they are not to *"make mention of the name of their gods, nor cause anyone to swear by them; you shall not serve them nor bow down to them"* (v. 7).

In some parts of the world, this still is a problem. My dear friend Bernard Muindi, who for many years has been the secretary general of the Presbyterian church in East Africa, has struggled with this problem. Not only did he and his fellow Christians survive the Mau Mau terrorism of the 1950s, but in the late 1960s, there was a resurgence of oath taking. Two of his elders who refused to take the oath of loyalty to their tribe, putting Christ first, were killed for their unwillingness to compromise.

Perhaps we'll never experience anything as dramatic as that in our lives. But I can assure you that creeping into the very life of any Christian community are the beginnings of pagan worship. We can worship our order of service or a particular kind of music instead of Jesus Christ. Believing that somehow we can buy salvation, we can lift up our good works in pagan offerings or present our money instead of ourselves. We can worship our understanding of theology instead of the God who has revealed Himself to us in the person and work of Jesus Christ. Our worship attention can be focused on our marriage partner, on our children, on our work, or on our nation. We are guilty of idolatry whenever we lift creature into the place reserved only for the Creator.

THE CONSEQUENCES OF UNFAITHFULNESS

[14] "Behold, this day I am going the way of all the earth. And you know in all your hearts and in all your souls that not

one thing has failed of all the good things which the LORD your God spoke concerning you. All have come to pass for you; not one word of them has failed. [15] Therefore it shall come to pass, that as all the good things have come upon you which the LORD your God promised you, so the LORD will bring upon you all harmful things, until He has destroyed you from this good land which the LORD your God has given you. [16] When you have transgressed the covenant of the LORD your God, which He commanded you, and have gone and served other gods, and bowed down to them, then the anger of the LORD will burn against you, and you shall perish quickly from the good land which He has given you."

—Joshua 23:14–16

Joshua moves from the positive promise of faithfulness to a negative direction and states the consequence of unfaithfulness.

People don't generally like negative thinking today. But to count the costs and draw conclusions isn't really negative thinking. Actually, it's a very positive, constructive approach to life. One is dealing with positive reality when one looks at consequences. To disobey is ultimately to run the risk of losing God's help. So Joshua sketches the bottom-line results that are very clear if we are unfaithful. In these final verses of chapter 23, Joshua points out the consequences of unfaithfulness—defeat, discomfort, disgrace.

Joshua, once again, underlines the fact that he is about ready to die when he says, *"Behold, this day I am going the way of all the earth"* (v. 14). This reminder of his impending death brings leverage to what he says. He reminds the people that if they reflect enough on it they will have to admit God has never failed; He has been good. But if God's people transgress the covenant, avoiding these very positive suggestions that lead to success, *"then the anger of the LORD will burn against you, and you shall perish quickly from the good land which He has given you"* (v. 16).

This bottom line is the flipside of the positive at which we have already looked. These negative consequences come when we don't give God the credit for all we have and when we don't obey the Lord with steadfastness. They come when we don't live lives of separation from the world and when we involve ourselves in pagan worship that doesn't understand the gift of God's grace and love and acceptance and His desire to forgive us and make us clean and pure.

Negative consequences also occur when we accommodate ourselves in ways that cause us to shift our priorities. We do it as a church when we forget we are called to be Christ-centered fellowships designed to lead men, women, and children to a personal faith in Christ; to nurture ourselves in that faith; and to deploy ourselves in Christian service for others. When we become narcissistically enamored with how nice we have it and forget our call to go into all the world in a sacrificial life of ministry and service, we are in trouble.

We can shift our priorities in our personal lives. Is Jesus Christ really first, our marriage partner second, our children third, our work fourth? How easy it is for these to become shifted in order of importance. I'm the first to face this struggle because I am a workaholic; I love my work. I can too quickly identify my commitment to God with my work; and, in the process, I neglect my wife, my children, and even my intimate relationship with the Lord.

How tragic it is when we transgress the covenant. This covenant has two dimensions to it. One half of it is always there. That is God's side. He never fails or forsakes us. The rest depends on us. The only part of the covenant at risk is our part. This is what Joshua was trying to tell the people. God would always be faithful. The question is, "How about us?"

The real issue is that of loving God. Joshua stated it bluntly, "Therefore take careful heed to yourselves, that you love the LORD your God" (v. 11). Hundreds of years later, Jesus gave the same teaching when the question was put, "What is the greatest commandment of all?" How did He respond? "Thou shalt love the LORD thy God with all thy heart, with all thy soul, with all thy might, and thy neighbor as thyself." Loving God comes first. Then the spinoff of that is the genuine desire to serve Him and others.

NOTE

1. W. Robertson Nicoll, ed., *The Expositor's Bible* (Grand Rapids: Wm. B. Eerdmans, Co. 1956), 1:729.

CHAPTER SEVENTEEN—THE BOTTOM-LINE CHOICE

JOSHUA 24:1–33

Scripture Outline

The Facts (24:1–13)

The Choice (24:14–15)

The Results (24:16–33)

I am convinced that we are living in the midst of exponential change that has totally destroyed the equilibrium of our lives. Daily I am battered by an array of stimuli. Each impulse demands a part of me and my time. There are so many competing ideologies and friendships claiming my allegiance. At times, I feel myself immobilized by the diversity, the complexity, and the changing dynamics of contemporary existence. I find it difficult to know what to do, how to think, and with whom to be.

The clutter on the desk of my life piles high, in astounding disarray, to the point that the options before me terrorize me into immobility, and indecision holds me in its grip.

Each generation tends to think that it is the first to experience this "future shock," but every generation has had it in one degree or another. In our era the complexity of life reflects itself in a restlessness of spiritual indecision and searching for answers to life's problems. It's not that Americans have never heard of Jesus Christ. No nation is more exposed to constant religious bombardment by radio, television, newspapers, and magazines. The name "Jesus Christ" is heard daily. But value systems are shifting, and old answers are not easily accepted. The church as an institution no longer commands respect without earning it. Spiritual restlessness also characterized the environment in which Joshua lived his final years, as the following Scripture demonstrates.

THE FACTS

24:1 Then Joshua gathered all the tribes of Israel to Shechem and called for the elders of Israel, for their heads, for their judges, and for their officers; and they presented themselves before God. ² And Joshua said to all the people, "Thus says the LORD God of Israel: 'Your fathers, including Terah, the father of Abraham and the father of Nahor, dwelt on the other side of the River in old times; and they served other gods. ³ Then I took your father Abraham from the other side of the River, led him throughout all the land of Canaan, and multiplied his descendants and gave him Isaac. ⁴ To Isaac I gave Jacob and Esau. To Esau I gave the mountains of Seir to possess, but Jacob and his children went down to Egypt. ⁵ Also I sent Moses and Aaron, and I plagued Egypt, according to what I did among them. Afterward I brought you out.

⁶ 'Then I brought your fathers out of Egypt, and you came to the sea; and the Egyptians pursued your fathers with chariots and horsemen to the Red Sea. ⁷ So they cried out to the LORD; and He put darkness between you and the Egyptians, brought the sea upon them, and covered them. And your eyes saw what I did in Egypt. Then you dwelt in the wilderness a long time. ⁸ And I brought you into the land of the Amorites, who dwelt on the other side of the Jordan, and they fought with you. But I gave them into your hand, that you might possess their land, and I destroyed them from before you. ⁹ Then Balak the son of Zippor, king of Moab, arose to make war against Israel, and sent and called Balaam the son of Beor to curse you. ¹⁰ But I would not listen to Balaam; therefore he continued to bless you. So I delivered you out of his hand. ¹¹ Then you went over the Jordan and came to Jericho. And the men of Jericho fought against you— also the Amorites, the Perizzites, the Canaanites, the Hittites, the Girgashites, the Hivites, and the Jebusites. But I delivered them into your hand. ¹² I sent the hornet before you which drove them out from before you, also the two kings of the Amorites, but not with your sword or with your bow. ¹³ I have given you a land for which you did not labor, and cities which you did not build, and you dwell in them; you eat of the vineyards and olive groves which you did not plant.'
—*Joshua 24:1–13*

As we have seen, the people of Israel had been led out of their horrendous captivity in Egypt. They had wandered for forty years in the wilderness. They crossed the Jordan, led by Joshua into the initial conquest of the land. Those were rugged years, and their faith was virile. Some believed the Lord. Others didn't. There was a kind of toughness of muscle, spiritually speaking. But a new day had come. Although the conquest was not complete, a spiritual unsettledness marked the lives of the people of God. Some owned the pagan ornaments of the Egyptians and Canaanites. There was a double-mindedness, the same kind of restlessness and indecision we can sense today. Some of the people remained strong in their faith, becoming catalysts for God in their society, making others think they were a religious nation. Others capitulated to contemporary thought-forms, doubts, and pagan practices. In between, there was that large group of Israelites without any kind of clear perception of who they were in relation to Jehovah.

Standing in stark contrast was Joshua. His life pattern had been set decades before as one of the twelve spies sent to look over the Promised Land. Only he and Caleb had come back with the confidence that God would fulfill His promise. Joshua was the long-haul veteran of a vital faith. He had endured the harsh realities of the wilderness experience, qualifying for a place of leadership. In a gutsy way, he stood before the gathered leaders of Israel at Shechem near Jacob's well, at the foot of Mount Gerizim and Mount Ebal, close to the worship center at Shiloh, surrounded by great symbols of Hebrew history. There he once again articulated the essence of God's covenant with His people, urging them in an exhortation that echoes all through human history to move beyond this indecision and restlessness, to a clear-cut decision for God.

This is one of the classic biblical texts. With all the energy that this toughened, godly, one-hundred-ten-year-old character could muster up, he cried out:

> "Now therefore, fear the Lord, serve Him in sincerity and in truth, and put away the gods which your fathers served on the other side of the River and in Egypt. Serve the Lord! And if it seems evil to you to serve the Lord, choose for yourselves this day whom you will serve, whether the gods which your fathers served that were on the other side of the River, or the gods of the Amorites, in whose land you dwell. But as for me and my house, we will serve the Lord" (vv. 14–15).

Joshua that day called for a decision that would help end the spiritual, intellectual, and moral restlessness that marked so many lives. Granted, some of the people had been faithful, and he commended them for that. But he had observed that, with the major part of the conquest over, many had reverted to old, traditional religious patterns. It is interesting to see how Israel constantly flirted with pagan idolatry.

Joshua's summons speaks as boldly today as it did then. Periodically, men and women of God have stood strong, making a clear proclamation of the Word of God, calling men and women to make a decision. Joshua had made his. He said, "And if it seems evil to you to serve the LORD, choose for yourselves this day whom you will serve" (v. 15).

This text gives the preacher an enormous opportunity to call persons to decision for Christ. Ask them if they have made their choice. Ask them if they are firm in this choice. Unfortunately, we can't take for granted that everyone in our sanctuary on a given Sunday morning is automatically a Christian. Represented within our congregations are all types of human experience. The call goes out, "Choose this day the one you will serve for the rest of your life." There are persons in our sanctuaries and classrooms who are in the valley of decision—restless, uncertain, bombarded with a multitude of impulses.

Hundreds of years later, Elijah on Mount Carmel gave a similar challenge. He said, "How long will you falter between two opinions? If the LORD is God, follow Him; but if Baal, follow him" (1 Kin. 18:21). The RSV translates this, "How long will you go limping with two different opinions?"

Peter, on the day of Pentecost, declared that the One promised by the Old Testament prophets had come—Jesus Christ, the Savior of the world. He was crucified, but He rose from the dead with a straightforward invitation to repentance and decision for Him. Thousands chose. Lives were changed, and the church was founded. Men and women were, in the words of Christ, "born again." This experience has continued through the centuries. Some have come gradually to the Lord, while others have had dramatic religious experiences. There is the promise of the assurance of salvation that can be ours if we have met the conditions, admitting that we are sinners, expressing genuine sorrow for our sins, and placing our trust in Jesus Christ as the One who has promised us His forgiveness.

Joshua knew that people caught up in indecision needed to be reminded of the facts if their choice was to be based on responsible data. He urged that they consider the options. They could dust off the old gods of Mesopotamia, the kind that Abraham and Sarah left behind and with whom their children and grandchildren occasionally flirted. They could pull out the old Egyptian gods, which some had smuggled, both in their memories and in their personal possessions, into the Promised Land. After all, they had lived in Egypt at the pinnacle of Egyptian power. There is an almost mystical excitement even today in seeing those artifacts that go back thousands of years in history. The Israelites knew them well. But if they preferred, they could adopt the gods of the Amorites, the Canaanites, among whom they now lived. The fertility cults were attractive. Jehovah could seem sort of dull, a cosmic killjoy in the way He sets up His law and instructs us in the ways of righteousness.

But Jehovah was still an option, and Joshua was not going to let that option get lost. So in the face of these other seductive options, and the potential indecisiveness and restlessness of that day, he gave a little history lesson. With the outline of some facts and the use of some strong verbs, Joshua placed in juxtaposition the gods of the Chaldeans, the Egyptians, and the Amorites, and the God who has acted in history. Jehovah is not some nebulous, divine entity who manifests himself in grotesque images made by human hands. He is a leader who has entered into conversation with the human race from the beginning. Humankind is His unique creation, which bears His very image. Then, in more specific ways, during the last thousand years, God had interacted with the "called-out" people, the Jews.

Joshua may have been an old man, but he knew his history. There at Shechem, he recited it for all to hear, mentioning names that triggered the Jewish memory and using verbs that described a God of action. He said, "I took" your father Abraham from beyond the river and led him through all the land of Canaan and made his offspring many. "I gave" him Isaac. To Isaac "I gave" Jacob and Esau. He said, "I sent" Moses and Aaron, and "I plagued" Egypt. He said afterwards, "I brought" you out. And "I brought" your fathers out of Egypt. He described the Egyptians pursuing with their chariots and horsemen and the Jews crying out to God. So God "put" darkness between you and the Egyptians and "made" the sea come upon them. He reminded the people how their eyes saw what God "did" to Egypt. Then "I brought" you to the land of the Amorites who fought with you on the other side of the Jordan. And "I gave" them into your hands. And "I destroyed" them before you. And "I delivered" you out of the hand of Balaam. And "I gave" the seven nations of Canaan into your hand. And "I sent" what helped you in battle. And "I gave" you a land on which you had not labored and cities which you had not built. And you now dwell in this land, and you eat the fruit of the vineyards and the olive yards which you did not plant.

Is there any other religion in the world that so clearly specifies the mighty acts of God? This is why the Apostles' Creed is so central to our faith. Ours is a God of action who has taken initiative on our behalf. This is the God who made heaven and earth; who loved us so much that He became a man in the person of Jesus Christ; who lived among us, teaching us how to live by setting a good example. But this is the God who knew that we cannot earn our salvation by good works. So He went to the very cross bearing our sins in His body, was buried in a borrowed tomb, and rose victorious from the grave. This is the God who, having promised His Holy Spirit, ascended into heaven and now has come into our lives in all the fullness of His spiritual power. This is the God who has built His church and is coming back in the form of His Son Jesus Christ to bring all human history to a point of final cataclysmic culmination in which the power of Satan will be destroyed, and Jesus Christ will reign for eternity.

THE CHOICE

14 "Now therefore, fear the LORD, serve Him in sincerity and in truth, and put away the gods which your fathers served on the other side of the River and in Egypt. Serve the LORD! 15 And if it seems evil to you to serve the LORD, choose for yourselves this day whom you will serve, whether the gods which your fathers served that were on the other side of the River, or the gods of the Amorites, in whose land you dwell. But as for me and my house, we will serve the LORD."
—*Joshua 24:14–15*

It is against this backdrop of a God who acts, a backdrop of facts and of testimony that can be given by millions of men and women throughout all human history that Joshua and the other prophetic voices throughout the centuries have called for us to make a choice. We are urged to stand in awe of this God, to serve Him in sincerity and faithfulness. We are challenged to put away our idols—husband, wife, child, sweetheart, boss, president, job, car, creature, whatever it is that so mesmerizes us. We are exhorted to let God be God.

Joshua puts it in even more specific terms in verse 15. What he is saying is, "For God's sake and for your sake, make a decision." He's urging the people not to get hung up in indecision and not to splatter little bits of faith all over the place. He is calling them to examine the facts and then choose. Updated to our contemporary times, he is urging men and women at the beginning of the twenty-first century to be willing to repent of sin and put their trust in Jesus Christ. Joshua was willing to model this. He had done it decades before. He could look back and say, "God has been faithful. I've made my decision. What about you?" Consider the options. What will bring you the greatest advantage? What will bring the greatest inner satisfaction and peace? What will exercise the best influence on your character? What comes best recommended by others?

This final chapter of Joshua offers a magnificent opportunity for the preacher and teacher to call for a decision for Christ. In my preaching on this chapter, I did precisely that. In the process of calling for decision, I sketched for the congregation the profile of such a decision, listing some of the elements that are present. I asked them to check this list and see if they had made or were willing to make a positive decision for Jesus Christ. I shared with them five ingredients that are required if one is to make a firm decision.

First, *one must be willing to quit straddling the fence.* There is something convenient about being a fence-straddler. This way it seems as if one has the best of both worlds. In fact, it is essential if one is going to make a substantial commitment to Jesus Christ that he or she has weighed the various options. I appreciate intellectual struggles of young men and women who are legitimately in the process of weighing the various alternatives. We need to understand them, appreciating the question mark that rests over their whole existence as they seek to find what for them is authentic commitment to a viable Christ. Unfortunately, though, some never get beyond the point of indecision. What is legitimate for a young person considering alternatives is irresponsible on the part of a forty- or fifty-year-old mature adult. One finally has to make a decision.

This will mean a change of lifestyle brought about by genuine repentance for sin. Change is tough, and repentance hurts. Fence-straddling habits need to be broken, setting one free to really serve the Lord who paid the penalty for sin.

Second, *one must be willing to exert influence on others instead of being pushed around by them.* It is so easy to float with contemporary fashions. Looking into store windows over a period of several years, we have seen all kinds of different fashions. Some spend small fortunes trying to keep up to date. My wife, Anne, and I are astounded both by the variety and the price tags attached to these symbols of fashion. As social, gregarious individuals, all of us are influenced by society to feel out of step if we wear a rounded-toe shoe when a pointed-toe shoe is in fashion, or if our suit has a narrow lapel when a wide lapel is in vogue. Adjusting to contemporary style is not harmful so long as we do not adjust ourselves to pagan religious thinking. There are certain absolutes that God has revealed to us about Himself. When Joshua led the people into the Promised Land, they picked up the contemporary religious fashions and mingled them with the Word of God shared through Moses on Mount Sinai. The result was spiritual trouble, indecision, a nation floating with the religious fashions of the day.

Joshua wouldn't be pushed around. He knew where he stood. He had stood there for years, faithful to the Lord, the God of Abraham, Isaac, and Jacob. He could see the appealing alternatives. Instead of adapting to them, he was willing to exert his influence on others. Boldly he pronounced, "Do what you want to do. As for me and my house, we will serve the LORD."

Third, *a decision for Christ must not be made lightly.* I alerted the congregation that, at the end of this sermon, they would have an opportunity to receive Jesus Christ as Savior or to renew their commitment to Him. I urged them not to make any decision lightly. I noted that once again this year we would have at least three classes for new members and one communicant's class for our young people where there would be instruction in the facts of the Christian life. Many who join these classes will be ushered into the membership of the church. I gave one major warning. I begged those who would be part of this not to take part in these membership classes just because their friends were doing it. I begged those considering joining that they make certain they were willing to commit their lives to Jesus Christ. If they did this, they could then have a meaningful relationship with Christ and His church. If they were just going along with the crowd, they would be in for trouble. It would be someone else's faith, not their own.

Joshua was hardened by battle. He bore the scars of a long-term commitment. His choice to follow the Lord was not made lightly, nor was it held lightly. Along with some other similar characters, he stood as a man of spiritual determination.

Fourth, *one must be willing to go public with one's faith.* Jesus had some words to say about those who had a private confidence in Him but were unwilling to acknowledge Him in public. He said, "He that denies Me before men, him will I deny before My Father which is in Heaven." That is a pretty terse statement. God wants our faith to be right out in front of us. A believer can get himself into enormous amounts of trouble if he is secretive about his faith. I urged those in my congregation not to decide for Christ unless they were willing to identify themselves as one of His disciples in their homes, in their businesses, in their social life, in fact, wherever they went. I reminded them that the Bible is not talking about the perfect lifestyle. None of us will be fully perfect in this life; this is why we need a Savior. At the same time, we are called to be public in our faith.

Fifth, *one must be willing to follow through with one's all.*

One of the most fascinating though tragic characters in the Bible is the Old Testament king, Saul. This man stood head and shoulders above his fellow countrymen. God had selected him for a place of leadership. Saul had all of the right qualifications and started off doing the job correctly. Then something happened. His pride became a problem. By the end of his life, he was a man overwhelmed with melancholy. He had made important decisions early in life only to backtrack on them later. He ended up a fearful, haunted man.

I urged those listening to this sermon to give their all to Jesus Christ throughout their whole life, beginning right then. This would mean that Jesus Christ be allowed Lordship over every aspect of one's existence.

When we preach evangelistically as this text mandates, it also is wise to give those whom we are addressing the knowledge that we understand that the choice may not be easy. Not only did I sketch some of the components making up the profile of a choice, but I also gave some of the many reasons one might not make a clear-cut decision.

One reason is that of *fear*. All kinds of fears can get in the way of receiving Jesus Christ as Savior, making it difficult to make a clear-cut decision for Him.

There is the fear of emotionalism. Many people state they don't want to be religious zealots. I once received a letter loaded with bitter, snide remarks about Billy Graham and others of us who call people to make a personal commitment to Jesus Christ. This person attacked the emotional excesses. I admit that some have manipulated others into decisions by such demagogic methods. Our evangelistic calls must not be marked by emotional histrionics. They should be straightforward, simple, deliberative declarations of the grace of our Lord Jesus Christ and His invitation to come to Him. I've noted, however, that some of the people who complain the most about emotional excesses are those who jump up and down like little children at football and basketball games but are scared to death of emotion when it comes to religion. Emotion is a basic part of life. We don't have to duplicate someone else's experience. But one who comes to Christ does not need to be afraid of emotion.

Some are fearful of oversimplification. I understand that we can only begin to probe the dynamics of God's grace in Jesus Christ. Theologians spend a lifetime examining what it means to be justified by grace through faith. That is a complicated subject. Fortunately, in His invitation to us God has reduced it to very simple terms so that even a little child can know and experience His love.

Some are fearful of this being too complicated. They don't want to receive Jesus Christ until they know everything about Him. That's like trying to say that one will not marry the woman or man one loves until that person knows everything about that prospective partner. What a dull relationship that would be; part of the joy of marriage is discovery. Part of the excitement of life in Christ is that of growth in relationship of increased knowledge as one walks through life with Him.

Another reason that some do not make a clear-cut choice for Christ is that it is *not a good time*. They say, "Someday, maybe I'll accept Christ."

There is never a better time than the present. Satan has a way of trying to put off the decision. Some people tell me that religion is for people who are in trouble. Like the rich young ruler, they come close to Christ and then turn away, afraid that He will cost them something. Looking from the outside at the life of the Christian, they see a call to conviction, self-denial, and humiliation. They don't want anything of that. They don't know how good it is to know Christ personally, to be intimately involved with Him. Some say things are too bad. They're not going to accept Christ when they are down. For others, things are in between. Life is on an even keel.

This kind of person has covered every angle. There is never a good time for him or her. They won't come to Christ when they are up because they don't sense the need. They won't come when they are down. They are too proud. They won't come when they are in between because they don't even take time then to think about it.

Another reason not to make a clear-cut choice is that *one wants to be an individual*, not one of the masses.

Fortunately, God doesn't deal with everyone the same way. One can make a commitment to Him. He then will stand by helping that life to unfold in a unique pattern. God is not in the business of cutting out baker-stamped cookies. He has a delicately beautiful, one-and-only plan for each individual life as that individual is willing to expose himself or herself to it.

I urged those present on Sunday morning who needed to make a decision for Jesus Christ to make the decision that morning. I begged them to not put it off any longer. I stated that I did not want to exploit anyone by emotional manipulation. It would be the Holy Spirit who would bring a harvest of men and women to trust in Himself. I reminded the congregation of this fact, suggesting that if the Spirit of God was probing inside of them, urging them to make a decision, they make it in their own quiet, still way.

But I urged them to not go on standing in the middle. The apostle John described a church made up of people who were neither hot nor cold. The Lord would prefer that we were cold rather than lukewarm. Better still, we are to be hot in our commitment to Him. John went on to say that the Lord wanted to spew the church of Laodicea out of His mouth because it was neither hot nor cold but lukewarm. Lot's wife stood at a point of indecision. She left Sodom and Gomorrah, fleeing from its wickedness. Then she stopped, paralyzed in her tracks, wistfully looking back at it. In these divided aspirations, she turned to a pillar of salt. What a graphic picture of the tragedy of indecision as her profile stands frozen between the world and God, not having the best of either.

THE RESULTS

16 So the people answered and said: "Far be it from us that we should forsake the LORD to serve other gods; 17 for the LORD our God is He who brought us and our fathers up out of the land of Egypt, from the house of bondage, who did those great signs in our sight, and preserved us in all the way that we went and among all the people through whom we passed. 18 And the LORD drove out from before us all the people, including the Amorites who dwelt in the land. We also will serve the LORD, for He is our God."

19 But Joshua said to the people, "You cannot serve the LORD, for He is a holy God. He is a jealous God; He will not forgive your transgressions nor your sins. 20 If you forsake the LORD and serve foreign gods, then He will turn and do you harm and consume you, after He has done you good."

21 And the people said to Joshua, "No, but we will serve the LORD!"

22 So Joshua said to the people, "You are witnesses against yourselves that you have chosen the LORD for yourselves, to serve Him."

And they said, "We are witnesses!"

23 "Now therefore," he said, "put away the foreign gods which are among you, and incline your heart to the LORD God of Israel."

24 And the people said to Joshua, "The LORD our God we will serve, and His voice we will obey!"

25 So Joshua made a covenant with the people that day, and made for them a statute and an ordinance in Shechem.

26 Then Joshua wrote these words in the Book of the Law of God. And he took a large stone, and set it up there under the oak that was by the sanctuary of the LORD. 27 And Joshua said to all the people, "Behold, this stone shall be a witness to us, for it has heard all the words of the LORD which He spoke to us. It shall therefore be a witness to you, lest you deny your God." 28 So Joshua let the people depart, each to his own inheritance.

29 Now it came to pass after these things that Joshua the son of Nun, the servant of the LORD, died, being one hundred and ten years old. 30 And they buried him within the border of his inheritance at Timnath Serah, which is in the mountains of Ephraim, on the north side of Mount Gaash.

31 Israel served the LORD all the days of Joshua, and all the days of the elders who outlived Joshua, who had known all the works of the LORD which He had done for Israel.

32 The bones of Joseph, which the children of Israel had brought up out of Egypt, they buried at Shechem, in the plot of ground which Jacob had bought from the sons of Hamor the father of Shechem for one hundred pieces of silver, and which had become an inheritance of the children of Joseph.

33 And Eleazar the son of Aaron died. They buried him in a hill belonging to Phinehas his son, which was given to him in the mountains of Ephraim.

—Joshua 24:16–33

The Book of Joshua ends on a note of affirmation. The people responded. When they said, *"The LORD our God we will serve, and His voice we will obey"* (v. 24), four great historical events took place.

First, Joshua took a large stone and set it up under the oak at Shechem that was by the sanctuary of the Lord. At several points in this book, Joshua has taken stones as reminders of the covenant. Joshua wrote down the words of witness. He declared that the witness stone would remain at Shechem, declaring that the people had heard the words of the Lord, reminding them never to depart from them.

Second, Joshua died. This man who had so faithfully served the Lord throughout his entire life and had just delivered a great benedictory address to the people died—as will all of us. No great memorial was built to him. The memorials were to the Lord. Joshua was buried within the border of his inheritance in the mountains of Ephraim.

Third, the bones of Joseph, brought up from Egypt, were buried at Shechem.

And fourth, Eleazar the son of Aaron died and was buried in a hill that belonged to his son Phinehas, which was given him in the mountains of Ephraim.

An era had come to an end. It was with a kind of melancholy that I shared a last message from the life of Joshua with my congregation. I'd like to think that Joshua's final message would have a permanent effect, just as I'd like to think that my preaching would change lives for the long haul. The fact is that there are cycles in the spiritual life of nations and of individual people. The next era would be that of the Judges. Again, it's important to emphasize that even though Joshua was dead, the positive results of his leadership lived on. The final word was not the stone of witness, the death of Joshua, the burial of the bones of Joseph, or the death of Eleazar. The final word is that the choice modeled by Joshua all of his life and the call to decision by the Holy Spirit of God had its impact. The Jews in future generations would have ups and downs spiritually, as has every generation. But the decisions made that day at Shechem were not flippant, casual, emotionally induced decisions. The bottom-line choice had a staying power. The Book of Joshua concludes on this very positive note that we must never forget: *"Israel served the* Lord *all the days of Joshua, and all the days of the elders who outlived Joshua, who had known all the works of the* Lord *which He had done for Israel"* (v. 31).

My prayer is that this can be said about those of us who are called to communicate the Word of God and also about those who will hear that Word from us and outlive us by decades, while at the same time remaining faithful to decisions made as a result of our faithful teaching and preaching.

BIBLIOGRAPHY

Armerding, Carl. *The Fight for Palestine*. Wheaton, Ill.: Van Kampen Press, 1949.

Bainton, R. H. *Christian Attitudes Towards War and Peace*. Nashville: Abingdon Press, 1960.

Boling, Robert G., and G. Ernest Wright. *The Anchor Bible*. Vol. 6, *Joshua*. Garden City, N.Y.: Doubleday and Company, 1982.

Butler, Trent C. *Joshua*. Word Biblical Commentary, vol. 7. Waco, Tex.: Word Books, 1983.

Calvin, John. *Commentaries on the Book of Joshua*. Grand Rapids: Wm. B. Eerdmans, 1963.

Craigie, Peter C. *The Problem of War in the Old Testament*. Grand Rapids: Wm. B. Eerdmans, 1978.

Deane, William J. *Joshua: His Life and Times*. London: James Nisbet and Co., 1889.

Dutka, Elaine, and Denise Worrell. "The Best Year of Her Lives." *Time*, May 1984, pp. 60–70.

Engstrom, Ted W. "The Price of Leadership." *Christian Leadership Letter*, January 1977.

Fosdick, Harry Emerson. *Guide to Understanding the Bible*. New York: Harper, 1960.

Garstang, John. *Joshua, Judges*. London: Constable and Co., 1931.

Gray, John. *A History of Jerusalem*. London: Robert Hale, 1969.

Halverson, Richard C. *Perspective*, November 4, 1970.

Hamlin, E. John. *Inheriting the Land*. Grand Rapids: Wm. B. Eerdmans, 1983.

Harmon, Nolan B., ed. Vol. II of *The Interpreter's Bible*. 12 vols. New York: Abingdon Press, 1953.

Iacocca, Lee, with William Novak. *Iacocca*. New York: Bantam Books, 1984.

Ironside, H. A. *Addresses on the Book of Joshua*. New York: Loizeaux Brothers, 1950.

Kaiser, Walter C., Jr. *Toward Old Testament Ethics*. Grand Rapids: Zondervan, 1983.

Lindsell, Harold. *Park Street Prophet: The Story of Harold Ockenga*. Wheaton, Ill.: Van Kampen Press, 1951.

Maclaren, Alexander. *Expositions of Holy Scripture: Deuteronomy, Joshua, Judges, Ruth, and First Book of Samuel*. Cincinnati: Jennings and Graham; New York: Eaton and Mains.

"Murphy's Decalogue." *Context*, November 1, 1983.

Nicoll, W. Robertson, ed. *The Expositor's Bible*, vol. 1. Grand Rapids: Wm. B. Eerdmans, 1956.

Peck, M. Scott. *The Road Less Traveled*. New York: Simon and Schuster, 1978.

Pesin, Harry. "A Polite Plea for Peace." *Time*, May 11, 1970, p. 66.

Pink, Arthur W. *Gleanings in Joshua*. Chicago: Moody Press, 1964.

Redpath, Alan. *Victorious Christian Living*. Westwood, NJ: Fleming H. Revell Company, 1955.

Schaeffer, Francis A. *Joshua and the Flow of Biblical History*. London: Hodder and Stoughton, 1975.

Soggin, J. Alberto. *Joshua*. London: SCM Press, 1972.

Spurgeon, Charles Haddon. *The Treasury of the Bible*. Vol. 1, *Old Testament* Grand Rapids: Zondervan, 1968.

Stewart, James S. *King Forever*. Nashville: Abingdon Press, 1975.

Tournier, Paul. *A Place for You*. New York: Harper and Row, 1968.

Woudstra, Marten H. *The Book of Joshua*. Grand Rapids: Wm. B. Eerdmans, 1981.